Emperor Qianlong

What policies did ↑ make to ensure that he
and the Manchus would retain their "foreign"
culture as the conquerers of China? How was
he able at the same time to integrate foreigners
and foreign culture elements into the socio-
political and cultural spheres of influence of the
Middle Kingdom?

Giuseppe Castiglione (1688–1766). *Study of the Qianlong emperor and courtiers* (preparatory sketch). ca. 1750. Ink on paper. © Musée de l'Homme, Paris.

Mark C. Elliott

Harvard University

Emperor Qianlong

Son of Heaven, Man of the World

THE LIBRARY OF WORLD BIOGRAPHY

Edited by Peter N. Stearns

Longman
New York San Francisco Boston
London Toronto Sydney Tokyo Singapore Madrid
Mexico City Munich Paris Cape Town Hong Kong Montreal

Library of Congress Cataloging-in-Publication Data

Elliott, Mark C.
  Emperor Qianlong: son of heaven, man of the world / Mark C. Elliott. — 1st ed.
      p. cm. — (The library of world biography)
  Includes bibliographical references and index.
  ISBN-13: 978-0-321-08444-6
  ISBN-10: 0-321-08444-6
  1. Qianlong, Emperor of China, 1711-1799.   2. China—Kings and rulers—Biography.
  3. China—History—Qianlong, 1736-1795.   I. Title.
  DS754.8.E455 2009
  951'.032092—dc22
  [B]   2008048382

Editorial Director: Leah Jewell
Publisher: Priscilla McGeehon
Executive Editor: Charles Cavaliere
Editorial Assistant: Lauren Aylward
Senior Marketing Manager: Laura Lee Maney
Marketing Assistant: Arthena Moore
Design Director: Jayne Conte
Cover Design: Margaret Kenselaar
Cover Illustration/Photo: Giuseppe Castiglione (1688–1766) and court artists. *Portrait of Emperor
    Qianlong* (detail from *Inauguration Portraits of Emperor Qianlong, the Empress and Eleven
    Imperial Consorts*). 1736. Handscroll, ink and colors on silk. Cleveland Museum of Art.
Map Creation: Alliance Publishing
Full-Service Project Management/Composition: GGS Higher Education Resources,
    A division of PreMedia Global, Inc.
Printer/Binder: RR Donnelley

Pearson Education Ltd., London
Pearson Education Singapore, Pte. Ltd
Pearson Education, Canada, Inc.
Pearson Education–Japan
Pearson Education Australia PTY, Limited
Pearson Education North Asia, Ltd., Hong Kong
Pearson Educación de Mexico, S.A. de C.V.
Pearson Education Malaysia, Pte. Ltd
Pearson Education, Upper Saddle River, New Jersey

Longman
is an imprint of

10 9 8 7 6 5 4 3 2

ISBN-13: 978-0-321-08444-6
ISBN-10:   0-321-08444-6

www.pearsonhighered.com

For Thomas, who cheered me on

Contents

Editor's Preface

"Biography is history seen through the prism of a person."

—LOUIS FISCHER

It is often challenging to identify the roles and experiences of individuals in world history. Larger forces predominate. Yet biography provides important access to world history. It shows how individuals helped shape the society around them. Biography also offers concrete illustrations of larger patterns in political and intellectual life, in family life, and in the economy.

The Longman Library of World Biography series seeks to capture the individuality and drama that mark human character. It deals with individuals operating in one of the main periods of world history, while also reflecting issues in the particular society around them. Here, the individual illustrates larger themes of time and place. The interplay between the personal and general is always the key to using biography in history, and world history is no exception. Always, too, there is the question of personal agency: how much do individuals, even great ones, shape their own lives and environment, and how much are they shaped by the world around them?

PETER N. STEARNS

Author's Preface

In the history of Europe, the eighteenth century is widely recognized as an era of unique importance. Characterized variously as the Age of Enlightenment or the Age of Revolution, the "long eighteenth century" is said to have lasted from the late 1600s through the early 1800s, during which time European social, political, and economic structures assumed recognizably modern forms. In fact, with various journals, societies, and academic centers dedicated to its study, the eighteenth century is so special it exists as a separate field of historical study: the French even speak of *dixhuitièmistes*, "eighteenth-ists"!

As it happens, the same period is one of great significance in Chinese history as well. In many ways China's eighteenth century was like Europe's, being both long and historically critical. Probably the most important single development was the doubling of the country's population, which grew from 150 million in 1700 to over 300 million by 1800. This demographic explosion reverberated throughout the human and natural environments and was accompanied by booming economic growth, especially in interregional trade, which did much to improve standards of living and stimulate cultural production, particularly in urban areas. At the same time, the eighteenth century witnessed the expansion of the empire to its greatest size in five hundred years; the coming of age of rigorous forms of intellectual inquiry; a flowering of culture; and the widespread growth of different types of popular religious beliefs and organizations. Finally, it was also during this time that contact between the Chinese and European worlds increased dramatically and the first modern diplomatic opening between China and the West took place.

All of this change occurred under the emperors of the Qing (pronounced *ching*, as in the second syllable of the word "searching") dynasty, the last imperial line to hold sway over China. It should be pointed out that, strictly speaking, the Qing ruling family was not itself Chinese—that is, it did not belong to the Han ethnic group. In fact, that family and the main body of the dynasty's people were Manchu. The Manchus were a people from China's northeastern border, a chunk of territory locked in between China, Korea, Mongolia, and Siberia (only later did it come to be known as Manchuria). This region, along with the Mongolian steppe to its west, was the historic home of various nomadic or seminomadic tribes whose military power posed a constant threat to the stability of Chinese states. By dint of military conquest and political compromise, for the better part of the period between 900 and 1400 CE, a number of different northern frontier tribes, including most famously the Mongols, made themselves masters over much or all of China. The empire was triumphantly reclaimed for the Han nation by the founder of the powerful Ming dynasty in 1368; but the peoples of the north were not through.

What began in the late 1500s as a loose conglomeration of feuding tribes had by the 1620s developed into a small but well-organized Manchurian statelet. Following the Mongol example, the Manchu leaders cautiously and deliberately expanded the area they controlled, building a sophisticated administrative apparatus to match the formidable army at their command. In 1636 they proclaimed the name "Qing" and by 1644 they and their allies were strong enough to sweep out the weakened Ming rulers and occupy Beijing. Qing success on battlefields around the country being interpreted as proof of their superior virtue in the eyes of Heaven, the Manchu claim to sovereignty over the Chinese realm was widely, though never universally, accepted. And while they ruled as an ethnic minority, far outnumbered by the Han Chinese, the Manchus combined uncommon political acumen and military muscle to forge one of the great empires in world history.

This imperial enterprise reached its apogee during China's "long eighteenth century." Since the custom of marking dates according to the Christian calendar did not become common in China until the twentieth century, the equivalent era is celebrated using the phrase, "the flourishing age of Kang and Qian." "Kang" is short for Kangxi (pronounced *kahng-shee*), the reign name of the emperor who reigned from 1662 to 1722. "Qian" abbreviates the name of the Qianlong (pronounced *chee'en-loohng*) emperor (1711–1799), Kangxi's grandson and the central figure in this book. Sixth in the line of Qing emperors, Qianlong reigned for sixty years, from 1736 to 1795, abdicating in 1795 but retaining behind-the-scenes control until his death in 1799. He thus held power longer than any other ruler in China's history. If it is difficult for us today to grasp what this means, imagine if John F. Kennedy were to have remained president of the United States from his election in 1960 until 2024.

Like Elizabeth I or Louis XIV, Qianlong, as we will refer to him,[1] bestrode the age. His tastes shaped its consciousness and his name defined its style. Like them, too, Qianlong was intensely aware of his image and took pains to shape it in the ways he deemed most flattering. His fame spread around the world: In the opinion of no less an authority than Voltaire, eighteenth-century Europe's most celebrated man of letters, the Manchu monarch approached the ideal of the true philosopher-king. Qianlong was as proud of his personal literary accomplishments, collected and printed in over thirty huge volumes, as of the military exploits that earned him the nickname, "Old Man of the Ten Perfect Victories." That he invented this nickname himself suggests that he was vainglorious and

---

[1]Strictly speaking, it is proper to refer to him as "the Qianlong emperor," since "Qianlong" was the name assigned to his reign, not his given name. However, for simplicity's sake, I will use the shorter "Qianlong" in this book.

egotistical (apart from being the longest-lived emperor in Chinese history, he was also the most-painted).

But there is no getting around the debt that modern China owes to Qianlong. During his reign, the empire grew to its greatest extent in centuries, assuming the basic geographic form it continues to have today. The incorporation of different domains—from Mongolia to the Himalayas, and from the Sea of Okhotsk to Lake Balkash—proceeded according to Qianlong's universalist vision, according to which he ruled benevolently and impartially over men and women of many languages and faiths. His active promotion of agricultural expansion and regional trade made for a time of broad prosperity. The domestic economy thrived, bringing a rising standard of living to the majority of his people, the richest of whom possessed some of the greatest fortunes on earth. Cultural production swelled. Nowhere else in the world were so many books published, and the masterpieces produced by the studios, kilns, and workshops of Qianlong's empire not only decorated its palaces and better homes but continue even now to to fill the world's museums and supply its auction houses with beautiful objects. China then was a trading power internationally as well—a position it would not enjoy again until the early twenty-first century.

Given Qianlong's undisputed importance, it is surprising that there is no biography of him in English or any other Western language. The only book devoted to him is Harold Kahn's classic *Monarchy in the Emperor's Eyes*, published in 1971, to which the present account is much indebted. Ultimately, however, that account is really more an anti-biography: for as Kahn elegantly showed, we cannot ever really know the emperor. We can only catch glimpses of his image in different mirrors, each one offering its own distortion of the imperial persona. In the end, it is impossible to say which image is the true one.

Image-making is a large part of the story told here. But in the thirty-eight years since Kahn's study was published, enough chinks have appeared in the public relations armor surrounding Qianlong that today we can, I think, get something of a sense of who he was. The opening of the vast archives of the Qing bureaucracy to scholars from around the world has stimulated an outpouring of scholarship on many aspects of eighteenth-century history, including political institutions, military campaigns, foreign relations, intellectual trends, and economic changes. I have done my best to integrate this new research into a snapshot of Qianlong and his age, relying most heavily on Chinese scholarship, which has produced more than ten book-length treatments of Qianlong since 1987. Notes on these sources and additional readings may be found at the back of the book. Throughout, my goal has been to provide a brief, accurate, and lively introduction to one of the most remarkable and influential figures of world history.

Like all authors, I have accumulated my share of debts in writing this book, most especially to other scholars whose books and articles have been so valuable to me. These are listed in the notes. Here, I will limit myself to expressing my gratitude to just a few people. First thanks must go to Donald Sutton, who suggested this book to me, and to my first editors at Longman, Erika Gutierrez and Janet Lanphier, as well as to Charles Cavaliere at Pearson, for their patience and encouragement over a considerably longer period than anyone expected. I would also like to thank the several readers whose comments resulted in vital improvements to the text and saved me from many mistakes: R. D. Arkush (University of Iowa), Jonathan Dresner (The University of Hawaii at Hilo), Huaiyin Li (University of Texas), Creston Long (Salisbury University), Mark W. McLeod (University of Delaware), David K. McQuilkin (Bridgewater College), David A. Meier (Dickinson State University), Daniel Meissner (Marquette University), Louis Perez (Illinois State University), Lisa Tran (California State University, Fullerton), John A. Tucker (East Carolina University).

On a more personal note, I would like to record here first the generous support so lovingly offered by my wife and son. My debt to them will be hard to repay. I owe special thanks to Blaine Gaustad, Michael Chang, and Dorothy Elliott, who read through the entire manuscript and provided much detailed and constructive criticism, as well as to Rena, who always made sure I had a place to work. My gratitude goes also to Nancy Berliner of the Peabody-Essex Museum, for her help with illustrations, as well as to Michael Chang, Bennet Bronson, and Chuimei Ho for permission to use their translations of Qianlong's words in Chapters 4, 5 and 7. All other translations from Chinese and Manchu are my own. I of course take responsibility for any mistakes—of translation, fact, or interpretation.

MCE
LEXINGTON, MASSACHUSETTS

List of Maps
and Illustrations

1

Emperor in the Making

We go back to 1735. In April, *Alcina,* an opera by King George's favorite composer, George Frideric Handel, debuted in London's Covent Garden. In Leipzig that September, Johann Sebastian Bach welcomed the birth of his eleventh son, Johann Christian, who would later be a teacher of Mozart. Shortly after the birth of the youngest Bach, the Swedish naturalist Linnaeus published the first version of his great taxonomical work, the *Systema Naturae,* in Leiden. In Philadelphia, a young Benjamin Franklin was busy penning new pieces to include in *Poor Richard's Almanack,* while in Edo (today's Tokyo), the experimental cultivation of the sweet potato by the shogun's botanist proved successful, resolving a long-standing crisis of food supply in Japan. And that October in Beijing, the Yongzheng emperor, ruler of the wealthiest and most populous realm in the world, lay on his deathbed.

Death of an Emperor

Years of overwork had taken their toll on the body of the Son of Heaven, who was fifty-seven. When he had become seriously ill a few years before, in 1729, it had not been easy for the emperor's counselors to persuade him to relax his demanding schedule—the first meetings beginning at five in the morning, the last memoranda drafted after midnight—and take some rest. Now, again, he showed signs of being unwell. At first he had been able to conduct official business from his bed, but after twenty-four hours he suddenly weakened and was too feeble to do anything except receive two of his grown sons, Prince Bao,[1] and one other, who attended him anxiously all day. By evening his condition had deteriorated still further. Two high-ranking princes, both brothers of the dying emperor, were called to where he lay in the Yuanming yuan, a secondary palace complex a few miles north of the capital. A little later these representatives of the imperial family were joined by five other men, all senior ministers and imperial chamberlains. The time had arrived, the emperor told those assembled, to name his successor.

---

[1]Pronounced *bow,* as in "take a bow." To guide the reader, a key to the pronunciation of proper names and terms appearing in the text is provided at the end of the book.

In an empire like the Qing, where there was no officially proclaimed heir apparent, the transfer of power was an awesome and unpredictable event. Unlike the Han Chinese rulers of the preceding Ming dynasty, the Manchu emperors of the Qing did not automatically assign the title of crown prince to the emperor's eldest son. Instead, they handled succession in the fashion of the Mongols and the Turks, whose political traditions lay closer to their own: After a ruler died, his closest relatives, together with leading nobles of the realm, convened a council to decide who among the emperor's sons or other male kin was most fit to become the next ruler. Though it risked infighting, such a method had the advantage of helping to assure that leadership fell into capable hands, and it was in this way that all Yongzheng's predecessors had been chosen to ascend the throne. But not Yongzheng himself.

Many years before, Yongzheng's father, the Kangxi emperor, had chosen to depart from Manchu precedent. He proclaimed his first-born son to be his successor, an experiment that ended badly when the crown prince turned out to be vicious, erratic, and inclined to abuse of power. In a stunning reversal of fortune, the ne'er-do-well was arrested, stripped of his titles, and thrown into prison. Deeply disillusioned, Kangxi bitterly swore he would never name any other heirs; and when he died in late 1722 there was much speculation about which of his remaining sons—there were more than twenty—would succeed to the throne. So tense was the atmosphere that Beijing was put under martial law for a week until the successful claimant had emerged from amid dark, and still today poorly understood, maneuverings to take control. That claimant turned out to be Kangxi's fourth son, the Yongzheng emperor.

Having come to power under what some considered questionable circumstances, Yongzheng had determined at once to find a way to prevent another uncertain succession in the future, while at the same time avoiding the problems that arose with an openly designated heir apparent. The solution he struck upon was to choose a successor himself—no more councils—and to make public the fact that a successor had been appointed, but to keep the successor's precise identity a secret, thereby minimizing factional politics between potential rival heirs. Thus, in September 1723, a year after becoming emperor, Yongzheng summoned his top counselors to the Forbidden City and explained that he had chosen the son who would succeed him and had written his name on a piece of paper which he was sealing in a small, damask-covered wooden casket that would be placed in the Qianqing Palace, one of the main audience halls in the Imperial City. But it would not be placed just anywhere in the palace. It was to be kept directly above the throne, some thirty feet up, behind a large wooden plaque bearing four Chinese characters exhorting good governance. Everyone would remember where the box was and what was inside it, but no one would open it until the proper time.

Unknown to all but two of the emperor's closest advisors, the name of the heir also was written on another piece of paper that the emperor kept with him when he was in residence at the Yuanming yuan. He had taken this precaution in 1730, after recovering from illness the year before. Now that the emperor was slipping fast, the chief eunuch was ordered to search the emperor's private quarters for this document, which was wrapped in a piece of yellow paper with the word "sealed" written across the back. Before long the edict was produced and, in the presence of the emperor and the others gathered in the emperor's chamber, the name of the future monarch was read aloud. Less than four hours later Yongzheng was dead.

In deep mourning and amid the tightest possible security, the imperial entourage returned swiftly to the confines of the Imperial City. There the identity of the new emperor was formally confirmed before daybreak the next morning. In front of all assembled, the chief of the imperial guard first retrieved the damask coffer from above the throne and presented it solemnly to the emperor's fourth son, Prince Bao, who, having been with his father all the preceding day and present when his name had been read out a few hours earlier, was prepared for what was about to transpire. At his side were two uncles as well as his father's top ministers, the Han Chinese Zhang Tingyu and the Manchu Ortai, all of whom also had been with the dying emperor the previous night. The twenty-four-year-old prince knelt, opened the box, and removed the edict within. He then broke the seal and opened the testament Yongzheng had written in 1723. The bright light of dawn left no doubt: the name, in his father's handwriting, was his own. Overcome, the new Son of Heaven collapsed on the floor (the official record says he wept) before quickly regaining his composure as the announcement of the succession was made to the court. The Qianlong reign had begun.

Rearing a Prince

Dramatic as it all was, few could have been very surprised by this turn of events. It was widely known that Prince Bao—or Hungli, to use his Manchu given name—was his father's favorite and that he had been well liked by his grandfather, the Kangxi emperor. He had been given the best possible education and was scrupulously trained in the arts of war as well as in painting, poetry, and calligraphy. In 1733 he had been granted a princely rank, which brought with it prestige and a significant income, along with new responsibilities. Other imperial sons, too, were assigned official duties. Some were made princes. But none of them enjoyed as much favor as Hungli.

The future Qianlong emperor was born in Beijing late in the night of September 25, 1711, just a year, in fact, before the birth of another famous monarch, Frederick the Great of Prussia. His father had already fathered three sons who lived beyond infancy, but by 1711 two of those three had died, leaving only one surviving son, who was then seven years old.[2] The excitement and relief in the household at the arrival of another potential male heir was considerable, although the fact that Hungli's mother was a low-ranking consort at the time did

---

[2]Ages in this book are presented following Western custom, i.e., calculated from the date of birth. Chinese ages are customarily measured in *sui*, and children are considered to be one *sui* old when they are born. Thus a child of three *sui* in China would be considered a two-year-old child in the West. Where a source indicates an age in *sui*, I have routinely subtracted 1 for the approximate age by the Western count.

not augur especially well for her son's future, since in elite households the status of one's birth mother very often influenced one's chances in life. Hungli's eventual succession guaranteed, however, that she would become one of the most celebrated and honored women in Chinese history, as Chapter 3 will show.

Very little is known about Qianlong's earliest years, apart from the time and date of his birth, which was recorded in the "Jade Register," the comprehensive genealogy kept of all members of the imperial family. No doubt he was shown every attention by his parents as well as by his wet nurse and others of the household staff charged with minding the children. We do know that Qianlong began his formal schooling at five, the age at which children might start to learn to read. In China, this was a more involved process than simply reciting one's ABCs. Young students—almost exclusively boys—began by memorizing a given text, such as the *Thousand-Character Classic*, an old text written in an antique style very different from the everyday spoken language. At first, students repeated after the teacher without the benefit of understanding the meaning of the words. Only once the student could say his lessons perfectly would the teacher instruct him in the meaning of each character in the text, as well as how to recognize and write every one. Normally this initial phase of one's education took a few years— in Qianlong's case, about three years, which we know because he once noted that he could read a book by the age of eight. After the acquisition of basic literacy, students proceeded to memorize and study the more challenging texts of the Confucian canon, the foundation of all higher learning and the basis for competition in the national examinations which qualified one for a career as an official, the one and only career that mattered in imperial China.

Though its members did not participate in the examinations, the imperial family, like other wealthy elites, took the education of its youth very seriously. For only by mastering the doctrines of China's great philosophers, the lessons of China's long history, and the subtle aesthetics of Chinese poetry and painting could the ruler understand what was required of him in his role as intermediary between Heaven and Earth. By the same token, only in this way could those whose role was to assist the emperor properly carry out their duties. As Qianlong commented later in his reign, "Everything one needs to know about self-cultivation and the government of men, about serving one's lord and being an official, is to be found in books." (Whether or not he really believed this is another question.) Since to promote talent and virtue was to ensure the dynasty's success, Beijing's princely households sought the very best teachers for its sons and, less frequently, its daughters. Such a teacher was Fumin, a Manchu scholar of distinction, who was Qianlong's first and longest-serving teacher. Fumin was brought in when Qianlong had just learned to read and stayed on after his father became the Yongzheng emperor. He later would teach Qianlong's sons, too. Under Fumin's tutelage, Qianlong made rapid progress, and within a couple of years had gained a solid foundation in history and poetry. Other teachers were soon introduced, and by the time he was twelve he had mastered the Four Books (the *Analects* of Confucius, the *Mencius*, the *Great Learning*, and the *Doctrine of the Mean*, texts dating from before the third century BCE that had been the backbone of the standard curriculum in imperial China since around the year 1100.

CH1.
#2.

Qianlong's education was not limited to this, however. In addition to the rigorous intellectual demands of the Chinese curriculum, he faced the challenges of learning to be a Manchu. This meant studying the Manchu language, with a grammar and writing system entirely different from Chinese, as well as Mongolian, another Altaic language similar to Manchu. To instill in them a sense of their own past, students also learned about early Manchu history, including the miraculous birth of a mythic ancestor in the peaks of the Long White Mountains far to the northeast, near Korea; the rise to power, centuries later, of a minor chieftain, Nurhaci, in defiance of his master, the Ming emperor; Nurhaci's creation of the vaunted Eight Banners military machine in 1615; the establishment of the Qing dynasty in 1636 by Nurhaci's son, Hong Taiji; and the fall of the Ming in 1644, followed by the Qing conquest of China, led by Hong Taiji's younger brother, Dorgon. For Qianlong and his peers in the early 1700s, these were not so much history lessons as family stories, since the principals were their own forefathers (Hong Taiji was Qianlong's great-great-grandfather). There was also intensive training in archery and horsemanship, skills that all Manchus, as a conquering people of martial origins, were expected to possess. Noble sons were no exception. Indeed, they were expected to set an example for others to follow. The days were thus long for the young Qianlong, beginning well before dawn and ending at dusk. The only holiday was at the New Year.

After his father succeeded to the throne in 1722, the elevation of Qianlong's status from imperial grandson (of whom there were easily 100) to imperial son (of whom there were three), meant that his education became that much more important. Famous classical scholars, all of them prominent officials with broad experience and extensive connections, were appointed to teach in the special study reserved for the emperor's sons inside the Forbidden City. From his distinguished tutors Qianlong received further instruction in the classics, the histories, and the many commentaries on these, all of which was aimed to make him aware of his obligations and responsibilities and to inculcate the correct values expected of a virtuous and just prince. Sloth and arrogance were vices to be avoided at all cost. To this end, and to assure the proper student–teacher relationship inside the classroom, Yongzheng ordered his sons to bow to their teachers when greeting them—a seemingly innocent command, except that imperial tutors, like other high officials, were *themselves* supposed to bow before the emperor's sons. (Before their first meeting the emperor was careful to warn the teachers that a bow was coming, so they would not attempt to prevent this reversal of the usual etiquette.) Qianlong never forgot having to do this. So deep was the impression his teachers made on him that in 1779, when he was nearly 70, he wrote a lengthy poem, "Longing for the Old Days," in which he reminisced fondly, as old men often do, about his schoolboy days more than fifty years before.

CH1.
#2.

CH1.
#1.

Young Hungli

It is difficult to know what kind of young man Qianlong was. Official chronicles tell us that he was intelligent, even-tempered, respectful, and courteous. This was in marked contrast to his older brother, who was not only greedy and lazy, but also treated ceremony lightly: It is said that he liked to organize mock funerals at which he played the corpse, and "guests" were asked to wail and mourn for fun. Such frivolity was wholly alien, even repulsive, to the serious Qianlong. We also know that Qianlong was fond of study and prided himself on his scholarly accomplishments even as a young man.

More information about his youth comes from a collection of juvenile poems and essays Qianlong published in 1730, to which his teachers contributed laudatory prefaces. If we are to believe what they said about him then, the future emperor was an exceptional student who applied himself earnestly to whatever material was set before him. One of the prefaces complimented him in these terms: "From the classical, historical, and philosophical writers to the abstrusities of the *Essential Metaphysics* to the origins of the various types of rhapsodies, there was nothing he did not comprehend." Another tutor was even more fulsome in his praise, writing, "The majesty of his deportment is that of the placid river and the mountain pass; the breadth of his heart that of the gusting breeze and burbling spring; the elegance of his prose that of billowing clouds and lush fog; the harmony of his rhymes the pairing of gold and matching of jade." From such hyperbole we might well conclude that Qianlong was something of a teacher's pet, but these raptures arose from more than simple favoritism toward a gifted student. By the early 1720s, popular wisdom already had it that Qianlong was being groomed for the throne. It would have been foolish for anyone to have written anything other than glowing compliments about his person and his accomplishments. Even at this early date, we can be sure that the imperial image-making machine was already at work.

Yet it must be said that the twenty-year-old Qianlong does seem to have been unusually conscientious and solemn. The preface he himself wrote to this collection of juvenilia contains many laudable, if perhaps predictable, statements that reflect the Confucian morality he had imbibed:

> I often look at what I have written and examine my own behavior by it. For if I were unable to reform my behavior through contemplation, such that my words and my deeds failed to correspond—if I were able to know but unable to act— well, what greater shame could I know than that?

There is also this startlingly honest admission:

> Each time I reflect on how I have received the generous favor of my father the emperor—who has instructed me in ways at once heartfelt and precise and has chosen for me wise teachers to relieve my ignorance through their tutelage— I redouble my efforts to correct my errors and aim for greater perfection. Idling about in a spirit of lethargy and doing nothing or getting fed up with poetry and books while there is yet so much I do not understand, and while I am yet so weak and the cultivation of my sentiments is still so immature—when I think about this in the middle of the night, I am terrified.

Knowing he would almost certainly become emperor one day seems to have provoked at least the occasional sleepless night and stirred in him fears of inadequacy.

That Hungli was tormented by such anxieties is understandable—he was, after all, only human. But that he should reveal his humanity in such a frank way is somewhat unexpected, especially in light of his later career, when he carefully cultivated an almost god-like image.

Destined to Rule

If in the early 1730s it seemed likely that Hungli would one day succeed to the throne, it was not just because of the formal preparation the emperor's fourth son had received but also because of the special relationship he had enjoyed with his grandfather, Kangxi. The bond between them formed very late in Kangxi's life but early enough in Hungli's to leave an unforgettable impression.

Their first formal introduction seems to have been in April 1722, when Yongzheng (at the time still Prince Yong) invited his elderly father to visit him at his suburban villa at the Yuanming yuan to enjoy the peonies, then in full bloom. There, beneath the unadorned beams of cedar and free from the usual court etiquette of the Forbidden City, Yongzheng presented his eleven-year-old son to Kangxi. Immediately taken with the boy, Kangxi insisted that the young prince take up residence in the imperial palace, where he would be close at hand and could attend school together with some of Kangxi's younger sons, who, though technically Qianlong's uncles, were his same age. From this time until Kangxi's death seven months later, grandfather and grandson were inseparable. At meals Kangxi gave him the tastiest morsels, and kept Qianlong at his side even when responding to official reports or meeting with ministers. He also saw to it that Qianlong received personal instruction in riding, archery and the use of firearms, and sent him off to practice in the small hunting park kept for the emperor's pleasure southwest of Beijing. Qianlong left a poem about one such excursion:

> Morning fog gathered in autumn sky, the heavens remote, watery-white.
> Forth to the hunt from walled gates we ride, through suburbs cold we weave astride.
> Our falcons spy pheasants rising in flocks; arrows fly, fleet like pairings of hawks.
> Upon his cane, we meet an old man on the way, who talks till the sun angles low with the day.
> Then, smoke from the village, distantly, hanging faintly purple on thin trees;
> Back in the saddle, riding into the evening wind—the hunt over, the heart still gladdened.

Did he show this modest composition to his grandfather? What did Kangxi think? Of this, regrettably, we have no record.

Come the summer, Qianlong was invited to go with the court on its retreat to the mountain villa in the forest at Chengde, a few days' journey north from Beijing, where the emperor would spend a month or two every year. At Chengde, Kangxi's fondness for Hungli became even more apparent. In these relaxed surroundings they shared the same residence and spent much of every day in each other's company. Qianlong watched with fascination as the emperor practiced his calligraphy, so Kangxi happily gave him some samples to keep, knowing that all would see in such a gesture a clear mark of the sovereign's partiality. The old emperor helped Qianlong with his studies and encouraged him with rewards for special accomplishments, as when Qianlong recited from memory all of a famous text in praise of the lotus, whose flowers emerge pristine and pure out of the mud and muck. Then there was the occasion one evening when, dining with Yongzheng at his son's separate quarters at Chengde, Kangxi made a point of asking to meet Qianlong's mother. He praised Lady Niohuru as a "lucky woman," implying that her son was destined to bring her "great honor." Everyone knew what *that* was supposed to mean.

The 1722 imperial visit to Chengde was a fateful one. In what would become one of the most famous incidents of Qianlong's life, he almost met an untimely end on an excursion to Mulan, the imperial game reserve located north of Chengde, just on the southern rim of the Mongolian steppe. The land at Mulan had been presented as a gift to the Kangxi emperor in 1683 by a Mongol tribe allied with the Qing. Hunts were organized here early every fall, a way of maintaining Manchu traditions that was very important to Kangxi, and would be later to Qianlong, too. Since all young men were expected to uphold this national custom, Kangxi included Qianlong in his own entourage and arranged a special demonstration of his grandson's skills so that everyone in the court could see for themselves that, even though he was only 11, he deserved to ride with the rest. Shooting from horseback, Qianlong hit the target with all five bolts, an impressive display. The emperor was so delighted that he presented him with a yellow riding jacket, an honor usually reserved for distinguished servants of the throne. Out in the field, though, tragedy nearly struck. Having shot a bear with his musket, Kangxi ordered Qianlong to finish it off with an arrow, planning in this way to let the boy return home covered in glory. Qianlong had just mounted his horse to approach more closely when the wounded beast suddenly reared up and charged right toward him. The horrified emperor quickly fired one more time and dispatched the animal for good, then turned anxiously to check on his grandson, who was still sitting calmly in the saddle, reins in hand, completely unfazed. The boy's composure under pressure was far more impressive than anything Kangxi could have staged. When he returned to his tent that afternoon, the emperor, agitated but undoubtedly relieved the bear had not waited longer before making his move, remarked to one of his wives, "This boy is destined to lead a charmed life."

Qianlong's brush with disaster became part of the official record and eventually acquired the status of legend. The symbolism of the youngster coolly staring down the charging, angry bear endowed the story with the message that Qianlong possessed special powers and that he was meant to rule over the empire, facing off against enemies internal and external with the same cool determination. This, plus Kangxi's sentimental attachment to the boy, was pointed to by some as the real reason that Yongzheng was allowed to succeed to the throne. Qianlong himself contributed to this tradition, writing fondly of his grandfather's special affection for him and composing sentimental poems in his tribute years later, such as one about a fancy gun he had gotten from him. But he pointedly distanced himself from the rumors about his father's succession, claiming that it was in fact owing to Kangxi's fondness for his father, Yongzheng, that he (Qianlong) became such a favorite.

Favorite Son   CH1. #3

Qianlong's complicated relationship with his father is much less celebrated than that with his grandfather, yet Yongzheng's influence on Qianlong was at least as great as that of Kangxi. Certainly Yongzheng held very high hopes for Hungli, or he never would have chosen him as heir or taken the trouble to introduce him to his father in the spring of 1722. Indeed, the evidence suggests overwhelmingly that Qianlong had always been the apple of his father's eye. For instance, in 1723, having for the first time as emperor led the Grand Sacrifice—the most important event of the annual ritual cycle, held at the beginning of the year to ensure a bountiful harvest—Yongzheng invited his son to share in the consumption of the meat used in the sacrifice. This gesture symbolized the confidence Yongzheng placed in Qianlong and foreshadowed the emperor's decision, carried out later that year, to secretly name Qianlong his successor. There is also the revealing testimony of Qianlong's younger brother, who once wrote, "When my older brother and I lived with father at his princely residence, morning and night we slept in the same room and shared the same food. Whenever father saw him, he was always pleased; whenever father heard his voice, he was always happy."

One witness to the closeness between Qianlong and his father was the noted court artist Giuseppe Castiglione, an Italian Jesuit in service to the Qing who painted an extraordinary portrait of the two of them, probably sometime around 1730 (more on Qianlong and the Jesuits may be found in Chapter 8). The painting depicts two figures, an older man on the left, who is Yongzheng, and a younger man on the right, Qianlong. They seem to be posing in a garden, an effect heightened by the small plum tree blooming in the foreground (partially hidden behind an unusually shaped rock), by the tufts of grass, and by the tall willows growing behind the two men. On the other hand, the deep blue background casts the whole scene into the realm of the abstract, removing it from any real landscape. The images, too, are idealized; Qianlong in particular is given such delicate features as to appear almost feminine. It is an intimate portrait, measuring only 30 inches high by 18 inches wide (76 cm × 46 cm), clearly something executed for personal, not official, use. (See Figure 1.1.)

This remarkable painting offers some clues to help us learn more about Qianlong and his father. The symbolic vocabulary of this portrait appears to be entirely Chinese. By depicting the present and future emperors dressed and coiffed like Chinese gentlemen from a previous age, the painting aimed not only to emphasize the intimacy of their relationship but also the instant "antiquity" of the future succession, something like the effect achieved by painting early modern European rulers in Roman garb. This emphasis on orthodoxy and classicism is seen also in the branch that Yongzheng extends to Qianlong, which symbolizes the continuity of legitimate rule that will pass from father to son. The hierarchy

寫真世寧擅繢我少
年時入室曙然者不
知此是誰
壬寅暮春御題

Figure 1.1 Giuseppe Castiglione (1688–1766). *Spring's Peaceful Message.* ca. 1730. Ink and colors on silk. Palace Museum, Beijing. This unusual portrait of Yongzheng (on the left) and the young Hungli—the future Qianlong emperor—symbolized both the close relationship between father and son and their hopes for a trouble-free succession. © Palace Museum, Beijing.

between throne and heir is further evident in Qianlong's much smaller size relative to Yongzheng and in his posture, bent as if bowing to his father's authority. When, in 1782, he saw the painting again after many years, Qianlong wrote an inscription at the top: "In portraiture Castiglione was masterful. He painted me [thus] during my younger days; the white-headed one who enters the room today does not recognize who this is."

As Qianlong reached his majority, Yongzheng took further steps to prepare his son for the job that awaited him. In 1733, as already noted, he bestowed on Hungli a princely rank, the title of Prince Bao, meaning "Precious Prince." In the decree he said, "Fourth Son was formerly dearly loved by my father [i.e., Kangxi]. Now not only is he already twenty, but his learning is also growing. This cheers my heart." By making Hungli a prince, Yongzheng gave him opportunities to gain hands-on experience in running the empire. On the one hand, he involved Qianlong directly in the planning of two military campaigns—one in the far west, the other in the south—campaigns that Qianlong would end up prosecuting further once he became emperor himself. In this way he became familiar with the exercise of power and learned the value of listening to experienced advisors and of having reliable information. He also learned of the primary importance of logistics and of knowing when to trust commanders. In the process, he became familiar with the Grand Council and the system of "palace memorials," institutional innovations his predecessors had introduced to make the management of the empire more effective (see Chapter 2).

On the other hand, on at least ten occasions Yongzheng also entrusted to Qianlong the job of taking part in important rituals, such as sacrifices to the ancestors, to the Altar of Grain, to Confucius, and to Guan Di, revered as the "patron saint" of war. Officiating in this capacity should not be thought of as the contemporary equivalent of christening ships or dedicating hospitals. In standing in for the emperor, Qianlong was charged with conducting rites that for two millennia had represented the connection between Heaven and Earth, a connection only the emperor could broker.

Qianlong knew from his reading what Confucius said of the ancient emperor Shun, that he "did nothing but gravely and reverently occupy his royal seat." As Prince Bao, it was precisely such reverence he had to demonstrate in carrying out the duties his father assigned. If the country encountered setbacks—a poor harvest, a rebellion, a military defeat on the frontier—one cause could be held to be a lack of sincerity in the performance of the rituals keeping the universe in proper order. As a young man, Qianlong could already feel the weight of the earth pressing upon him. Soon he would feel its full burden. He was as well prepared and as well suited for the job that awaited him as any emperor in history.

2

Qianlong Takes Charge

Two years' practice was all Qianlong got before becoming monarch for real. Yongzheng's sudden demise came as a shock, and rumors spread either that he had been poisoned by Daoist (Taoist) masters promising him an elixir of immortality or that he had been secretly assassinated. Of these conspiracy stories, the most popular involved the daughter of Lü Liuliang, one of Yongzheng's most hated critics. Supposedly she had received training in ninja-like techniques and stole into the emperor's room late at night to murder him and gain revenge for her family's suffering. However fanciful these and other such tales may have been, it *was* true that two days after Yongzheng died, Qianlong turned all the Daoist priests out of the palace. It was also true that the main figures involved in the Lü case, including those who earlier had been pardoned by Yongzheng, were arrested on Qianlong's orders and put to death. These facts lent just enough credence to the popular pseudo-histories that circulated widely.

In spite of these tremors of unease, the transfer of mandate happened without any of the uncertainty that had accompanied Yongzheng's succession. People who wondered whether the mechanism the late emperor had put in place would work were no doubt greatly reassured when the damask box was taken down, Hungli's name read out, and the young prince acclaimed as the new emperor. Ten days later, on October 18, 1735, Qianlong was formally enthroned in an impressive early morning ceremony in the grandest building of the Forbidden City, the Taihedian, or Hall of Supreme Harmony, at which time a new reign name was announced, to take effect the first day of the New Year.

The New Emperor

In China, the selection of an auspicious name under which an emperor would rule was an integral part of the inauguration of a new reign period. In principle, the name invoked divine assistance and augured the ruler's success. We do not possess any explanation of why the Chinese name "Qianlong" was selected. The character *qian* figures prominently in the *Classic of Changes* (*Yijing* or *I-ching*), where it represents the primal force of the universe; it is also associated with male energy and with heaven. It had been used many times before in reign names, as had the Chinese character *long*, which has a variety of meanings, including "great," "majestic," and "prosperous." Together, "Qianlong" translates roughly as "Heaven's Flourishing" or "Cosmic Prosperity." The corresponding Manchu reign name, "Abkai wehiyehe," literally means, "By Heaven Supported." In both cases, the intent was to convey the essential unity of Heaven's will with the emperor's own rule.

His given name now taboo, Qianlong ascended the throne. By Western reckoning he was just twenty-four years old. Unlike his grandfather and great-grandfather, he was not so young that he needed the help of a regent from whose influence he would later need to free himself, yet he was young enough that, unlike his father, he carried little political baggage with him. His enemies were few and his mandate clear. As much is reflected in the portrait we have of him at this moment, painted on the first anniversary of his rule by the Italian Jesuit Castiglione (see Figure 2.1). We see Qianlong dressed in a formal fur-collared court robe embroidered with dragons, clouds, and waves, the symbols of imperial power. He looks out at us confidently, without pretense. The face is a longish oval, the features regular and handsome, the expression poised and intelligent. The lips are distinctively full, the ears and chin prominent, the complexion fair, with no trace of facial hair (later depictions would show him with a hint of a moustache). Compared to the formal portrait painted the year before, reproduced on the front cover, we can detect a certain hardening of the lines around the mouth, but this is obviously the face of a young man optimistic about his future and confident of his ability to rule a magnificent empire.

Overview of the Qing Imperium

The realm over which Qianlong presided was not a nation in the modern sense, but an empire comprised of different domains and peoples incorporated in distinct and inherently unequal ways under the authority of a single, universal sovereign. The provinces of China proper formed its core. Here were the richest agricultural zones, the densest commercial and transportation networks, the largest cities, busiest ports, main centers of industry, and a vast number of artisanal factories and workshops. Over 200 million people lived here, constituting 90 percent of Qianlong's subjects, most of them ethnic Han Chinese densely settled in villages, towns, and small cities. The country's few large cities—Beijing, Nanjing, Guangzhou—were home to only about 7 percent of the population.

The Chinese provinces, sometimes referred to as the "inner lands," were surrounded by the "outer lands" of Manchuria, Mongolia, Tibet, the southern provinces of Yunnan, Guizhou, Guangxi, and the island of Taiwan (conquered in 1683 and made part of Fujian Province). These peripheral zones (another zone, East Turkestan, was yet to be added to the empire when Qianlong took power) were more sparsely populated and generally far less prosperous than the Chinese heartland. Their climates exhibited greater extremes of heat, cold, and altitude, and their populations, which in many cases were dominated by non-Han ethnic groups such as Mongols, Tibetans, Turks, and Miao, were more diverse than

Figure 2.1 Giuseppe Castiglione (1688–1766). *Coronation Portrait of the Qianlong Emperor.* 1736. Ink and colors on silk. Palace Museum, Beijing. Qianlong was 25 years old when he sat for this large formal portrait by his favorite court artist, the Italian Castiglione. He holds a bead of a Buddhist rosary between the fingers of his left hand. © Palace Museum, Beijing.

those of China proper. Communication and transportation in the frontiers were more costly and less efficient than in the inner provinces, making life harder both for those who lived there as well as for those who would govern there. Poor as they were, these far-flung regions were very important to the empire's security, especially those in the north and west. These were regarded as strategically vital zones because they shielded China's heartland from unmediated contact with the world beyond (See Map 2.1).

By the last third of his reign, forty years after he took power, Qianlong had enlarged his domain to include a vast territory that stretched from the rich port cities on the coast of the Yellow Sea to the prosperous oasis towns on the old Silk Road, from storm-swept Sakhalin in the northeast to the snowy Himalayas in the southwest, from the southeastern tropical jungles of Sipsongpanna (on the Burmese border) to the northern deserts and grasslands of Mongolia. His rule was enabled by a complex combination of civilian and military administrative institutions, and his authority supported by a range of different ideological systems. The territories and inhabitants of inland China were ruled from Beijing via a civil bureaucracy operating at central, provincial, prefectural, and county levels, each level staffed by officials who held degrees earned through an extraordinarily competitive examination system. These officials, of whom there were not quite 25,000, held their posts at the pleasure of the emperor. They carried the emperor's directives down to the populace, reported regularly on local conditions, executed the laws of the land, and oversaw the transfer upward of tax revenues back to the government.

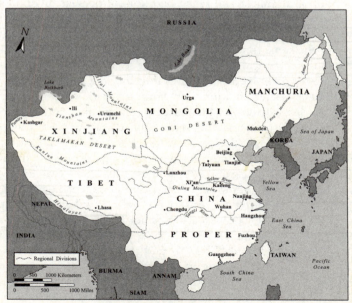

Map 2.1 The Qing Empire CA. 1780

In contrast, the frontier regions were mostly governed by quasi-military administrations staffed by members of the Eight Banners, the elite Qing military force (see Chapter 4), who kept order in part by threat of violence and in part through collaboration with local power-holders. Important exceptions to this pattern were the southeastern zone, which was a patchwork of standard administrative structures and imperially sanctioned tribal chieftaincies, and Tibet, which the Qing governed with the assistance either of allied Tibetan aristocrats, Tibetan prelates such as the Dalai Lama, or a combination of both. Some frontier lords paid taxes, while others offered valuable local goods (furs, ginseng, horses, jade) to the court instead. Many were required to pay homage to the emperor in person, either according to an established calendar or on an ad hoc basis. Political expediency dictated, and carefully structured ritual governed, most of these interactions. Throughout the realm, written records were maintained on just about everything—from population censuses to grain prices, tea harvests to snowfalls, horse farms to dike repairs—millions upon millions of pages of documentation, most in Chinese and some in Manchu, much of which has survived. Certainly as far as systematization and effectiveness of administration, no pre-modern state approached the Qing in terms of scale or sophistication.

In many respects, the constitution of the empire was broadly similar to the other great early modern land empires such as the Romanov, Ottoman, and Mughal. All were geographically extensive conglomerations of diverse peoples governed from a core state; all involved disparate hierarchies of status and privilege; all depended on a composite, flexible ideology of legitimation centered on the person of the ruler; all were modestly decentralized, combining direct with indirect rule (in general, the farther away from the center, the greater the reliance on the loyalty of native elites); all relied on a mix of persuasion and coercion to effect and maintain imperial unity; and all were hybrids, demonstrating relative tolerance with respect to internal differences of ethnicity, religion, language, and culture while at the same time striving to contain such differences, which carried potentially strong centrifugal forces that might tear the state apart. The encompassing principles of early modern empires thus differed radically from the ideals of autonomy and self-determination that characterize the modern nation-state.

Two things distinguished the Manchu empire from these other empires. One was that, as the successor state of the Han (206 BCE–220 CE), Tang (618–907 CE), Song (960–1276 CE), Yuan (1260–1368 CE), and Ming dynasties, the Qing inherited an imperial structure that presupposed a high degree of continuity with the past. Even as it opened certain possibilities, this 1,800-year legacy imposed certain limitations and expectations. Because in eighteenth-century China the ideals of good government were uniformly held to inhere in prior models, Qianlong—unlike, say, Peter the Great—was not free to innovate on too great a scale or to introduce sweeping changes in such time-honored institutions as the civil service, which had already been around for some one thousand years by then. This is not to say that innovation did not happen, only that when it did, it usually occurred in a tentative, unofficial, and indirect manner. History taught that dramatic political reforms usually ended up reversed, and history mattered too much for Qianlong to have dispensed with it casually. After all, historical precedents furnished a powerful legitimating force for interlopers like the Manchu emperors, who needed (or felt they needed) to convince skeptics that they were the true heirs of the Way passed down by earlier generations of Sons of Heaven, even though they were not Han Chinese.

Han awareness of Manchu differences and their occasional resentment of them is sometimes pointed to as one sign of a latent "nationalism" in early modern China that, while it obviously differed substantially from modern nationalist beliefs, greatly complicated life for Qing rulers. This points to the second distinguishing aspect of the Qing empire, which is that the Manchus were minority rulers, outnumbered by their subjects 250 to 1. While mindful that they had to share power with the majority Han Chinese, they were at the same time wary of sharing too much. Caught between needing to preserve their own special interests as a conquering elite and needing to admit educated Han literati to the ranks of the governing, Qing rulers had to negotiate a balance between pro-Manchu nativism and assimilationism. For example, when the Manchus took over, they forced all Han Chinese men to cut their hair in Manchu style (the top half of the pate shaved, the hair in the back gathered into a long plait) as a sign of their submission. Many viewed such an act as a violation of their loyalty either to the fallen Ming ruler or to their parents: one's body was regarded as having been a gift from one's mother and father, and to shave one's scalp, even halfway, amounted to a rejection of that inheritance. As a rule, those who were unwilling to comply with the haircutting order kept their hair but lost their heads. At the same time, the Qing court showed its willingness to stick with the tried-and-true civil service examinations as a way to recruit officials and adhere to the familiar curriculum of Confucian learning.

Having to balance ethnic particularity with sovereign universality was not a problem faced either by the Romanov tsars or the Ottoman sultans, who either came from the same ethnic stock as the ruled or who governed a population that lacked a single dominant ethnic group that could materially affect the terms under which outsiders might rule.[1] It was, however, a concern for the Mughal emperors of India. Under the broadminded Akbar (r. 1556–1605), the Mughals initially succeeded at balancing their interests as Muslim minority rulers with the expectations of their mostly Hindu subjects, who made up some 80 percent of the population. Their empire disintegrated in the seventeenth century, however, when later rulers tilted strongly toward their Persian Sufi roots, alienating all but a few local supporters. The Manchus, like the Mughals, found themselves operating in an adopted natural and cultural environment, but managed better than the Mughals in most respects. This success came, however, at the price of having to make far greater compromises with indigenous customs than the Mughals—who never adopted the Hindu religion—had to make.

---

[1] While the very idea of accepting a foreigner as a monarch might seem strange today, the practice was common enough in world history. For examples, recall that the "English" kings William III (r. 1689–1701) and George I (r. 1714–1727), though related to the British royal line (William through marriage), were both foreigners who never really learned to speak English.

His Father's Legacy

If in his coronation portrait Qianlong appeared optimistic, it was not without good reason. Thanks to his father, the Qing realm was in good shape. This state of affairs contrasted sharply with the alarming situation Yongzheng had inherited when he took over thirteen years before. At that time, corruption was rising, tax revenues were falling, and factionalism was rampant. Lost was the confidence of the last third of the seventeenth century, when a still-vigorous Kangxi had succeeded in consolidating Manchu rule, quelling the last threats from Ming loyalists in the south and Mongol chiefs in the north, recruiting scholars, expanding cultivable land, and providing tax relief. Heartbroken by the apostasy of his appointed successor and embittered by revelations of treachery among Chinese officials at court as well as among Mongol lords on the frontier, Kangxi was no longer able to devote the same energy as before to the management of the state. Though Qianlong was then too young to have sensed it, in those anxious years of the 1710s the question hovered in the air: Could the early promise of Qing rule have been exhausted so quickly?

After taking the throne in 1723, Yongzheng managed to reconsolidate the dynasty's fortunes through a combination of intimidation, attention to detail, and imaginative reforms. First and most important, he restored the empire's fiscal health, instituting policies that substantially improved tax collection rates by specifying exactly how much officials could tack on as a surtax percentage, collecting that money, and then applying part of it toward funding a new system to annually reward those who demonstrated a modicum of honesty. Fearlessly and ruthlessly seizing illegally gotten assets, Yongzheng also significantly increased penalties for corruption and abuse of position and, in general, tried to ensure that, wherever they might be in the hierarchy, officials would be too afraid to carry on the usual schemes of enriching themselves at the expense of the local peasantry and the national treasury. As a result, during the Yongzheng reign the imperial treasury grew from 8 million ounces of silver[2] to over 60 million, a vast fortune that would enable Qianlong to carry out projects that his father and grandfather only dreamed of. No wonder he appeared so serenely confident for his portrait.

Yongzheng had been active on other fronts, too. In addition to settling upon a new method for choosing a successor, he took further steps to root out factionalism, which he saw as the single greatest cause of weakness in his father's court. For instance, he stripped Manchu nobles of most of their special privileges and turned the Eight Banners military system into a tool of central imperial power. He also attempted to influence Chinese attitudes toward the Manchus. A good example is his handling of the case of the scholar Lü Liuliang, mentioned at the beginning of

---

[2]The Qing employed a bimetallic system of currency. Taxes and larger sums of money were usually rendered in silver, in units of one Chinese ounce or *liang* (= 1.41 oz. or about 40 grams), called a "tael" in English (from the Malay word *tahl*, "weight"). Payment of everyday sums was typically made using copper alloy cash, which were round coins with a square hole that allowed them to be strung together. Conversion rates between copper and silver varied; the ideal ratio was 1,000 cash to 1 tael.

this chapter. Like many of his contemporaries, Lü (1629–1683) despised having to adopt the Manchu tonsure and had written disparagingly of the Manchus as inferior "barbarians" who were unfit to rule China. When, forty-odd years after his death, Lü's racist attitudes surfaced publicly, Yongzheng was so enraged that he had Lü's body exhumed and profaned, executed his surviving son, and enslaved all the women in his family. Furthermore, he wrote a detailed refutation of Lü's arguments, titled, "A Record of Great Righteousness to Dispel Confusion." The emperor's tract was for a time required reading for every student in the country. Yongzheng wanted to force the Han to respect the Qing mandate, or, if not, to make sure they would be too afraid to challenge it openly. This political legacy was at least as important to Qianlong as the fiscal muscle he inherited. At the same time, like his father and grandfather, he never entirely shed the fear that the Chinese were ready at any moment to sabotage the Manchus should he lower his guard. In the 1760s, when reports reached him that, for mysterious reasons, peasants in a few counties in central China were snipping off their queues, fears of sedition and rebellion immediately seized Qianlong, who instigated an enormous witch hunt that turned up no signs of any conspiracy at all.

Though Yongzheng's accomplishments were many, the suddenness of his death meant that he left behind unfinished business: most notably, a rebellion in the southwest and negotiations with the Dzungar Mongols on the northwest frontier, matters Qianlong needed to address as soon as he became emperor. How would he proceed? What would be his ruling style? Would he be an autocratic micromanager like his father? Or would he be more like his grandfather, content to set an example and entrust the rest to his ministers?

First Steps

Qianlong was quite conscious that his first moves would be closely scrutinized. He also recognized the limitations of his own narrow experience in governing and relied heavily for advice on Zhang Tingyu and Ortai, the experienced counselors his father had named to guide him through the transition period. Both had been close to Yongzheng and enjoyed his absolute trust. Under Qianlong they would continue to enjoy extraordinary imperial favor, at least for a while. Guided by the advice of these statesmen, as well as his own reading of his father's record, Qianlong announced that he would not be continuing the politics of intimidation that marked the Yongzheng years.

He let this be known in an ingenious way, publicizing his intentions in what was advertised as Yongzheng's last testament. Such a testament was traditionally a forum for the late ruler to pass judgment on himself and lay the ground for his successor to change direction if he wished. In it, Yongzheng said—or, more likely, was made to say, since this kind of proclamation was frequently the work of others—that the harsh measures he had enforced had been necessary to stem the rot he found when he took power and were not meant to be permanent. Now that these abuses had been put right, the will read, "it was fine to think about restoring the old norms," that is, to revert to a more forgiving approach. By releasing this document just a few days after his father's death, Qianlong was promising to turn over a new leaf in government. Furthermore, by making it seem that his father had authorized such a shift, he avoided accusations of being unfilial, the worst charge that could be laid at the door of a monarch who claimed to base his rule on the teachings of the sages.

Many at court welcomed the announcement of a change in court policy. If some members of the lettered elite (to whom this document was mainly directed) were suspicious, there was quite a bit of evidence to suggest that Qianlong meant what he said. Within a few days of taking power, the young emperor pronounced an amnesty for scores of people who had been imprisoned or disgraced by Yongzheng. Those freed included some of Qianlong's uncles and other members of the imperial clan implicated in plots to oust Yongzheng in the mid-1720s, capable generals who had failed the emperor's trust, and otherwise competent officials who found themselves on Yongzheng's bad side and had been summarily cashiered, humiliated, expropriated, and in some cases exiled to the frontiers. By these actions, Qianlong hoped to heal the pain that went along with the rancor over the succession in 1723 and to close ranks among the Manchu elite split by that factionalism. To the extent he could, he wished to foster an atmosphere of clemency, unity, and goodwill that he could then turn to his own advantage. The grand-scale pardons of 1735–1736 also gave him the opportunity to demonstrate magnanimity and benevolence—another reason why, for centuries, newly enthroned emperors like Qianlong had routinely proclaimed amnesties. But Qianlong did not stop there. He forgave taxes, relaxed the law on salt smuggling (the sale of salt was an extremely lucrative state monopoly), and made a special effort to recruit talented scholars who had so far failed to make it through the regular examinations. In these ways the Qianlong era indeed marked the dawning of a bright new day. As one popular rhyme of those days ran, "Qianlong's a treasure, his grandfather's pleasure; Qianlong's cash, may it last and last."

Had our suspicious scholars looked a little more closely, however, they might have seen that Qianlong was not departing as far from his father's precedents as it first seemed. Even as he distanced himself from negative aspects of Yongzheng's rule, he made clear he was *not* looking to return to the "good old days" of the late Kangxi reign, when abuses of power went on virtually unchecked. Such was the message of the edict Qianlong issued one month after his enthronement:

In ruling, the important thing is to find the middle path. Generosity must thus be rectified by severity, and severity must be tempered by generosity. My revered ancestor [the Kangxi emperor], a man of deep humanity and great benevolence, ruled for sixty years. He nourished all living things such that everyone and everything was tranquil and at peace. So accustomed did he become to this that it might be said excessive generosity was a failing of his. When my father succeeded to the throne, he strictly enforced regulations and cleared up corrupt practices until all matters were properly ordered. If people fear the law they will avoid crime and will dare not be greedy. In this way my father was able to change things in time and bring them back to the middle way. His criticism of officials was nothing but his own way of showing utmost concern for the people. Now I am at the beginning of my reign.

I shall at every moment keep my father's principles as my principles, his policies as
my policies. But I shall also be mindful of balancing the stern and the mild, and of
moving deliberately, in order to achieve peaceful and righteous government.

This diplomatic decree reveals Qianlong's debt to his father and his grandfather
alike, while still respectfully criticizing their faults. For example, though Yongzheng
is said to have achieved the "middle way," the comment on Yongzheng's treatment
of officials ("nothing but his own way of showing utmost concern for the people")
implies that, in fact, Qianlong felt his father, despite his good intentions, was too
harsh. At the same time, he acknowledged that Kangxi had been too lax. The task
Qianlong set for himself was thus to find the right balance between mercy and
discipline, persuasion and coercion.

As he made clear elsewhere in the edict, even if he was aiming to err on the side of
leniency, the leniency he spoke of was not an "anything goes" attitude: "When I say
'generous' I mean the consideration appropriately reserved for soldiers and the pro-
tection appropriately offered to common people, not blanket forgiveness of all crimes
or the softening of all punishments." His intent, he explained here and in three more
edicts issued to officials within the next few months, was to offer his generosity in
exchange for a promise from those who served him that they would be strict with
themselves. Should they fail in this, he warned, he could and would be harsh himself.

We can conclude that Qianlong was somewhat torn as to precisely where the
"middle way" lay. He doubtless recalled the popularity that his grandfather had
enjoyed in his later years, but realized that without the edge of fear that
Yongzheng's authoritarian efficiency inspired in people, it would be difficult to
rule effectively. The dilemma was a classic one, rooted in different views of human
nature. The prince would always be faced with a choice, whether to entrust his
rule to strict laws and harsh penalties or to a belief in the exemplary power of his
own moral rectitude. Qianlong hoped to split the difference, and achieved his goal
for a while. But in the end, it seems, he came to resemble Kangxi more than
Yongzheng. As the years wore on, the same sort of decay set in, bringing to the late
Qianlong era the same scandals and corruption, while the lack of an obvious heir
(see Chapter 9) provoked the same worries over an uncertain future.

Experiments with Authority

These developments were still far in the future in 1735. In fact, despite
Qianlong's promises of mildness and his desire to create the impression of a break
with the past, the tone of the first years of his reign represents more than anything a continuation of the Yongzheng era. Rivalries did not disappear overnight.
Even as he soothed those whom his father had alienated, Qianlong emulated his
father in many ways, sounding much like the sardonic Yongzheng, for instance,
in ordering provincial officials to stop sending condolences, fruit, and other presents in sympathy for his father's passing:

I have received your memorial of condolence. Over the last two months
I have many times decreed that provincial officials should stop sending such

memorials, and I thought that by now you would have understood. Since you feel so bereaved by my father's death, the appropriate thing for you to do to repay his favor would be to put all your energies into administering local affairs!

Or in reprimanding officials who arrived late for audience:

Whenever I am due for audience, we send someone out to first ascertain whether everyone is already present [before I enter]. However, only after we have done this several times do we find that all are accounted for. Today was the same thing again. If you officials are late like this when it comes to imperial audiences, I can just imagine what it is like when you go to your offices every day!

More seriously, Qianlong was anxious, as his father had been, to ferret out new factions that might threaten his authority. One such was the clique led by his cousin Hungsi. The son of the "mad" crown prince who had died in custody under Kangxi, Hungsi had been treated well enough by Yongzheng, who offered him titles and an estate but did not give him an official position. This snub evidently frustrated him greatly. Around Hungsi gravitated other might-have-beens, all also Qianlong's cousins (in keeping with Chinese naming styles, everyone of that generation had names that began with the same character, in this case, "Hong," rendered "Hung" in Manchu), including Hungpu, the son of Prince Zhuang, Yongzheng's brother and a top advisor to Qianlong. As early as 1737 Qianlong had noted the potential problems posed by the Hungsi faction but resolved to wait before moving against them. His opportunity came in late 1739, when Hungsi showed up at Qianlong's birthday celebration in a sumptuous canary-yellow sedan chair of unmistakable imperial design and color. The chair was ostensibly a gift for the emperor, but Qianlong was not fooled. Within weeks Hungsi was accused of treason and brought before the Imperial Clan Court for trial, where it came out that he had approached a soothsayer with suspicious questions such as, "How long will the emperor live?" and "Will I still rise higher in the future?" Qianlong responded to this outrageous act much as his father would have. He commanded that Hungsi be placed under house arrest for the remainder of his life, that he and his entire family be expunged from the imperial genealogy, and that other members of the clique be deprived of their titles and stipends. Prince Zhuang was thrown out of office in disgrace and stripped of his ranks. The soothsayer was executed. "However much I would like to be big-hearted about this affair," Qianlong opined in passing his rulings, "I absolutely cannot pardon it."

Qianlong was equally stern in his treatment of lofty political veterans. When it emerged a few years after the Hungsi affair that one of Qianlong's tutors, Ortai, had lent his name to cover the formation of a secret caucus high in the government, the emperor reacted sternly. As a Manchu, Ortai (1680–1745) was able to enter official service without passing through the examinations and, thanks to a reputation for incorruptibility, had risen quickly under Yongzheng's patronage to become the most powerful Manchu in the land after the emperor. His prestige ensured that he, along with Zhang Tingyu, stayed on to assist Qianlong after 1735. This gave him the chance to win followers and gain more clout. Indeed, not long after becoming emperor, Qianlong noticed that among his leading officials, "the Manchus all depend for their thinking on Ortai, the Han all on Zhang Tingyu." This was a bad sign. China's was a political system without parties, where indeed the very idea of a political party was anathema (hadn't Confucius said, "The superior man is not a partisan"?). Qianlong warned his other officials not to trust everything they heard from these two power brokers. For him, as for earlier emperors, the only political tie that mattered, the only one that could be permitted, was the individual tie of loyalty between him and each official. Any group that held consistently similar opinions and acted in a coordinated fashion was branded a clique, and by definition a clique could only have private, selfish interests in mind, not the greater public good. That the divide between Zhang and Ortai fell broadly along ethnic lines only made things worse.

Thus, when it was brought to his attention in early 1743 that Ortai's son was mixed up with a certain ambitious official who had made a career out of charging others with corruption and that Ortai had protected him even when such charges proved false, he felt betrayed and accused him of partisanship. Qianlong warned Ortai, "I have used you in the past and I am forgiving you now, but this is hardly a guarantee that I will not punish you severely in the future!" From these cases we can see that even as he claimed to be the spiritual heir of the generous Kangxi, Qianlong was very much the son of his stern father. The same can be said of his handling of the two most pressing problems of these early years, the Miao rebellion and the Dzungar question. Qianlong's quick and effective resolution of both these matters, detailed below, concluded likely as they would have under Yongzheng, suggesting the labor of a son anxious to please his late father.

The Emperor's Schedule

Being emperor was hard work. Distracted as we moderns tend to be by the trappings of imperial power—grand palaces, servants, luxury, privilege—it is easy to forget how demanding the tasks of ruling could be, especially if one were determined to take them seriously, as Qianlong was.

The emperor's day began early, usually around five a.m., by which time the routine morning sacrifices to the shamanic spirits worshiped by the imperial clan had already happened. After rising and going through his morning ablutions, the emperor, attended by eunuchs, would dress, have breakfast, and then spend a short while reading history. This put him in the right frame of mind for the day ahead. By no later than seven o'clock he was prepared to greet his ministers. Depending on the nature of the day's business, this meeting might happen in the Qianqing Palace or just to the west, in the emperor's private study, the Yangxin Palace. Not surprisingly, discussions of official business took up a great deal of the emperor's day. Typical items on the agenda included reviewing reports from provincial officials about weather conditions, natural disasters, river conservation, land reclamation, harvests, and local prices; passing final judgment on the most serious legal cases—that is, those in which the recommended sentence was execution; directing and confirming the appointments, transfers, and demotions of all civil and military officials; and checking the status of ongoing special projects, such as big construction projects (temples, dikes, palaces), large-scale celebrations, or the editing of major publications.

Additionally, Qianlong had to read and respond to scores of petitions and formal reports to the throne. Most of these dealt with routine business, in which case the emperor's secretaries already had discussed what action he needed to take. If Qianlong agreed with their assessment, he only needed to sign off and an edict ordering that action would be issued. Not infrequently, however, there were instances when he disagreed, or thought that his officials had failed to consider a matter fully. In those cases he would write his own decision or send the matter back for further investigation and deliberation. Naturally, if there were a military campaign underway, as there often was, the emperor had to work even harder. Together with his most trusted ministers, the grand councilors, he developed strategy, plotted campaigns, oversaw logistics, and evaluated reports from the field. Depending on the timing and urgency of such reports, meetings could happen almost anytime and the emperor's usual schedule disrupted.

By early in the afternoon, the day's most pressing business would have been completed. Around one o'clock time was set aside for audiences with new appointees to office. For each man a special green-topped wooden tally was prepared in advance, a kind of résumé on a stick, on which were written his name and brief record; a full dossier on each person was also kept on hand, to be consulted once he was conducted into Qianlong's presence. Armed with this information the emperor was in a position to conduct that day's personal interviews, of which there might be as many as fifty, in a relatively efficient manner. He might ask an appointee about his family, his hometown, or some other topic, or he might choose to ask him a more serious question about local administration, a pressing economic issue, or the nature of truth. Once the audience was concluded, the emperor was then able to confirm the proposed appointment. Establishing direct contact with officials in this way was a practice that inspired confidence and a personal connection between the emperor and those who served him. It also allowed the emperor to identify new talent that he might want to recruit to higher positions in the future—as well as to weed out those he felt lacked promise or dedication. Qianlong ended this part of the day in private conference with his senior grand councilor, reviewing personnel decisions.

At three p.m. it would ordinarily be time for the emperor's main meal of the day. In the imperial kitchens a staff of 370 people would have spent the better part of the day preparing all manner of food for him and the rest of the imperial family. Against the unlikely event of his falling ill after a meal, a careful record was kept of everything the emperor ate, who had fixed it, and which eunuchs had served it. The use of silver platters and utensils, which were believed to turn black in the presence of poison, further insured against any foul play. (Lest the reader think that such measures reflect some sort of excessive caution on Qianlong's part, recall that his contemporary, King George III, fell victim to poisoning beginning in 1788, which probably caused his "madness" and certainly his death in 1820.) On any given day several dozen dishes might appear on the emperor's table, the idea being that something of all that plenty ought to appeal to him. Since he was not in the habit of ordering specific items, it is hard to know for sure, but records suggest that among Qianlong's favorite foods were bird's nest soup and anything that included duck, though he also showed a preference for traditional Manchu dishes of venison and other game. He professed that he was not extravagant in this department, noting that annual expenses for the imperial kitchens amounted to "only" 100 taels a day. But as this was twenty-five times the monthly salary of a cavalryman in the Manchu army (and an even greater multiple of a typical peasant income), we should take this claim with a grain of salt, as it were.

After dinner the emperor took some time away from official business to paint, practice calligraphy, write poetry, and to spend time with his art collections. As the reader will see in Chapter 7, Qianlong was a world-class collector of paintings, antiques, and ceramics; examining fine art objects was a passion for him, not some idle preoccupation. One imagines that the early evening may well have been his favorite part of the day. Occasionally he might take in some theatre. Unless there were urgent business to finish up, the emperor would retire for the night at around nine p.m. in order to arise rested the next morning.

Early Successes on the Frontier

In his first years on the throne, urgent matters concerning the frontier crowded the young emperor's morning schedule. In the south were the Miao, who, like the Manchus themselves, were a non-Han people living on the border of the traditional Chinese state. The territory they inhabited, mainly in modern Guizhou Province, had been incorporated gradually into the empire during the Yuan and Ming dynasties, and governance of the region long remained vexatious. Apart from the tropical climate, which was held to be unhealthy, the mountainous terrain hindered mobility and large-scale military operations. Beyond that, few Miao spoke Chinese, fewer still could read it, and the Miao language itself lacked a writing system. Imposing Chinese-type governmental structures and installing Chinese officials here was considered out of the question. Instead, the emperor confirmed hereditary local chieftains in their positions and extended various privileges in exchange for a promise of loyalty. The Qing embraced this system at first, but in 1726, in response to reports that chieftains were unfairly exploiting their fellow Miao, Yongzheng decided to replace them with Chinese officials and bring the administration of the Miao territories into line with the rest of provincial China. The state would also redistribute the chieftains' considerable landholdings more fairly among the population and would begin to collect a land tax from Miao farmers instead of accepting the tribute that Miao leaders brought to the court every year.

Predictably, Miao tribal chiefs resisted this change. The new policies were implemented only thanks to the energetic (some might say ruthless) leadership of Ortai, who had several thousand troops at his disposal, and even then it required more than a year to overcome initial opposition. Ortai remained in Guizhou until 1731. Not long after he returned to Beijing the fragile peace he had made began to fall apart. By early 1735 central authority had collapsed in the area, which was now under the leadership of a new Miao "king." To make things worse, the official deputed to quell the uprising, Zhang Zhao, used his position to score political points, actively heaping blame upon Ortai, whom he disliked, but doing little to curb the rebellion. This was the situation when Qianlong took over.

Having served on the special council his father had formed to deal with the emergency when he was still Prince Bao, Qianlong was already familiar with the issues at hand. He wasted no time. The day after Yongzheng passed away he recalled Zhang Zhao to Beijing, replacing him with a capable military commander who had been Ortai's assistant in Guizhou. The dismissal was very much in Yongzheng's style, as seen in the caustic tone of his response to Zhang's suggestion that the new policies be abandoned:

> Moreover, especially ridiculous is your saying that because the recently opened Miao frontier is violent we should give up trying to rule there directly. [. . .] In your report you blow hot and cold, saying here that we should abandon the fight, saying there that we should root out [all the rebels]. These are two extremes of opinion! How am I supposed to know what you really mean? This is muddle-headed thinking indeed.

Within nine months, Qianlong's man had defeated the rebels in a bloody campaign, leaving no doubt that he possessed the decisiveness to pursue the enemy to the bitter end and complete the job Yongzheng had begun. The policies Qianlong put in place thereafter were aimed at accommodating the Miao generously—their land would never be taxed and they could follow their own legal statutes for settling disputes—while his settlement of troops in military colonies in the region was designed to forestall future rebellion. The reward was decades of (relative) peace in this part of the empire.

In the west, Qianlong was also fast off the blocks with respect to the Dzungar Mongols. He grew up hearing all about the wars his grandfather had commanded against the Dzungar leader Galdan in the 1690s. Among the largest-scale military operation seen anywhere in the world since the days of Khubilai Khan, these campaigns had required provisioning three large armies as they moved across the Gobi. The triumph was as much political as it was logistical. Kangxi succeeded in breaking the power of Galdan, who led a tribal confederation composed of the descendants of hardy steppe nomads whom not even Chinggis Khan (i.e., Genghis Khan) had been able to bring to heel. The Qing victory lasted a generation; in the 1730s, the Dzungars were once again on the move. Though the new Dzungar chieftain, Galdan Tsereng, was not as formidable a foe as his great-uncle had been, Qianlong knew not to underestimate the challenges of engaging nomadic armies, especially when the battleground would be in inhospitable desert two thousand miles away.

Nor was it simply the military threat that troubled the emperor. Faithful followers of the Dalai Lama, the leader of the Gelug (or "Yellow Hat") school of Tibetan Buddhism, Dzungar leaders were all too willing to become involved in Tibetan politics if they thought it would give them an advantage in their century-old struggle to achieve domination over the steppe. True, their Manchu rivals had the upper hand, but the Qing foothold in Tibet was still precarious and offered opportunities for the Dzungars to destabilize the Manchu imperium. Three times—in 1720, 1723, and again in 1727—Qing armies had marched into northeastern and central Tibet to prevent Dzungar chieftains from consolidating their political position. Finding the religious hierarchy unreliable (it, too, eagerly sought powerful allies), and unwilling to consign Manchu soldiers to a permanent garrison in Lhasa, Yongzheng installed a loyal Tibetan aristocrat, Polhanas, as an unofficial Qing regent and appointed two Manchu councilors to assist him and keep an eye on things. This arrangement brought twenty years of stability and contributed much to the integration of Tibet and Qinghai (the northeastern region of Tibet, also known as Amdo) into the Qing realm. But another expedition sent in 1727 to deal directly with the Dzungars in the Altai region (what is now the extreme northwest part of China's Xinjiang and the extreme southwest part of Mongolia) ended in disaster when in 1730 nearly half the army was wiped out in a surprise attack and the other half forced to retreat the following year. Peace initiatives were floated in 1734 and negotiations with the Dzungars—in which Yongzheng had presciently included his fourth son—were ongoing when Yongzheng died.

Thus it was that, the week after his enthronement, Qianlong took advantage of the arrival of a Dzungar embassy to carry on further discussions over the frontier. The embassy came with gifts, a letter from Galdan Tsereng, and two Qing prisoners who were being returned as a sign of good faith. Satisfied that the Dzungars were sincere in their desire for peace, Qianlong authorized the demarcation of a border between Dzungar lands and Qing territory—which he noted had been his father's original intention—and pulled most of his troops from the region, save for a few thousand to be kept on at key garrisons. The final terms of the treaty between the Qing and the Dzungars were settled in early 1740 after four years of negotiations over the precise boundary lines, the location of Qing guard posts, the size of Dzungar embassies that would be permitted to travel to Tibet and Beijing, and the conditions for border trade.

Along with the settlement of the Miao rebellion, Qianlong's successful conclusion of the dispute with the Dzungars was a major milestone of his first years. Like the 1689 Treaty of Nerchinsk negotiated under Kangxi and the 1727 Treaty of Kiakhta negotiated under Yongzheng, the 1740 Dzungar Treaty exemplified the importance to the Manchus of settling the northern border of the empire and maintaining correct relations with their Russian and Mongol neighbors. It also showed the willingness of the Qing to make use of such early modern tools as treaties, embassies, and maps to carry out foreign relations. As it happened, while the Russian treaties remained in force for a remarkably long time (lasting well into the nineteenth century), the treaty with the Dzungars did not. It was broken in the mid-1750s when a power struggle broke out after the death of Galdan Tsereng. At this point Qianlong decided to deal with the Dzungars once and for all, and with force. The final resolution of the Dzungar question in 1759, discussed in Chapter 6, would be one of Qianlong's most celebrated achievements.

Consolidator or Innovator?

That Qianlong at first followed in his father's footsteps suggests that, unlike his father, Qianlong was more a consolidator than an innovator. He was happy to make use of the institutional framework that Yongzheng had developed, most notably the palace memorial system and the Grand Council, which from the early 1700s were indispensable in the conduct of the empire's most important business. It was in large measure thanks to these two innovations that Qianlong's military legacy was so impressive. They also enabled Qianlong to keep his ear close to the ground in the day-to-day job of governing China. Their importance in the exercise of imperial power in the eighteenth century warrants a brief outline of their development.

Arising out of imperial dissatisfaction with existing means of communication, the palace memorial system was one of the most outstanding of several improvements the Manchus made on the political structure they inherited from the Ming. Within that older arrangement, all imperial officials, whether those working in the central government in Beijing or those assigned to posts in the provinces, reported to the throne via a rather indirect route. Their reports, known as "memorials" in English, were submitted first to a secretariat, who summarized them, prepared a draft response for the emperor to approve or disapprove, and handled the reporting of imperial decisions to all concerned. Careful records were kept of everything that came in and went out. It was an impressive chancellery system, but it had its shortcomings. For one thing, there was no way to guarantee the confidentiality of reports, which passed through many hands before reaching the emperor. For another, the emperor's autonomy to act was frequently at the mercy of the powerful men, the grand secretaries, who framed his responses and influenced his decisions.

To circumvent these problems, Kangxi devised a new system that allowed for greater secrecy. The way it worked was simple. When a particularly pressing or delicate matter arose, an official would write a report (the format was somewhat different than for routine memorials, which continued to be sent to the secretariat), lock it in a box, and send it by special messenger directly to the emperor, who was the only other person to hold the key to the box. After reading the secret memorial, the emperor would pick up his brush, dip it in the vermilion ink reserved for his use, respond, and return it in the same box. No secretary prepared it, no scribe translated it, no minister perused it, no messenger glanced at it. With confidentiality assured, it was suitable to send intelligence of the most sensitive sort—military preparations and scouting reports, accusations of corruption or malfeasance—as well as news that needed to be communicated to the emperor rapidly, including weather and crop reports, natural disasters, market prices, and the like, upon which the emperor could act directly in whatever manner he thought appropriate. It was precisely through these secret memorials, for instance, that Qianlong received information on his cousin Hungsi and on the unscrupulous careerist whom Ortai had been protecting, and it was through them, too, that Qianlong kept in touch with developments on the Guizhou and Dzungarian frontiers.

Assuring confidential and quick delivery of information is a challenge for any regime, but for an empire as sprawling as the Qing in a world without advanced communications technology the challenge was especially great. Because the secret memorial system effectively compensated for the emperor's separation from the local scene and a local official's distance from the emperor, it emerged as a vital means of transmitting news to the throne. Originally limited to a handful of Manchu officials, by the 1720s scores of people were using this channel, leading Yongzheng to seek its regularization. He ordered the return of any memorials that people had received from Kangxi and stipulated that thereafter, at the end of every year, officials were to send back all the memorials in their possession to the palace, where they would be stored (hence the name "palace" memorials). A few years later it was further decided to keep reference copies of every such memorial that went out—a compromise in the system's confidentiality, to be sure, but an administratively unavoidable step. This was done partly with later chroniclers in mind, but primarily for the convenience of the recently created Grand Council, which had simultaneously evolved into a major decision-making body.

The Grand Council was another important Qing addition to the central bureaucracy that matured under Qianlong's rule. In imperial China there was no division of government into executive, legislative, and judicial branches, and no division of church and state. Responsibility for public affairs was divided up according to different principles. The central administration in Beijing was made up of six ministries or "boards" (Rites, Revenue, Civil Appointments, War, Punishments, and Works), each directed by a pair of executives, one Manchu and the other Chinese. The province-based administration consisted of a ranked set of governors and commissioners, many of them Manchus, under whom served local officials (prefects and magistrates, almost exclusively Han). The activities of all these officials were under the watchful eye of the Censorate, whose duty it was to detect and report on corruption and malfeasance. Matters relating to the emperor personally, including his household finances, as well as the imperial factories for porcelain and textiles, were handled by a special bureau, the Imperial Household Department, which also oversaw other special palace workshops and agencies, including one just to provide milk and cream, which the Manchus adored, for the imperial kitchen. Administration of the capital city fell to another independent office, as did oversight of the Eight Banners. Supervision of affairs with Mongolia, Tibet, and Russia was left to the Bureau of Colonial Dependencies, the closest thing the Qing government had to a foreign office.

Chief authority over this massive structure, of course, was vested in the person of the emperor. But there was far too much business for a single man to monitor on his own, no matter how energetic or conscientious he might be. At one point there had been a prime minister, but this key position was eliminated in the four-teenth century. After a time the head of the palace administration, the first grand secretary, assumed something of this role. Lacking formal authority, however, he did not always have the emperor's ear and often found himself outmaneuvered by someone else, very often a member of the staff of eunuchs who were charged with handling matters pertaining to the imperial bedroom and had the run of the palace. When they assumed power in China, the Qing drastically reduced the size and importance of the eunuch staff, but stopped short of restoring the prime minister. Instead, the emperor, who was used to deciding matters in council form (as mentioned, this had been an important feature of early Manchu government), turned for advice, as we have seen, to men around him whom he trusted—uncles, brothers, cousins, experienced commanders—along with a few trusted Chinese civil officials. It was out of this tradition that the Grand Council eventually formed.

Initially, the Council's main role was as a war cabinet, a small group of advisors entrusted with overseeing the conduct of military campaigns in the northwest. Because the Grand Council was outside the regular bureaucracy—it had no official name and no description of it appeared in any government handbooks until 1819—its members held their appointments unofficially, and on top of whatever regular positions they held in the government. Precisely because it was so secret, it acquired virtually unlimited discretion. When Yongzheng died, the council was temporarily disbanded, but in January 1738 Qianlong reinstituted it and brought back most of the people who had served under his father. From this time forward the Grand Council rose to unsurpassed prominence. Though their offices (located just a minute's walk from the emperor's study) were spartan, grand councilors became the most powerful ministers of the realm. They charted Qianlong's campaigns, supervised important investigations, planned his publications and travels, debated his policies, and provided advice on just about every type of business. If the palace memorials circulated blood and oxygen around the empire, the Grand Council was its heart and lungs. Without it, Qianlong's power would not have been nearly so great. Ironically, later in his reign, as his power waned, some might say that this was precisely because of the Grand Council.

Finding His Stride

Whether in terms of fiscal strength, governmental reform, or institutional innovation, Qianlong's debt to Yongzheng was considerable. He took pains to publicize this debt, which leads us to one final aspect of the tenor of Qianlong's first years, namely, his concern to remain filial and to be *seen* as being filial. For instance, when he threw the Daoist priests out of the palace in late 1735, he insisted that the low regard he had for these "comedians" was an attitude his father had shared, too, and that Yongzheng had never taken their rites seriously at all. He had to be even more careful when ordering the arrest and execution of the two men responsible for publicizing the calumnious essays of Lü Liuliang, since Yongzheng specifically promised them that his descendants would never exact retribution. As to why he was violating this guarantee, Qianlong explained that as Yongzheng had destroyed Lü for having insulted his father, Kangxi, so he was destroying the men who had insulted his father. Interestingly, however, he offered no explanation for his simultaneous decision to recall and destroy Yongzheng's "Record of Great Righteousness," though one suspects Qianlong feared that its intensely defensive tone had done the dynasty more harm than good.

That Qianlong took this step reveals one very important difference between him and his father: Qianlong was more confident and secure than Yongzheng.

These qualities emerged, as we have already remarked, in contemporary portraits of him, and in time they would make their mark as well on the empire as a whole. Though in some of his early edicts his words retained something of the same mordant flavor of Yongzheng's rescripts to palace memorials, it is not found in his later edicts, when his authority was already well established. It would seem that Qianlong did not have the same need as his father to speak cruelly to people (though he might well treat them cruelly). As time went on, it seems he did not have the same need to speak to them at all, as he ceased to do as his father had done in writing lengthy screeds and sharp asides. Corrections of spelling errors, on the other hand, do, suggesting that, as in his schoolboy days, Qianlong always remained something of a pedant.

In carrying to fruition the uncompleted work left over from the Yongzheng era, Qianlong should not be seen as a slavish imitator. When he felt that his father had been wrong, he was not afraid to take steps to correct those mistakes, as when he recalled the official Zhang Zhao from Guizhou (a famous calligrapher, the disgraced Zhang was nevertheless retained in imperial service). He was also sure enough of himself that in certain instances he reversed his father's policies altogether. The best example of this might be his halting the drive to increase the amount of arable land by opening up untilled mountainsides and tracts of the frontier for farming. Yongzheng had initiated this policy originally to augment agricultural output and give landless peasants a new beginning, and showed great pleasure when it brought good results. In a pattern that would be repeated in 1950s China, provincial officials discovered that it was to their advantage to inflate their reports of reclaimed land just to win the emperor's approval. Since tax collection was calculated according to the amount of land farmed, there was a price to be paid for these lies, and that price was paid by an overburdened peasantry.

Very soon after he came to the throne, Qianlong was informed that, among other things, the reports of land brought under cultivation in Sichuan and Guangxi provinces were false, and that in Henan people were selling their daughters just to pay the new taxes levied on utterly barren land. He was urged by his advisors to end the program, and in late 1735 he did just that. Before long the young emperor ran into resistance. The governor of Sichuan Province, Wang Shijun—one of those chiefly responsible for creating the overreporting problem in the first place—submitted a memorial in August 1736 in which he wrote, "The recommendations that are being submitted these days are only about overturning past precedents. The word is being passed around that all you have to do is throw out some precedent dating from the days of Yongzheng and it will be approved. It's shocking how quickly this has spread throughout the empire."

Here was a bold challenge. Wang dared not say point blank that he thought the emperor's decision to cancel the program was a bad one, so he availed himself of the old tactic of "pointing to the mulberry to revile the locust tree," and phrased it instead as a criticism of other officials, without naming anyone or saying which precedents were being reversed. Nonetheless, the message came through loud and clear. Qianlong was furious when he read Wang's memorial and no doubt very worried. If Wang felt brave enough to put this in a memorial to him, there must be many others who felt the same way and who opposed

Qianlong's efforts to trim the sails and chart a different direction. The next day Qianlong summoned the members of the Grand Council and several other high officials to inform them of this turn of events. In high dudgeon, he accused Wang of sedition and of having offended the throne. He recounted how, when Kangxi and Yongzheng came to power, they had gone about amending or changing things, just as he had: "How can this be said to be 'overturning precedents'? If this kind of thing had happened when my father was alive, would he have forgiven Wang? Of course not!" Wang, who had just returned to Beijing, was detained forthwith and sentenced to decapitation.

The Wang Shijun affair showed how determined Qianlong was to put his stamp on things and just how difficult that could be. Wang's execution sent a warning to others who might have harbored doubts about the new ruler's judgment. With time, of course, people forgot how things had been before and grew accustomed to Qianlong's ways, his preferences, concerns, petty worries, and foibles. A new cohort of officials emerged, beholden only to him. As this happened, the old stalwarts who had known him from his youth, teachers before whom he had once bowed, gradually departed the scene. When in 1749 Zhang Tingyu finally retired, an era truly came to an end.

Zhang (1672–1755) was from a noted family from Anhui Province that had been producing famous scholars for several generations. He had earned the top examination degree half a century before, in 1700, and had risen high under Yongzheng to be one of the founding members of the Grand Council. Before he died, Yongzheng had promised him that a memorial tablet with his name on it would be installed in the Ancestral Temple one day, an unheard-of honor for someone who was not part of the imperial clan and was not even Manchu. In part for this reason, and as the loyal servant of three emperors, Zhang's eminence was unrivaled by any other Chinese official and he gathered to his side many up-and-coming officials who sought his counsel and patronage. Yet Zhang was not above reproach.

The trouble started in 1749, when Zhang, now retired, made bold to approach the emperor for a written note assuring him that when he died his spirit would indeed be enshrined in the Ancestral Temple. The emperor grumbled but acceded to this highly improper request, even writing a short poem to make him feel better. He lost his temper the next morning, though, when the seventy-seven-year-old Zhang sent his son to convey his gratitude instead of coming himself. "So he is well enough to come in person when making his request, but he cannot be bothered to show up to thank me?" the emperor fumed, "Whoever heard of such a thing? His house is in the capital, close enough that, no matter how sick he was, he should still have come crawling in to say thanks." Qianlong was even angrier the next day when Zhang finally did show up, correctly guessing that he had been tipped off, and berated him in the most severe manner, calling him among other things a "useless antique." After this time there was only bad blood between Zhang and his master, who seems never to have forgiven him for his lack of respect. The emperor even went so far as to strip Zhang of his rank of earl, repossess his Beijing house, and seize a good part of his fortune shortly before Zhang died at the age of 83. It was only out of loyalty to his father that he did after all enshrine Zhang in the Ancestral Temple. Before Qianlong found it possible to think fondly of Zhang again, he would be an old man himself.

Part of the reason for Qianlong's extreme behavior with respect to his former teacher may have been that he wished to crush the influence at court of the "Zhang faction," just as previously he had eliminated the Ortai faction. In this he was unquestionably successful, though he was unable to prevent other coalitions from forming later to take its place. At the same time, one wonders whether his actions did not also stem from some deeper desire simply to be rid of the old man and of the last reminders of his father's rule. For among the many challenges that the young emperor faced, few were more formidable than dealing with the legacies of Kangxi and Yongzheng and living up to the expectations people had of him. In time the veneration and fear they had inspired would be his, too.

3

Family, Ritual, and Dynastic Rule

We usually think of monarchical dynasties as purely political institutions, mechanisms that allow exceptionally powerful families to maintain their hold on power and pass it on to succeeding generations. The cry, "The king is dead! Long live the king!" neatly conveys the durability of monarchic authority in the face of transient mortal life and underscores the mystery that lay behind the transfer of dynastic power in premodern times, when, for better or worse, sovereignty was vested in a single person. This sovereignty typically was soaked in a rich ideological stew, in which floated ideas as to the nobility, moral superiority, and divine right of the ruler, his ancestors, relatives, and descendants. These beliefs, and the acts they imposed upon the emperor, helped legitimate the power and wealth enjoyed by the dynasty and hid from view the obvious political calculations and deal-making with other wealthy elites that were critical in the operation and preservation of authority. For these reasons, it is easy to forget that dynasties were first and foremost families in which personal relationships mattered a great deal—the difference being that family quarrels within a dynastic house could have repercussions of serious national importance. Not just symbolically, but organically, too, the fate of the country was therefore linked to the fate of that one family.

The complex relationships between Qianlong, his father, grandfather, and other male relatives detailed in the preceding chapters are indicative of the ways in which powerful families around the world, such as the Habsburgs, the Bourbons, or the Sauds, develop from generation to generation. In his relations with others in his family—his mother, his many wives, and his children—we can see that Qianlong took very seriously the classic dictum of the *Great Learning* that good governance of the realm was rooted in good governance of the family. He believed that the maintenance and transmission of correct ways within his family held the key to the future of Qing rule and that he had no greater duty than to assure its perpetuation. Examining how personal relationships and public politics mingled in Qianlong's life provides us a way to better understand him and also a way to better understand political culture in eighteenth-century China.

Filial Son

As the previous discussion of Qianlong's schedule has made plain, the demands made on the person of the emperor were significant. Even for one as confident as Qianlong, there was a lot to do. To meet these obligations Qianlong received help from many quarters. But nothing was more useful to him, nothing as central to his actions, as the wide repertoire of ritual available to him as the head of an imperial system that, by the eighteenth century, had already been around for two millennia. These rituals, and the beliefs out of which they grew, had accumulated an authority every bit as weighty and unquestioned as the authority held by Christian belief and ritual in early modern Europe. Even for a Manchu—perhaps *especially* for a Manchu—to be emperor meant to subscribe to an ancient code of behavior rooted in classical writings that enshrined and glorified certain particular virtues, which the monarch was expected to practice scrupulously.

Needless to say, these were not the same as Christian virtues. Where the Christian king was to rule in fear of God (and sometimes the pope) and live following the example of Christ, or where the Ottoman sultan was to rule as the defender of Islam, the emperor of China was to rule in accordance with Heaven, to display reverence to his ancestors (direct and metaphorical), and to live following the example of the ancient sages. The standard of morality was high in all cases. As far as Confucian orthodoxy is concerned, its most striking characteristic was its strong emphasis upon filial piety.

Filiality—which we may define as behaving properly toward one's parents while they are alive and honoring them correctly when they are dead—was arguably the single most important virtue the emperor needed to demonstrate. It underpinned the entire hierarchy of Chinese society, in which nearly all relationships were structured in terms of superior and inferior, implicitly on the model of father and son. Filiality ranked foremost in the "Sixteen Maxims" issued by Kangxi, didactic moral prescriptions that were read aloud in every village twice a month. Having grown up with them, Qianlong was quite familiar with these maxims. His grandfather's position, that filiality was the very basis of good government, mirrored texts like the *Great Learning*, which Confucius regarded as a source of great wisdom and which Qianlong had memorized by the time he was eight years old:

> It is not possible for one to teach others when he cannot teach his own family. Therefore, the ruler, without going beyond his own family, completes the lessons for the State. There is filial piety—therewith the sovereign should be served.

The belief that the family was the model for the empire was thus a primary tenet of Chinese political philosophy, and it escaped no one's attention that even the Son of Heaven was still a son. We have already seen the importance of filial imagery in Chapter 1 and have alluded to Qianlong's filial duties toward his father and grandfather. Formal sacrifices of food, wine, and incense to the spirit tablets of Yongzheng, Kangxi, and other ancestors were a regular part of the ritual calendar. If Qianlong did not perform them himself, he assigned the task to a worthy proxy. Many of his policies were consciously grounded upon the precedents set by his forebears. He took this code so far that, as discussed in Chapter 9, late in life he abdicated the throne (technically, at least) so as not to surpass the record set by his grandfather as the longest-reigning emperor in history.

Qianlong and His Mother

Qianlong's filial sentiments were by no means restricted to male relatives. For as long as his mother was alive, it was incumbent upon him to guarantee her well-being. He took this responsibility extremely seriously, as it offered him an excellent means of modeling filial behavior for the rest of his subjects.

We have already met Qianlong's mother, the "lucky woman" who was introduced to Kangxi in Chengde during that charmed summer of 1722. Lady Niohuru—she is known to us only by her family name—was then twenty-nine years old, the fourth of Yongzheng's nine wives. The story is told that in her early teens, as part of the triennial draft of young women for palace service, she was sent to work in Prince Yong's residence in northeast Beijing, where her pretty face and conscientious ministrations once while he was ill earned her his favor, and she was thereafter promoted to the lowest rank of imperial consort. Less colorful records indicate that she was recruited to his household directly as a concubine. The former story is not impossible (about one-seventh of imperial wives started out as palace maids), but the latter is more likely true, given that Lady Niohuru's great-grandfather was a famous hero of the Qing conquest, and that her own family, though it may have enjoyed only modest means, was one of the most respected Manchu lineages. One of her distant aunts had even been a consort of Kangxi. (We must discount the legend that Qianlong was really the son of a Han woman, surnamed Chen, as the fond imaginings of early twentieth-century Chinese nationalists who wanted to claim Qianlong as one of their own.)

In either case, whether as maid or as wife, the means of selection—namely, the "daughters' draft"—was the same. The terms of this draft, a relic of the feudal rights enjoyed by early Manchu nobles, applied to all healthy young women between the ages of 13 and 16 in the Manchu banners, who were required to present themselves at the palace for official review. For each girl there was a brief dossier containing basic vital statistics such as banner registration, family line, and appearance. With this information officials decided whether or not the girl before them was suitable for employment in the palace or, if she were from a more distinguished background, perhaps for marriage to some member of the imperial clan. If she were not chosen for either of these roles within five years of her interview, she would be free to marry as her family wished (the approval of the captain of her banner company was still required); girls who had not presented themselves for review never received such a dispensation and were in principle ineligible for matrimony. If indeed the story that Lady Niohuru was selected as a mere servant were true, she could have expected to serve in that capacity until she was 25, at which time she would have regained her personal liberty, along with a token amount of silver as payment for her services. Selection as a secondary wife to an imperial prince, however, bound her to his household for a lifetime and greatly restricted her mobility; after that time, even to have received permission to leave the residential compound to visit her family would have been nearly impossible.

After the birth of Hungli in 1711, Lady Niohuru advanced to a higher, more privileged position, with three maids and a modest allowance of food, fabric, and money. She never had any other children. Luckily for her, however, the one she had ended up being the most talented of Yongzheng's sons and the only one by a Manchu consort to live to maturity. Once her husband became emperor and chose her son to be his successor, her standing rose further and she became a concubine of the second degree. She rose to the rank of empress, however, only after Qianlong's enthronement, at which time, as his mother, she was formally designated an empress dowager, Qianlong's own wife having become the new empress. At this time she was given a private residence within the palace (the "Mansion of Motherly Tranquility"), a large staff of her own, and a very generous stipend.

In all probability Qianlong's contact with his mother was very limited when he was a boy, and we have no stories of the lessons she taught him. But this did not seem to diminish his affection for her, and it certainly did not keep him from bestowing upon her every possible sign of respect and lavishing her with honorary titles. For forty-two years, from the time he took the throne until she died at age 84 in 1777, he served her faithfully, greeting her first thing in the morning nearly every day, presenting her with magnificent gifts and catering to her tastes and wishes with unflagging thoughtfulness and devotion. Knowing of her devout Buddhist piety, he built her a special temple and filled it with religious paintings and objects, including a fantastic set of 787 figures constituting the entire Buddhist pantheon. When she died, he had a Tibetan-style reliquary made to hold the combings of hair she had saved over the years, in accordance with Buddhist practice. The resulting object, in the shape of a stupa,[1] was made entirely of gold and silver. Weighing 237 pounds (107.5 kilograms) but only 20 inches (53 cm) tall, it is today one of the most breathtakingly beautiful objects in the palace collections.

If Qianlong's attentiveness to his mother became legendary even in his own lifetime, this was in part because of the splendid birthday celebrations he organized for her sixtieth, seventieth, and eightieth birthdays. These anniversaries, paid for largely out of the emperor's private purse and from more-or-less voluntary subscriptions raised among the Manchu nobility and the top levels of civil and military officialdom, were seasonal sensations in Beijing society, each more elaborate than the previous one. At the main celebration banquet for her fiftieth birthday, Qianlong himself waited on his mother at dinner. After the meal, he disappeared for a moment before reemerging, attired in colorful garb decorated

---

[1]A stupa (pronounced "stew-pah") is a religious shrine of Indian origin, typically consisting of a bulbous, high-shouldered dome on a square pedestal surmounted by a tall, decorative cylinder that narrows at the top. Some are small enough to be portable, while others are the size of buildings. Stupas might contain the relics of monks, nuns, or devout followers of Buddhism, and often marked sacred sites. Since to build a stupa was itself to perform an act of devotion, Qianlong's commission of the stupa for his mother thus had both religious and filial dimensions.

with feathers, to lead his brothers, brothers-in-law, sons, and grandsons in a dance expressing their filial sentiments toward the empress dowager. (Such theatricals were by no means unknown in other royal courts: Louis XIV once danced the part of Alexander the Great in a court ballet written just for him.)

For her sixtieth and seventieth birthdays, in addition to festivities in the capital, Qianlong arranged extensive sightseeing tours to the temperate climes and picturesque cities of southern China. On her eightieth birthday, in 1771, feeling she was too old for the journey to Jiangnan, her son took the extravagant step of bringing Jiangnan to her, ordering the reproduction in Beijing of a shopping district from her favorite tourist destination, Suzhou, in today's Jiangsu Province. Stretching along the road between the Forbidden City and her own summer residence north of the city, this ersatz "Suzhou Street" was like a Qing version of Disneyland, with mile upon mile of shops and restaurants, theaters, and teahouses, some newly built, some refurbished at government expense. In addition to this, Qianlong authorized the construction of a number of Suzhou-style restaurants, stores, inns, and theaters within the palace grounds—all staffed by appropriately costumed eunuchs—and saw to it as well that the canal route leading from Beijing to the Summer Palace was bordered by colorful tents, stages for opera and musical performances, and decorated with festoons, trees, and potted flowers. Enormous sums of money went to the construction of arcades, pavilions, bridges, theaters, food stalls, and miniature landscaped gardens meant to recall the South.

Even more remarkable, perhaps, was that until advancing years interfered with her mobility, Qianlong took her with him everywhere he went: to the Yuanming yuan when the occasion presented itself in Beijing, to Chengde and Mulan in the summer, to the ancestral lands of Mukden, even on his extended tours of the South (described in Chapter 5). Indeed, he presented his wish to please her as the main reason for these grand-scale imperial progresses in the first place:

> Whenever and wherever I have traveled, I have always done so in the company of my esteemed mother, and the sights of Jiangnan are first-class, famous throughout the world. Truly, I would wish to carry her sedan chair myself to show her the beauties of its landscape and the abundance of its products, thus to cheer her maternal bosom.

Such was his enthusiasm—and hers, for that matter—that even something so formidable as the ascent of Taishan (Mt. Tai, elevation 5,000 feet/1,524 meters) did not discourage either of them. Maybe because of this constant activity, she remained vigorous and healthy well into old age, her hair reportedly not beginning to gray until she was sixty-six years old.

In escorting her all over the country, one wonders whether Qianlong did not do so out of a desire that she should share in some of the freedom of movement he enjoyed. Manchu women, after all, were accustomed to greater liberties than those enjoyed by Han women. Foreign visitors to Qing Beijing often observed women on horseback, and remarked on the relative ease with which Manchu women were able to move around the city, making social calls, shopping, and so on. Manchu authors of the seventeenth and eighteenth centuries included in their

works descriptions of winsome Manchu maids on horseback along with memorable portrayals of take-charge Manchu females, confirming the impression held
by many Han Chinese that Manchu women carried themselves in a masculine
style. Some females in Qianlong's household even took part in the Mulan hunts.
Perhaps the most obvious symbol of the Manchu woman's distinctive, "liber-
ated" status was her feet, which were not bound. Indeed, foot-binding was one
Chinese custom that Manchu women apparently never sought to emulate; it was
a Manchu woman (Empress Dowager Cixi) who, in the early twentieth century,
decreed a legal end to the practice.

Married to the Emperor

If Qianlong and his mother got along well, this was in part because, unlike the
senior women of the preceding Ming dynasty, she rarely involved herself in court
affairs. Shortly after becoming emperor, Qianlong gave orders that his mother
was not to be informed of any matters of state policy, and there are no signs that
she influenced him politically in any way. Not that she was entirely a passive
creature. We know, for instance, that she took to reprimanding him quite pointedly for his excessive expenditures on her behalf. We also know that she
expressed strong opinions on more than one occasion when it came to her son's
wives, no doubt because she felt that this was too important a matter to be left to
him alone.

For indeed, in China, as in most of the rest of the world where power and
wealth were transmitted hereditarily through sons, the selection of a wife was a
very serious business. No man could be considered of much consequence without
an honorable—and fertile—woman at his side. Much depended on her. She played
a vital role in family ritual, often acted as the practical manager of the household,
and, through her children, ensured the permanence of a man's fortune and name.
If she were to die, the family would likely disintegrate. For this reason, and also
because rates of infant and child mortality were relatively high, a well-to-do man
might take more than one wife to ensure he had a son, especially where much was
at stake in assuring the survival of an heir (daughters could not inherit property or
titles). In such cases, however, the first wife continued to occupy the position of
senior female; secondary wives, sometimes called "concubines" in English, were
informal additions to the household and enjoyed no ritual place whatsoever. Their
children were legally considered the children of the first wife. Owing more to economic rather than sexual considerations, then, about 10 percent of men in China,
mostly from the upper classes, were polygamous. But where a rich man might have
one, two, or even three secondary wives, the emperor took many more. After all,
what stakes could be higher than the succession to the throne? In fact, through the
eighteenth century, no emperor had been born of his father's empress, so imperial
secondary wives (called "consorts")—who differed from ordinary concubines in
that, like the first wife, they were the emperor's legal spouses and their children
were counted as their own—were quite important.

Qianlong ended up with forty-one consorts. He married his first wife in 1727
and acquired seven more by the time he became emperor in 1735; he brought the

last two consorts into the palace in 1777. With very few exceptions, these women were chosen through the daughters' draft described earlier. Teenagers when they entered the palace, they lived the rest of their lives in its strictly guarded inner sanctum, every compound surrounded by insurmountable fifteen-foot-high red plastered walls and separated from other compounds by a maze of passages. Unless she was chosen to accompany the emperor on trips outside the Forbidden City (which were not infrequent), a consort's contact with the outside world was extremely limited. Other than festivals and special occasions, the only women she saw were members of the staff of 200–300 maids and ladies-in-waiting (somewhat fewer than at the court of Louis XIV), and the only men she saw were eunuchs, of whom there were about 2,000 in the palace. Usually hired in their teens, these castrati were charged with the task of securing the women's quarters and running communications back and forth to the main palace. The reasons for such careful measures are obvious: the emperor, and the empire, had to have absolute certainty that any son born of an imperial wife was truly the emperor's son. Sequestration of the emperor's wives was the only way to guarantee this, which it did: wild rumors aside (and in contrast to the comparatively libertine situation in contemporary Europe), there are no substantiated accounts of illegitimate births to any Qing royalty.

Not all of the emperor's wives were equal. Once joined to his household, a woman was assigned a specific rank that placed her in the hierarchy of palace ladies. Each of the eight ranks of consort came with its own standard of support, perquisites, and sumptuary restrictions; positions in the top four ranks were limited, but one's place in the hierarchy was not age-specific. That is, a woman might rise in the hierarchy independently of how long she had been there if circumstances favored her—if the emperor were for whatever reason particularly fond of her, or if, say, she had given birth to a son who outlived infancy and who pleased his father. Some consorts also enjoyed preferential treatment in terms of the gifts they might receive from the emperor (usually jewelry, precious objects from his art collections, clothing, fabrics, and the like). All of these things reverted to the imperial household when a consort died, however, and did not become her personal property.

Nor was there a strict ethnic hierarchy. It was understood that the emperor's main wife—the only one who held the rank of empress—should be Manchu, but other wives could be drawn from the Mongol and Chinese banners. None were from the civilian Han population. At least two of Qianlong's wives were Korean, and one, Lady Khoja, was Turkic, from a prominent Sufi lineage in Kashgar, an oasis city in eastern Turkestan (for more on Lady Khoja, see Chapter 6). Qianlong's own mother, it will be remembered, was Manchu, and his grandmother (Yongzheng's mother), who started out as a palace maid, was as well; yet one great-grandmother hailed from a distinguished family in the Chinese banners and one great-great-grandmother was a Mongol. The children of all these women were considered to be Manchu themselves, the ethnic standing of their families modified through elevation into the Manchu banners.

We know little about the specific details of how women were chosen to be wives of the emperor. We may suppose that Qianlong had more or less a free hand in deciding whom he might take as a secondary wife. However, as mentioned, the choice of a primary wife was too weighty to leave to his judgment and would likely have been decided for him by his parents while he was in early puberty. They selected a young woman of the Fuca (pronounced "foo-chah") clan, a descendant of one of Nurhaci's bravest companions, to be Qianlong's main wife. Succeeding generations of the Fuca family had produced a number of men of distinction, titled aristocrats who served as high ministers and councilors in the government. Lady Fuca's uncle, Maci, had held a number of important positions, including imperial chamberlain, and her younger brother, Fuheng, later became one of Qianlong's right-hand men, rising to the post of grand councilor in the 1760s.

Death of an Empress

When the young Hungli wedded the Lady Fuca he was sixteen years old and she fifteen—seemingly young, but in fact average ages for first marriages at the time. Before it was cut short by tragedy, their marriage of twenty-two years was by all accounts a happy one. The two were similar in many ways and seem to have been truly a well-matched pair. Lady Fuca was Hungli's steady companion and accompanied him on all his travels; when he was ill, she remained near his side until he recovered. He in his turn secretly named as heirs the two sons she bore him, though both succumbed to illness as children. The empress was dutifully solicitous of her mother-in-law, and her ability to maintain harmony within the emperor's harem won her universal admiration. Like Qianlong, Lady Fuca seems to have been a serious person who placed a high value on traditional Manchu frugality. Not given to ostentation or excessive luxury, she preferred artificial flowers of straw and silk to crowns of pearls and iridescent kingfisher feathers. A vivid illustration of her devotion and economy is provided by the story of how in 1747, on a trip to the Mulan hunting grounds, she once sewed for her husband a flint pouch. This was after Qianlong had told her of the custom, common in the days of their grandfathers, for men to carry on their belts pouches with flints and steel for striking fire. But, he noted, unlike the fancy pouches of their own day, which were made of brocade and decorated with gold, silver, ivory, rhinoceros horn, and other precious materials, the old-style flint pouches were much simpler and decorated only with the fine hair from a deer's tail. In response, she made him a pouch of plain indigo silk that she embroidered herself with a plain flower design. When, six months later, she died suddenly, Qianlong had a special box made to house this last gift from his wife. He explained its origin (which is why we know this story) and enclosed a poem with the words, translated here from the Manchu, "Seeing an old thing of hers, I lament, for it brought shapes and sounds before my eyes and filled them with tears" (see Figure 3.1).

The death of Qianlong's first empress was a major turning point in his reign, but the causes of Lady Fuca's untimely demise are not entirely clear. She was only thirty-six years old. The recent loss of their second son, who, despite having been inoculated, had contracted smallpox and died on the very eve of the lunar New

Figure 3.1 Giuseppe Castiglione (1688–1766) and court artists. *Portrait of the Empress* (detail from *Inauguration Portraits of Emperor Qianlong, the Empress and Eleven Imperial Consorts*). 1736. Handscroll, ink and colors on silk. Cleveland Museum of Art. A young woman of 24 at the time of this painting, her happy marriage to the emperor came to a tragic end with her death just twelve years later. The triple earrings she wears were a typical style of Manchu jewelry. © Cleveland Museum of Fine Arts.

Year, may have left her psychologically vulnerable.[2] After this sorrowful event, court astrologers warned the emperor of unfavorable movements in the skies that boded ill if the empress remained secluded in the palace. So in February 1748, Qianlong, accompanied by a modest entourage, took her and his mother on a tour of Shandong Province, not far away to the southeast, hoping that such stirring sights as Confucius' birthplace and majestic Mt. Tai would revive his wife's spirits. Indeed, the change did seem to do her good, and she even felt well enough to make the ascent and pray at the temple of the goddess of the mountain. On the return trip, however, things took a turn for the worse. The party was quartered at the provincial capital on the first of April when a spring snowstorm struck unexpectedly. The empress showed signs of having caught a chill and took to her bed. Her condition seemed not to warrant any special concern, so Qianlong went

---

[2]As in many other parts of the world, smallpox was endemic to China, and the disease's high fatality rate was always a concern. To protect members of the imperial lineage, in the 1680s the Kangxi emperor, a smallpox survivor with the pockmarks to prove it, instituted mandatory inoculations for children, who were deliberately infected with a light case so as to provoke immunity. Under Qianlong, this practice was expanded to include most Manchu children in Beijing, causing a sharp drop in infant mortality—though some children, even the emperor's own, still succumbed.

about his ritual activities in the city as planned. A week later, on the final leg of the journey back to Beijing, as the party was transferring to barges at the town of Dezhou (where the main road meets the Grand Canal), the empress' condition suddenly worsened. Hundreds of officials who had gathered on the banks to send off the imperial visitors now fell on their knees to pray for her recovery. Later that evening, with the emperor by her side, she died.

Grief at his wife's passing seems to have driven Qianlong slightly mad. Ultimately it provoked a political crisis of no small proportions. His first order was that her remains, along with the entire barge on which they lay, be transported immediately back to the capital. Moving the barge up the canal to Beijing was not a problem, but engineers had to devise a way to get it out of the water and through the city gates. They finally hit upon a plan whereby the vessel was hauled out of the canal onto a wooden track greased with vegetable leaves, then pulled by laborers through the streets. Once it was brought before the eastern entrance to the Forbidden City, the empress, already encoffined, was borne into her own residence, the Palace of Eternal Spring, where she lay in state for one week. After that, her coffin, made of rare, indestructible catalpa wood, was removed to a special building elsewhere in the palace complex, there to remain until preparations for burial were complete. This would not be for some years, however, as construction on the imperial mausoleum was not finished until the winter of 1752.

Meanwhile, Qianlong declared national mourning on an unprecedented scale for his late wife, now formally known as the Xiaoxian (loyal and wise) empress. For nine days after her death, no official business was to be transacted. For one month, everyone in the imperial household, along with all members of the nobility and high officialdom, was to dress in white mourning garb and to abstain from eating meat. Concurrently, the court enforced a ban on all weddings in the capital and a ban on music at civilian weddings in the provinces. Officials in the provinces were to remove their regalia, gather at the yamen,[3] and carry out three days of lamentation. In addition, strict tonsorial regulations were announced. Imperial sons were to cut their queues and their wives were to cut their hair short. All males, Manchu and Han, were to abstain from shaving their heads for one hundred days, as dictated by Manchu custom. Manchu women, on the other hand, were to abstain from putting their hair up, and could choose either to leave it long on their shoulders or cut it short; they were also enjoined to reduce the number of earrings they wore from three in each ear to two. Thus the edicts—their drafts emended in the blue ink of mourning, not the usual vermilion—poured forth from the palace.

Most officials responded appropriately, obeyed these commands, and the tactful among them speedily conveyed their condolences to Qianlong at the empress' passing and extended their sympathy. Though he must have realized that at least some of these memorials were submitted *pro forma*, still it bothered the emperor when certain people, particularly Manchus, failed to write. Because their indebtedness to the throne was greater than that of Han officials, he reasoned, "by rights they should have been howling in sadness and rushing to come forward."

---

[3] "Yamen" is a Chinese word that refers to a compound of buildings and courtyards where an official conducted business and lived with his family.

Qianlong quickly punished fifty-three thoughtless ingrates who had neglected to submit their condolences by demoting them two ranks. A month after the empress' death, he went further and denounced two of his sons for mourning insincerely. Accusing them of the worst crime possible in his eyes—lack of filiality—he removed them from the line of inheritance. Shortly thereafter, he was informed of many minor blunders made by officials charged with managing the empress' obsequies—including an error in the Manchu translation of a proclamation in her honor, which gaffe earned its author a delayed death sentence.

All of this was nothing when it came to the emperor's attention that a considerable number of officials had flouted the mourning requirements he had set forth by shaving their heads before the one hundred days' sanction was up. Only then did the full extent of Qianlong's anger, bitterness, and pain become apparent. Not only had these officials dishonored his beloved empress, but they had disgraced the emperor as well and shown flagrant disregard for the native ways of the ruling house. Once again, Manchu officials who ought to have known better were the main object of his wrath. Han officials who came forth to admit their crimes were forgiven, but no such clemency was shown to those in the Eight Banners. Many in the summer of 1748 lost their jobs, their titles, or their salaries, or, in a few cases, even their lives, as the atmosphere at the top levels of government became increasingly tense. Who would report on whom? What would the consequences be? Qianlong was showing a mercuriousness that few had seen before: even officials close to the throne were puzzled, and trod cautiously. This sort of unpredictable vindictiveness, hitherto not characteristic of the emperor and uncomfortably similar to the temper of his father, would show itself repeatedly over the next forty years of his reign.

More Hair-Cutting

One person who did not fear riling the emperor was his mother. Just five months after the death of Lady Fuca, the empress dowager approached her son about raising his third-rank consort, Lady Ula Nara, to fill the now-empty position of empress. This woman, from a much less illustrious family than Lady Fuca (her father was merely the captain of a banner company), had been part of Qianlong's household before he was emperor. Ultimately, she would give birth to two sons and a daughter, but in 1748 this still lay in the future, so there was not much reason to suppose she was one of the emperor's favorites. Nor do we know why the empress dowager backed her so forcefully. There was no absolute need to name a new empress, as other consorts could be called on to perform at rituals and sacrifices at which the emperor's wife had a role, provided they were of a high rank. His loss still fresh, Qianlong would have preferred to leave things as they were, but relented in the end to his mother's demands on the condition that Lady Ula Nara's elevation to empress be postponed until the mourning for Lady Fuca was over.

Lady Ula Nara, seven years younger than Qianlong, was thirty-two when she was finally named empress in 1750. For about fifteen years things went well. Though two of their children died before their second birthdays, one of the boys born to the new empress survived infancy and was growing healthily. Lady Ula

Nara got along well with the empress dowager, and the emperor liked her enough to include her on his fourth trip to Jiangnan in 1765, the first such trip he had made since the death of Lady Fuca. While touring Hangzhou that spring, however, a quarrel of some sort erupted between the emperor and the empress—perhaps over the emperor's fancy for another woman (the popular view) or over her disrespectful treatment of his mother (Qianlong's version of events). Such a quarrel would never have been made public, except that in her boudoir one night the empress made the extraordinary gesture of unceremoniously cutting her hair short in protest. This was not a fashion statement, but – as she herself certainly realized–a serious violation of court etiquette, as grave a challenge to Qianlong's authority as would Dudley's declaring himself a Catholic have been to the authority of Elizabeth I. Lady Ula Nara's outrageous act did not go unnoticed. Informed of it the following morning, Qianlong packed her off to Beijing instantly and ordered her to be held under house arrest until further notice. A little over a year later, in the fall of 1766, she died of an unspecified illness.

The emperor's reaction to the death of his second empress could hardly have differed more from his reaction to the death of the first. He did not decree national mourning, and he denied her the funeral that would have been due an empress, limiting her honors to those of a consort of the first rank. Even more shocking, the emperor decided that she should be buried in a separate tomb apart from Lady Fuca, and not, as would have been normal, in the imperial mausoleum. It was impossible for Qianlong to take actions of this nature without justifying himself. In an edict written a few days after her death, he explained that Lady Ula Nara had become psychologically unstable and had behaved in an unforgivable way toward his mother. Her death, he said, resulted from the worsening of her mental condition; under the circumstances, he had shown her leniency. Not all were convinced by the emperor's account. One official wrote from the provinces to say that failure to observe mourning was not in keeping with proper ritual; for his impertinence he was punished by exile to a penal colony in the far west. A similar fate befell the Imperial Household Department official Ayongga, a member of the imperial clan, who protested the emperor's decision to posthumously demote Lady Ula Nara. Much to Qianlong's consternation, Ayongga's earnest remonstration won a sympathetic hearing among the emperor's top advisors, who shared his feeling that the emperor had behaved immoderately and in violation of ritual propriety. This did not calm the emperor's fury. Accusing him of grandstanding, the emperor wrote, "How is it that you, an imperial relative and a close official, should dare stoop to that offensive habit the Han Chinese have of trying to make yourself famous?" Over the objections of his ministers, Qianlong sent Ayongga to live the rest of his life in the harsh climate of northern Manchuria.

Still, the affair of Qianlong's second empress would not go away. Ten years after her death, a minor provincial official submitted a letter to the court saying that he felt the emperor had been wrong in failing to formally announce mourning for the empress, and that it was his duty to speak out on her behalf and restore her honor. As soon as his complaint reached Beijing, the author was arrested and haled in for questioning: Surely he had not acted alone? The wording of his letter suggested he had been fed information from the inside. Who had put him up to this foolhardy act? Confessions extracted with the help of finger presses, extended kneelings, and other forms of torture shed no light on any sort of conspiracy, but they made it clear that the letter-writer was not alone in believing that the real reason Lady Ula Nara had cut her hair because she was displeased at Qianlong's wish to take another secondary consort. The emperor dismissed such notions as absurd and injurious, but—significantly—did not rebut them specifically.

This was still not the last of it. Two years later, in 1778, a slightly deranged young scholar brazenly approached Qianlong during an imperial procession and lodged a petition asking for the restoration of Lady Ula Nara to the rank of empress. For the last time the emperor was forced to defend his actions, repeating that she had wantonly violated a serious taboo and thus merited the punishment she received. The matter was not raised again, but Qianlong could not have been deceived that people had forgotten about it. True or false, the word on the street was that he had wronged his empress, and the emperor, for all his majesty, was powerless to persuade anyone otherwise. There was nothing chivalrous in these protests. As in preceding controversies over ritual violations at court, the fear was that the emperor had failed to discharge the ritual obligations he owed Lady Ula Nara and that a displeased Heaven would bring misfortune upon the dynasty and the country at large. Similar concern at the court of the Ming emperor 250 years before over the proper rites to honor his ancestors had resulted in an enormous controversy that left seventeen officials beaten to death on the steps of the palace and 170 others stripped of their posts and sent to the frontier. In that case, loyalty to the institutions of the dynasty outweighed loyalty to the person of the emperor, at least in some minds. The controversies at Qianlong's court, first over Empress Xiaoxian and then over Lady Ula Nara, were only superficially about hair. They were really about correct rites, family precedents, and cosmic order.

The Lonely Widower

After the catastrophic episode with Lady Ula Nara, Qianlong never took another consort to be empress. (Technically, a third empress was named in 1795, but this was done simply in posthumous honor of the birth mother of the new emperor.) Anyone who was bold enough even to suggest to him that he ought to name another empress was put to death. He also seems to have lost interest in sex, for he had only one more child after 1766, his tenth and last daughter, Princess Hexiao, who was born in 1775. Instead, as he grew older, Qianlong seems to have become increasingly devoted to the memory of his first wife, Lady Fuca. From the day she died, he never stopped writing poems to her. These verses come across as genuine expressions of melancholy, nostalgia, and loneliness. The following lines he wrote on his way through Shandong, traveling back from Hangzhou in 1765, just after he had sent Lady Ula Nara home in disgrace:

Four times have I gone by Ji'nan, but never do I pass through its gates;
I fear to enter, lest my many sorrows unfold.
Ah, that ill-fated third month of spring!
Seventeen years have passed, yet my grief remains unappeased.

Seventeen years, thirty years, forty years, fifty years—it seems he never quite got over his loss. By the time Qianlong died in 1799, he had written over one hundred poems lamenting Lady Fuca's death. This is the last one, written in 1798 after what would be his final visit to her tomb:

> I wanted to drive past without stopping;
> But hiding my feelings earns no comfort, either.
> No harm in offering three cups;
> The four seasons announce another winter.
> The pine trees I planted are old now, tall and scaly;
> They open to the clouds and the broad blue sky.
> Holding hands, I lead you back to the house;
> What joy is there in [solitary] longevity?

All My Children

When he wrote the above lines, Qianlong had already passed the throne on to his fifteenth son, Yongyan. The choice of this son was not an easy one. Behind it lay a long, checkered story of failed hopes and halfhearted compromises.

Qianlong fathered many children—twenty-seven, all told—of whom fifteen (ten sons and five daughters) lived to adulthood. Ten of his children died before the age of five and only eight lived into their thirties; by the time he himself died, in 1799, Qianlong had outlived all but four sons and one daughter. Infant mortality was naturally higher in premodern times, of course, but this did not make the early death of children an easy thing to deal with (the reader will recall that it was the death at age two of her second son that may have led to Lady Fuca's frail nervous condition). As noted earlier, two sons, the first and third, were reprimanded for failing to mourn their mother's death properly and were struck from the list of possible candidates for the throne. Even so, when they succumbed to illness while still in their twenties, Qianlong mourned their deaths bitterly. A few years after having disqualified these two, Qianlong visited the princes' school; he had not yet decided on a new heir and was no doubt curious to see how his boys were faring. It seems this was an unannounced visit, for he caught some of them truant. We can imagine his chagrin when he discovered that his children were failing to take their studies as earnestly as he once had, and that some did not even bother to attend their lessons.

The lack of talent among his sons troubled Qianlong because it represented a limitation on his power, a failing of some sort. True, a few, such as the eighth and eleventh sons, shared ample artistic gifts, but they also turned out to be playboys, showing greater interest in the delights of the capital's entertainment district than in politics. In Qianlong's eyes they lacked the necessary gravity required of the Son of Heaven. (Later in life, the eleventh son, at first merely eccentric, eventually became mentally unstable and unable to care for himself.) At one point, the fifth son seemed to have good prospects. Qianlong even granted him a princely title, the first to go to any of the sons in that generation. But just four months after receiving this distinction, he died. His death at age twenty-five left only two sons in possible contention for the throne, the fifteenth and the seventeenth. Both were born of the same mother, the Consort Wei. The latter son was a classic idler who devoted himself wholly to sensual pleasures rather than to the classics, sometimes slipping out of the palace at night in disguise to meet with drinking companions—hardly a likely choice for emperor. So out of seventeen sons, in the end, Qianlong had no real choice but to designate the fifteenth, Yongyan, as his heir. He postponed doing so for some time, however, waiting until December 1773 (just five days after the Boston Tea Party) to announce that he had chosen a successor and that the casket containing Yongyan's name had been hidden in its proper place over the throne. Beginning in 1796, this son reigned for twenty-five years as the Jiaqing emperor, and proved to be an intelligent and responsible monarch.

In fact, though, it seems that Qianlong's favorite "son" was actually his youngest daughter, Princess Hexiao. Qianlong was sixty-four years old and a great-grandfather when she was born in 1775. Perhaps because she was the only little girl left in the palace (all of her sisters having already married), the young princess became the apple of the emperor's eye, much as he himself had been Kangxi's darling as a boy. For her first birthday, her father presented her with precious toy animals, including a jade lion and a swan made of white coral. As Hexiao grew older, it became apparent that she had inherited not only her father's looks, but also his confidence and his skill with a bow. Dressed in men's clothing, she often went hunting with Qianlong and acquitted herself quite well in the field. "Had you but been a boy," he is supposed to have told her, "I would have made you my heir!" When she came of age, she married Fengšeninde (his name, which in Manchu literally means, "good luck to him," was chosen by Qianlong), the son of Hešen, the most important minister of the later years of Qianlong's reign. By then Princess Hexiao was a serious young woman, scolding her husband for behaving childishly when she caught him once playing games in the snow.

Princess Hexiao's marriage, like the marriages of her fourteen siblings who lived to adulthood, was arranged by her father when she was still very young. It might be thought that imperial matches were made with only politics in mind, but this was not the case in the Qing. Unlike European monarchies, the Manchu ruling family did not depend so much on ties with other families for stability or money or prestige that it needed to marry all of its sons to the daughters of political rivals or powerful nobles. (Indeed, after the time of Yongzheng, there were no more truly powerful nobles.) It did, however, sometimes marry its daughters off with alliances in mind, most commonly with Mongol princes. Two of Qianlong's five daughters married this way; the other three married the sons of influential Manchu political or military figures. All of them lived in Beijing, even those married to Mongols. In the case of Princess Hexiao, the emperor no doubt felt that by marrying her to a trusted and powerful court figure, he was securing her future, which he knew he would not be around to guarantee personally.

The wedding took place in January 1790, when she was fifteen, her husband fourteen, and her father seventy-five. It was a grand event, starting off with a banquet in the main throne hall, from which the princess departed by sedan chair for the residence of her new husband. An escort of twenty guardsmen cleared the way through Beijing's streets, past the crowds who had come out to observe the excitement. The procession was long, and included a splendid wagon train carry-ing wedding presents the emperor was giving his daughter: gold, silver, gems, furs, furniture, servants, clothing, countless bolts of silk and satin, jewelry boxes, combs, cosmetics, clocks, teapots, even spittoons. No daughter in the realm had ever brought such a dowry. Its extravagance—a Korean ambassador who had witnessed the marriage of an older princess remarked that Hexiao received ten times as many gifts—attested to the very strong affection Qianlong felt for his youngest daughter.

Her good fortune declined dramatically only a decade later, however, when her father-in-law, Hešen, was executed on charges of corruption in 1799 (see Chapter 9) and the new emperor, Jiaqing, deprived her husband of most of his titles and posi-tions. Still, it could have been much worse, since he might well have been executed himself (truly, he was "lucky"). Not only did Jiaqing (her elder half-brother) spare her husband's life but he even allowed them to keep part of their estate so they would have something to live on. When she died in 1823, the last memories of a golden age vanished with her

As a young emperor, Qianlong strove to emulate the ideals he had observed as a boy at the courts of his grandfather and father. For all his efforts, it seems he was only marginally successful in passing those ideals on to his own children. Especially after the death of Lady Fuca in 1748, his direct involvement in the edu-cation of his sons diminished, leaving him for many years despairing of a suitable heir. We can thus appreciate the pride he felt in Princess Hexiao, who—except for her gender—embodied the essence of those qualities he felt made his people fit to rule China. The emergence of a strong character such as hers may have reassured him that, however disappointing his other children were, he was still capable of siring a worthy offspring. Had his sons by Lady Fuca survived, things might have been different. As it was, he found no son or grandson to place his hopes in as Kangxi and his father had been able to place their hopes in him. To be sure, their lack of dedication to the Manchu family business was not entirely Qianlong's fault. Some of it was the usual thing that happens to spoiled children of wealthy families, and some of it was plain bad luck. Yet his treatment of his mother and the lavishing of gifts upon Princess Hexiao suggest a trend toward increasing extravagance as the Qianlong era progressed. By putting on ever grander and more magnificent displays of wealth, the emperor does bear some responsibility for creating an atmosphere of permissiveness. Even if it was done in the name of filiality, Qianlong ended up transgressing the boundaries of modest simplicity that, as he himself once professed to Lady Fuca, were so important to Manchu virtue. His strong attachment to strict old-fashioned ritual contrasted sharply with this growing profligacy, and must have left some confused.

4

The Dilemma of Manchu Success

A preoccupation with continuity dominated not just Qianlong's family life, but almost all aspects of his waking existence. If as a father his basic duty to his family was to ensure the perpetuation of the family name, so as emperor his basic duty was to ensure the prolongation of the family's rule. On top of this, as the leader of his people, Qianlong had another, similar, obligation to ensure the survival of the Manchus and of Manchu traditions. On a fundamental level, these various duties were interconnected: Manchu rule, represented in the person of the Qing emperor, could only continue if the emperor had sons *and* if the emperor's family retained those things that made it recognizably Manchu. On the former count, in Chapter 3 we have already seen evidence of Qianlong's concern over finding a suitable heir. The situation on the latter front was also the source of considerable anxiety, particularly if we understand "family" as Qianlong did, to mean the broader community of Manchu men, women, and children.

Condemned by Success

By the time Qianlong became emperor, the Manchus were in danger of becoming victims of their own success. A century of living among the Han Chinese and the combined effects of high living, imprudence, inflation, and underemployment were threatening to turn a redoubtable, highly competent military elite into a class of parasitic has-been warriors who could not really speak their native language. Qianlong's reign thus coincided with a major crisis in Manchu identity in which the future of Qing rule hung in the balance. The emperor was preoccupied by the example of the Manchus' ancestors, the Jurchens of the Jin dynasty (briefly described later), whose excessive acculturation to the Chinese way of life led, it was widely believed, to their fall from power.

History is littered with cases that show the difficulty of preserving the original spirit of vital world-making that characterizes the origins of all great political regimes. The pattern, of course, is that success breeds complacency and with complacency comes ruin. The Greek historian Xenophon warned Greek soldiers that to remain in Persia would inure them to a life of ease and turn them from Hellenes into barbarians. Later, the Romans claimed the Greeks had lost their "manly virtue" and that it had been reborn in the hearts of the descendants of Aeneas; but in the speeches of Roman senators one finds countless references to falling standards and lost ideals. Similar refrains have been sung in other times and places. The great Arab historian Ibn Khaldun (1332–1406), for example, would have understood Qianlong's predicament well. He believed that the secret of political power lay in what he called *asabiyya,* or "group feeling," that sense of cohesion and belonging that binds individuals together in the pursuit of a common aim, usually bettering their lives by earning supremacy over others.

Had he lived in the eighteenth century Ibn Khaldun would certainly have recognized the importance for the Manchus of hanging on to their group identity. He also would have insisted that Qianlong's chances for success were not good. According to Ibn Khaldun, royal authority always decayed in the space of four generations:

> The builder of the family's glory knows what it cost him to do the work, and he keeps the qualities that created his glory and made it last. The son who comes after him had personal contact with his father and thus learned those things from him. The third generation must be content with imitation and, in particular, with reliance upon tradition. The fourth generation is inferior to the preceding ones in every respect. Its member has lost the qualities that preserved the edifice of its glory. He imagines that the edifice was not built through application and effort. He thinks that it was something due his people from the very beginning by virtue of the mere fact of their descent.

In the Qing case, the builder was Hong Taiji and his brother Dorgon, who engineered the Qing conquest. The builder's heir was Kangxi, and the third-generation traditionalist Yongzheng. Qianlong thus represented the fourth generation, which would be responsible for the destruction of the dynasty. Qianlong's rearguard actions were by this logic doomed from the start.

Qianlong never read Ibn Khaldun's writings. Still, he seems to have known that time was not on his side. This chapter lays out the long struggle conducted by Qianlong in the name of sustaining Manchu ways, Qing power, and his own identity as a non-Chinese ruler of China.

The Jin Precedent

If history was any guide—and, as we shall see, history was Qianlong's guide in almost everything—holding on to Manchu ancestral traditions while governing China would be a very tough challenge. In thinking about the Manchus, Qianlong's most important baseline of comparison was the Jin dynasty, which ruled the northern part of China from 1115 to 1234. The Jin dynasty shared a number of key similarities with the Qing. Like the Qing, the Jin was founded by a northern frontier people, the Jurchens, from whom the Manchus were in fact quite likely descended; like the Qing, the Jin, too, came to power through military conquest. Also like the Qing, the Jin had debated whether, as outsiders, their claims to rule China were as legitimate as claims made by ethnically Chinese rulers, and decided they were. But probably the most obvious similarity shared by the Jin and the Qing dynasties was the basic problem of how to rule over the vast Chinese empire when their own people were so few in number.

The lesson that Qianlong read in the history of the Jin boiled down to the fairly simple proposition that a minority group needed to maintain its own particular identity if it was to continue to stay in power. If over time the distinctiveness of the group was allowed to fade and the conquering people left to assimilate to the ways of the majority Han Chinese, then—so the thinking went—the vitality of the ruling elite would be dissipated and the dynasty was doomed to collapse. Qianlong noted that Jin rule lasted only a little over one hundred years and connected it with reports in historical chronicles (which formed his reading at breakfast) of widespread assimilation among the Jin-dynasty Jurchens.

That his own reign coincided with the hundred-year mark in Qing rule over China was surely one reason Qianlong took so seriously a speech made in 1636 by Hong Taiji, the second Qing emperor. Hong Taiji raised the Jin experience as a cautionary tale of the fate that would befall the Manchus if they allowed themselves to be seduced by the charms of Chinese culture. Pointing out to his followers the ways in which some Jin emperors centuries before had adopted the pampered, "dissolute" lifestyle of the Chinese, he warned that this led inevitably to the neglect of native language and traditions. "What I fear," Qianlong's great-great-grandfather had said, "is that the children and grandchildren of later generations will abandon the Old Way, neglect shooting and riding, and enter into the Chinese Way!" Should this come to pass, he predicted that the fall of the dynasty would be hard to avoid. The point of this story was that the "Old Way" of the Manchus must be preserved at all costs.

Such dire warnings might have remained for Qianlong merely an abstract lesson, except that by the 1730s the Manchus were indeed showing telltale signs of assimilation. Among the grandchildren of the tough soldiers who brought the Qing to power, many had succumbed to the pleasures of urban life, setting aside their swords and lances for dice and paintbrushes. Some were unable even to ride a horse and took instead to moving around in that most effete of conveyances, the sedan chair. An ever-growing number of Manchu soldiers were living beyond their means and were forced to pawn their weapons and armor to pay debts piled up at restaurants, gambling dens, and shops. On top of all this, the Manchu language was losing ground to Chinese as the dominant language at court, and even among his own imperial guard Qianlong heard Chinese spoken with alarming frequency.

But Qianlong had no intention of presiding passively over the disappearance of the Manchus or the demise of the Qing. As he wrote forcefully on one occasion,

> Today I happened to be looking through the *Veritable Records* for the Kangxi reign and read: "Although all under Heaven is peaceful, military preparedness cannot be abandoned. If Manchus themselves continuously fall into formation, follow on the hunt, practice diligence, and endure hardship, only then will they become accustomed to exertion. This is something that the Han Chinese, with their love of daily ease and comfort, simply cannot accomplish." Upon reading this I was trembling and fearful. Would I dare forget this even for one day? (Translation by Michael Chang, *A Court on Horseback*.)

To remind his people of the stakes involved, Qianlong went so far as to have Hong Taiji's cautionary words engraved on stone and put on display in major cities all around China where Manchus could read them. Because after 1644, Chinese cities were in fact where most Manchus lived—and that was a big part of Qianlong's problem.

The Creation of the Manchus

Before the Qing armies invaded China, the people who made up the core of those armies, the Manchus, had lived for generations in villages scattered throughout the frontier region northeast of China. This region lacked a single name (by 1800 it would be called "Manchuria") and the Manchus did not have a unified name for themselves then, either. The name "Manchu" did not even exist yet; using the old Jin name, people called themselves "Jurchen," if they called themselves anything at all. There were three separate groups: the Jianzhou Jurchens, the Haixi Jurchens, and the Yeren (or "wild") Jurchens, each of which occupied a distinct geographic region and was subject to further tribal or lineage subdivisions. With no formal political structure, responsibility for decisions on important affairs was left to hereditary lineage headmen. Most headmen held titles and privileges bestowed by the Chinese government in Beijing, confirming their roles as local leaders. In exchange, they declared loyalty to the Ming emperor and agreed to render to his court locally produced goods (mainly furs and ginseng, but also horses) in lieu of taxes. This loose tributary arrangement allowed Beijing to claim authority over these peoples and kept a relative peace.

The separation into different groups of the Jurchens, whom the Chinese saw as occasionally troublesome, was a deliberate consequence of a policy that aimed to prevent alliances from forming among lineages or tribes. Beijing feared that such a development might threaten Ming dominance. Indeed, the court sometimes took the trouble to deliberately cultivate instability in the region, which made their peacekeeping presence there seem all the more necessary. At the end of the sixteenth century, however, the very sort of alliance the Ming had long dreaded began to take shape under the leadership of a junior member of a Jianzhou lineage named Nurhaci (Qianlong's great-great-great-grandfather). Though he started out as a headman like the others, Nurhaci showed himself to be the most skillful political and military leader any Jurchen tribe had seen in over five hundred years. By the 1590s he had brought most of the Jianzhou Jurchens either directly or indirectly under his rule and set about expanding his control to include other Jurchens as well. Taking inspiration from the way villagers formed temporary armed groups to hunt together in season, he organized the households under his authority into small units called in Manchu *niru* ("arrows") and put several "arrows" together into larger units known as *gūsa*, called "banners" in English. Along with companies, these banners, which were distinguished by color, became the defining structures of Manchu society. They proved a superb means of marshalling soldiers for battle and also provided an efficient, flexible framework for bringing people of different backgrounds into a permanent, unified, militarized social order of "bannermen" and "bannerwomen."

As Nurhaci became more powerful, more and more Jurchens—along with Mongols, Koreans, and Chinese living on the frontier—joined him. All of them required a place in the nascent regime, and the banner system provided an institutional home that conferred upon them a new status clearly identifying them as Nurhaci's followers. When his son Hong Taiji took over in 1626, the last opposition from the Haixi Jurchens had been quelled and two of the Yeren tribes had also been incorporated into an alliance of tribes, an alliance not unlike the sort of confederation that Chinggis Khan had assembled some four centuries before. After it absorbed the territories of southern Manchuria in the early 1620s, Nurhaci's confederation had already begun to assume greater responsibilities, such as collecting taxes and administering justice over the local civilian Chinese population. Under Hong Taiji's leadership the confederation began to look more like a state, acquiring alongside its powerful military a rudimentary administrative apparatus with lettered officials who issued decrees, instituted laws, translated documents, and kept records. Finally, in 1636, Hong Taiji took a dramatic step toward the final unification of all the Jurchens under his authority by proclaiming that henceforth they would all be known by a new name, *Manju*, in other words, "Manchu."

The origin and sense of this name remain unclear to this day; it seems it might once have been the name of one Jurchen sub-tribe, or perhaps it was originally the name of a river. Wherever "Manchu" came from and whatever it meant, Hong Taiji insisted that everyone use it and threatened harsh punishment for anyone applying the old name "Jurchen." Part of his thinking may well have been that he wanted to avoid a name associated with the days of being subjects of the Ming, whose supremacy he was now preparing to challenge. Another motive, however, seems to have been to provide a unifying label for all Jurchens that was free of the connotations of old rivalries. Needless to say, merely assigning a new name did not instantly create unity, and disagreements between certain Manchu lineages lingered. Nonetheless, it must be said that the creation of the "Manchus" was an unusually successful experiment in ethnic engineering—so successful, in fact, that there are still many millions of people who identify themselves as Manchus in China today, even though the Manchu dynasty and just about everything associated with Manchu culture, including the spoken language, are long gone.

The Dilemma of the Manchu Occupation

Part of the success of the newly christened Manchu people can be explained through the effective institutional integration of Jurchens from different backgrounds into the Eight Banners and the weakening of earlier tribal ties. How great these original differences were is difficult to say. Written records from the preconquest period—records in which Qianlong later took a keen personal interest—suggest that Jurchens in the early 1600s indeed did share something of a common identity and culture and that they were very conscious, moreover, of the things that made other people (Chinese, Koreans, Mongols) different from them. That the name "Manchu" stuck leads one to suppose that it may actually have expressed a widely shared sentiment that they, the various Jurchen peoples, had come to constitute a new people. If so, that feeling was surely reinforced by the simultaneous introduction of a new name for the state, "Qing," in 1636. Hong Taiji chose this name to replace the name "Jin" that his father, deliberately patterning himself after the earlier Jin dynasty, had chosen in 1616. Again, we are not entirely sure what the name Qing was supposed to mean, apart from its literal sense in Chinese, "pure." But we should note that in the Manchu language the new name was *Daicing*, which in both Manchu and Mongolian means "warrior." For those who could understand it, then, Hong Taiji was sending a clear signal as to his intentions for the future.

Sure enough, eight years after the reforms of 1636, Qing warriors poured through the Great Wall. Few ever went back. Instead, they and their families took up permanent residence within China, making their homes in cities like Beijing, Nanjing, Hangzhou, and Xi'an, where walled military garrisons were established to secure the new regime's control. After the conquest, bannermen came to constitute a special class of subjects, ruled separately from civilians. In exchange for a lifetime of dedication, the Qing court (relying on China's vast wealth) guaranteed their welfare and the welfare of their families from cradle to grave. Legally classified as members of a hereditary professional military caste—it is important to remember that one had to be born into the system—bannermen could not enter any line of work other than the military or the bureaucracy (farming was another option, but few considered it an appealing choice). What we would regard as purely personal choices (e.g., marriage) were routinely subject to official approval by banner officers. If war broke out, men might be summoned on short notice to take up the fight on the frontier, which entailed grueling marches and prolonged deprivation, and where death or serious injury was always a real possibility.

Despite such restrictions and demands, for many decades, life in the banners was quite attractive. For one thing, it meant that one had a steady income provided by the state, paid four times a year in silver and in grain. In addition, one enjoyed a variety of privileges, such as disability payments, pensions, frequent bonuses, free housing, and interest-free loans. Bannermen paid no taxes and were immune to prosecution by local Chinese civilian officials. Even when arrested, they were held in separate jails, and if they were convicted of wrongdoing they got off with lighter penalties, when they were punished at all. Moreover, their access to official positions, especially for those who lived in Beijing, where about half the population of the Eight Banners lived, was far easier than it was for Han Chinese, since most of them did not need to have examination degrees to fill posts in the imperial bureaucracy. With these various privileges as an attraction, not surprisingly, more and more non-banner Chinese tried to find ways to join the system, often going so far as to change their names and pose as Manchus. The additional influx of people created an overwhelming burden for the Eight Banners administration, which could barely cope with the natural increase of the original banner population.

The looming bankruptcy of the banner system—in both the literal and moral senses—was thus one of the most serious issues Qianlong faced in his first few decades on the throne. "The Eight Banners are the root of the nation and dynasty," Qianlong blustered soon after taking power,

> . . . but long years of ease have gradually led to wasteful extravagance. On top
> of this, population has increased. Yet people fail to attend to basic household

economy and fritter away everything they have instead of being frugal. Soldiers and bannermen not actively employed think only of pretty clothes and fine food, and get into the habit of throwing their money away on those things without thinking twice. This is the real reason for poverty among bannermen.

This statement spells out Qianlong's view of the problem: the livelihood of the conquest group was imperiled by wastefulness and too much easy living. These trends had the potential to destroy the dynasty's "root."

Equally alarming was the pace of Manchu acculturation, the other consequence of the occupation of China. Daily contact with the Chinese world—in markets, restaurants, theaters, and the corridors of power—brought with it exposure to a culture that was older, vaster, and richer by far than anything to be found in the frontier world the Manchus had left behind. Over time that harsh frontier world became little more than a memory, and life within China became the real world for almost all Manchus. It was only a matter of time before Hong Taiji's fears of Manchus "entering the Chinese Way" were realized. Qianlong was obviously unable to shield people from the delights of urban life or get them to revert to the lifestyles of a century before. To have removed bannermen from the sources of temptation by closing the garrisons and sending everyone back to Manchuria was not an option, as it would have meant surrendering control over China altogether and would have defeated his purpose.

Concern that the continued erosion of native institutions and the loss of clear distinctions between conqueror and conquered compelled Qianlong to act to defend the basis of Qing authority. Faced with a dual crisis, he pursued two strategies. One was to shore up the institutional structure of the Eight Banners, which we will come back to later in this chapter. The other was to promote a renaissance of Manchu ethnic awareness. Following his father's example, Qianlong never tired of promoting Manchu ancestral traditions and Manchu virtues as bravery and frugality along with skills such as marksmanship and horsemanship. He adopted a variety of approaches toward the preservation of a separate Manchu identity, including advancing the Manchu language, collating and editing historical materials, writing poems that glorified the Manchu homeland, codifying religious rituals, and celebrating Manchu martial culture. Examining these different activities can help us better understand Qianlong's perspective on his rule, his place in history, and his understanding of the Manchus' role at the head of the empire.

The Power of Words

For Qianlong, the most crucial element of Manchu identity was language. The centrality of language to ethnic identity is widely observed around the world, and this was no less true among the Manchus. In letters written to Mongol chieftains more than a century before Qianlong's reign, Nurhaci had made frequent reference to his followers as "the people of the Jurchen tongue," implying that all those under him spoke Jurchen and, just as important, that Jurchens were Jurchens by virtue of their shared language. Hong Taiji's warning of the dire consequences that would follow if the Manchus' native tongue were allowed to decline is another sign that the Manchu elite had long recognized the importance of language. This concern was shared by emperors after 1644, but few rivaled Qianlong in their attention to this issue. In his many pronouncements exhorting Manchu subjects to devote themselves to the study of their native language, he noted that "the keystone for Manchus is language." He linked the growing preference for speaking and writing Chinese with "the loss of our old Manchu customs." When Manchu officials were unable to converse with the emperor in their formal audiences with him, or when they took Chinese-sounding names, Qianlong scolded them for having "forgotten their roots" and for allowing themselves to have become seriously tainted by Han customs. "How can someone who calls himself a bannerman not speak Manchu?!" he once fumed.

Qianlong tried various means to stimulate broader interest in the Manchu language, such as instituting formal language schooling and offering attractive career opportunities for adept translators. Though these efforts had limited effect, the emperor was not discouraged. He furnished scholars with more and better aids for learning and using Manchu, including new translations of the major Chinese classic texts. In 1771 he published a revised and enlarged version of a Manchu-Chinese dictionary, first published by Kangxi in 1708, explaining in the preface his hope that "by disseminating this to my descendants, the officials, and the people, [Manchu] writing will be standardized and passed on generation to generation, and thereby made everlasting." Later in his reign, expanded versions of this dictionary appeared successively with the Mongolian, Tibetan, and Turkic translations of Manchu terms and phrases added in. But Manchu, as the official "national language," always took pride of place.

The emperor's obsession with language and text is seen also in concordances of pronunciations and standard transcriptions of Chinese and Manchu proper names and in specialized works on the early Manchu language written in the 1740s at Qianlong's direct orders and published by the palace. In sponsoring these works, the emperor may have imbibed some of the philological spirit current among Chinese intellectuals at the time (discussed in Chapter 7), but above all he was acting out of a sense of duty to history, especially Manchu history. Just a few years after becoming emperor he had had the *Veritable Records* (the title of the official chronicles) of the earliest Qing rulers recopied using the newly standardized system he advocated for writing place names. In the process, it was discovered that a portion of the dynasty's earliest archives was in tatters. Not only that, there was hardly anyone left who could still decipher the old script in which these records were written. Fearing that the dynasty's early history might one day prove unrecoverable, Qianlong ordered the immediate compilation of a comparative dictionary of old and new Manchu. Later, in the 1770s, he went further and commanded that these archives be recopied in the reformed script. At the same time, he ordered scholars to edit and revise the early chronicles, taking advantage of the opportunity to produce an officially sanctioned (and somewhat sanitized) version of early Qing history.

Qianlong's preoccupation with language was in considerable measure responsible also for his decision to have the main Buddhist canon translated into Manchu. This enormous body of Indian religious texts, originally written in Sanskrit, existed in many languages, but the continued lack of a Manchu version suggested to Qianlong that his efforts to achieve parity between Manchu and other, older scriptural languages still came up short. As he wrote in the preface:

> The Sanskrit scriptures have been translated into Tibetan, into Chinese, and into Mongolian. Our Qing dynasty has ruled China for over one hundred years now, with these three groups long beholden to us as officials and servants. How can it be that the scriptures are lacking in the national language [Manchu] alone? Having them translated from Chinese into Manchu will lead all people everywhere to study Manchu; even if they do not learn the Buddha's first truths, they will still learn to respect their lord and love their superiors, to abandon evil and pursue goodness. Is this not also worthy? Our primary intent in translating the Buddhist scriptures into Manchu is precisely this and nothing else.

If we examine this text closely, we see that in rendering the foundational texts of Buddhism into Manchu, Qianlong's primary wish was to encourage people to learn Manchu and to elevate the language's standing, enrich its vocabulary, and bring it prestige. Whether they took up Buddhist practice themselves seems to have been a secondary consideration.

A devout believer himself in esoteric (Tantric) Buddhism, another of Qianlong's aims doubtless was to gain karmic merit through an act that, as it glorified the Manchu language, also glorified the teachings of the Buddha. In 1771 Qianlong therefore organized a group of about one hundred experts to translate the entire canon (called the Kanjur) into Manchu. This became the most massive translation effort of Qianlong's reign. Great care was taken in the transliteration of religious terms, which were put in forms as close as possible to the Sanskrit original rather than to their Chinese translations. Another part of the process involved the use of an entirely new set of Manchu letters, created at Qianlong's behest, that could more accurately render *dharani*, mystical Buddhist incantations that relied on sound rather than meaning for their efficacy. When it came to this (or any) language project, no detail was too small or unimportant as far as Qianlong was concerned: He personally reviewed the translations of many sutras himself, pointing out errors and making improvements. Later he even went back to double check that his emendations had been followed and added further corrections if they had not been. The scale and thoroughness of the project gave it a life of its own; when it was done, nineteen years later, Qianlong was past his eightieth birthday. Only three sets of the translation were ever printed, each set filling 108 large volumes, beautifully printed in red ink. One set is preserved today, divided between museum collections in Beijing and Taipei.

Inventing History

Qianlong's desire to rewrite the past and celebrate Manchu language and history ran deep. It led him to compose or sponsor two entirely original works in very different genres, the *Ode to Mukden* and the *Researches on Manchu Origins*. The first of these was a 1743 poem he wrote to commemorate his visit that year, described in Chapter 5, to the ancestral tombs in Manchuria. Encircled on its southern periphery by a palisade of willows and on its eastern rim by the snow-capped Changbai

Mountains, Mukden was the mythical locus of Manchu origins, a preserve of ancient memory closed to Chinese settlement. Qianlong's poem, conceived in the classical Chinese form of the *fu* or "rhapsody," which traditionally lent itself to ornate description and romantic invention, consisted of a lengthy consideration of the wonders of the Manchu homeland, a "country blessed by heaven, [whence] khans arose." Under his brush, Mukden's sky and earth, its teeming wildlife, dense forests, and fertile fields combined to create an auspicious environment:

> Majestic Mukden was founded along the north bank of the Shen waters. Its mountains are high and its rivers broad. It is fixed as a universal model, a most wondrous place, great as a tiger or a dragon. Established on a grand scale, it promulgates the rule of great kings. It surpasses and humbles all [other] places and has united [lands] within and [lands] without.

It was only natural, according to Qianlong's view, that so majestic a dynasty as the Qing should have arisen in such a setting. Five years after it was first published, the emperor ordered the *Ode* reprinted in a special edition that required the carving of woodblocks for the entire text sixty-four times: thirty-two times in different Chinese antique seal scripts, and thirty-two times using the same seal scripts as adapted to the Manchu alphabet. He thus managed to inject further political meaning into the *Ode*, writing in a new preface that he desired to promote the "ancient" forms of Manchu writing, which he claimed were superior to Chinese in their "perfect combination" of sound and form. This was a far-fetched claim, because Manchu did not even have its own script before circa 1600. We can see that, for Qianlong, extolling the virtues of the Manchu language and the Manchu past trumped such prosaic considerations as mere fact.

Much the same spirit can be found in the *Researches of Manchu Origins*, published in 1783. This work, which reprinted in its pages the preface to the *Ode to Mukden*, aimed to establish a grand narrative of Manchu history linking the founders of the Manchu Qing dynasty to those of the Jurchen Jin centuries before, both in terms of ancestry as well as in terms of shared geographical origins in the Changbai Mountains. In causing this account of Manchu history to be written and published, Qianlong had a number of things in mind. First, by proving the antiquity of the Manchus as a people, he hoped to demonstrate the Manchus' own imperial heritage and thereby underscore the legitimacy of Qing rule. Second, by arguing that the Manchus had never in fact been subservient to the Ming, he wished to show that it was the Chinese emperor who had betrayed Manchu leaders, and not Manchu leaders who had proved disloyal to the Ming, a line of reasoning that also reinforced the justice of the Manchu claim to the Mandate of Heaven. Third, by furnishing a holistic account of the rise of the Manchu state based on written records, Qianlong aimed to dispel any doubts regarding the Manchus' own political and cultural vitality and to endow his people with a more "authentic" history than the legends of the early Manchus, mentioned in Chapter 1.

Interestingly, Qianlong did not seek to hide the Manchus' "barbarian" origins, and even quoted from early Chinese descriptions of the Jurchens that portrayed them as crude and violent. However, he drew the line at citing equally uncomplimentary accounts dating from the Ming, which hit too close to home. In fact, he banned most of these writings from circulation altogether at just this time, because of his wish to demonstrate that the Manchus represented the culmination of centuries of development that had reached initial fruition under the Jin and now had achieved its full flowering under him; to have sixteenth-century Manchu forebears described in terms equally as insulting as those used for sixth-century forebears would have violated the idea of a smooth historical progression from ancient times to the present that Qianlong wished to convey.

The power of this narrative was such that even though little archaeological evidence has ever emerged to support its main claims (such as descent from pre-historical peoples who dwelt in the area), many modern accounts of the Manchus written in the twentieth century continue to make reference to the very same landmarks first pointed out by Qianlong. By grounding the Manchus firmly in Chinese antiquity and by framing the rise of the Manchus to imperial power as the outcome of inexorable historical process, Qianlong succeeded in providing all Manchus with their first coherent "national" history. But the *Researches* did more than just this. Because it included sections on geography, genealogy, and customs, Qianlong's compilation, like his earlier poem on Mukden, fleshed out other aspects of the Manchu heritage and helped in the construction of a more stable (so he hoped) identity that would endure beyond his own reign and serve to perpetuate Qing rule for generations to come.

Taming Shamanic Rites

Thoughts of future generations, the wish to extend imperial authority as far as possible, and a seemingly irrepressible urge to regulate and codify led the emperor to attempt to insert himself into every aspect of Manchu life. This included not only language and history but also religion. For most Manchus, "religion" meant not Buddhism, which had come to them relatively recently, in the early 1600s, but shamanism. Shamanic beliefs and practices were among the most enduring elements of native Manchu culture and set Manchus apart from non-Manchus in Qing society.

Shamanism in fact originated in the Manchus' own backyard, in northeast Asia. It may be loosely characterized as a system of beliefs in a world of spirits inhabiting the natural environment, with whom specially gifted human mediums, called shamans, are able to communicate. Very often, the shaman was a woman. Her communication with the spirit world took various forms, including sacrifice, dance, music, and incantation, and was employed toward various ends, such as curing disease, ensuring prosperity, and preventing harm. The most common shamanic rites among Manchus in the Qing aimed simply to propitiate the spirits. Sometimes referred to as "bright rituals," these occurred on a regular basis and involved sacrifices to different deities as well as to heaven and to one's ancestors. Less common was "transformational" shamanism, with darker, more unpredictable ceremonies that were intended to heal the sick or to exorcise demons in specific cases of possession. For both types of ritual, shamanistic practice occurred within two rather distinct cults, one imperial and the other common. Each cult was distinguished by the specifics of the ritual, including the chants used, spirits invoked, and so forth.

In codifying Manchu shamanism, Qianlong may have been trying to replace the common cult (meaning the whole range of rituals practiced by lineages other than the imperial clan, the Aisin Gioro) through the promotion of the orderly imperial cult as the standard ritual for all Manchus. To achieve this goal Qianlong characteristically resorted to a textual strategy, issuing a standard version of the "bright rituals" of the Aisin Gioro in a 1747 publication titled *Manchu Rites for Sacrifices to the Spirits and to Heaven*. In the preface to this work, Qianlong made it clear that his purpose was to preserve native Manchu customs by rectifying variant practices among the different clans. The elaborate rituals of patriarchal shamanic sacrifice carried out by his family were therefore advanced in the *Manchu Rites* as the model for all Manchu families to follow. In particular, Qianlong was concerned about the influence of the Chinese language, because shamans frequently no longer understood the meaning of the chants they performed in Manchu. Some continued to use them, but badly mangled the pronunciation and therefore the meaning of the chants; others were switching to chanting in Chinese. By providing a standard liturgy, Qianlong hoped to bring greater uniformity to shamanic traditions and at the same time bring them within imperial control, thereby gaining a measure of influence over the spiritual lives of his Manchu subjects.

In this regard, it is noteworthy that no liturgy was included in the *Manchu Rites* for transformational ritual. Indeed, the very title of the work suggests that this kind of ritual was not to be treated, perhaps because Qianlong saw in this aspect of shamanic tradition remnants of an "uncivilized" Manchu past, and therefore wished to sweep it under the rug. How successful he was in this effort it is difficult to say. The formalized protocols contained in the *Manchu Rites* are not the only shamanic texts that have survived from the Qing, suggesting that in spite of Qianlong's desire to supplant it, the common ritual endured. In this regard, we might note, Qianlong ultimately *did* supply a model for other Manchus, just not the one he meant to supply; that is, where he meant for people to follow the ritual he published for their use, they went him one better and instead imitated his larger strategy, writing their own rites down for their own posterity.

Warrior Ways

Whatever the long-term threat to dynastic continuity posed by the deterioration of Manchu cultural identity, there was no more immediate and tangible problem than the loss of warrior ways. Eight Banner soldiers were personally responsible for the emperor's own security, and they bore the lion's share of the burden of empire, staffing garrisons around China proper as well as fighting the wars on the ever-expanding Qing frontier. These duties required utter dependability, bravery, and grit—qualities that Qianlong celebrated as defining Manchu traits, and which he thought were lacking in Han Chinese. It was these qualities that had given the Manchus an edge in 1644 and under Qianlong they still figured in the overall calculation of Qing power. All governing regimes rely to some extent upon coercion, but for a minority regime like the Qing the question was more urgent. From where Qianlong sat, it mattered a great deal that the Chinese populace—the 98 percent of the empire's population outside the Eight Banners—be at least somewhat in awe of Manchu military might.

That people *were* afraid was unquestionably the case in the early years of the dynasty. Even a generation or more after the conquest, Manchu soldiers were often accused of exploiting their superior position as conquerors: cheating Chinese merchants, enslaving peasants, and raping women. The mere presence of a Manchu soldier or officer on the street inspired respect and caution, if not outright dread. In those days, meetings of the emperor's top ministers were often as not conducted in the Manchu language; Han Chinese officials were left outside the door to nod their assent to whatever was decided by the powerful bannermen close to the throne. Such fear was regarded by the emperor as a necessary and healthy thing. It gave the Manchu elite a political edge which they would not otherwise have had, since they were not nearly as experienced in government as the Han officials who worked alongside them, and who they suspected secretly held their Manchu overlords in contempt. Since they could not realistically hope to compete with Han Chinese in erudition, it made sense to retain war-making as the Manchus' strong suit.

This worked well for quite some time. But, predictably enough, the toughness and dedication of the founding generation slowly gave way to softer, more self-interested ideals in their grandchildren. Aspirations to achievement in Chinese cultural terms were not long in spreading among Manchus living in such flourishing urban centers as Beijing, Nanjing, and Hangzhou. Bannermen joined literary societies, where they could practice painting and poetry writing, or they became collectors, playwrights, even novelists (the author of China's most famous novel, *The Dream of the Red Chamber*, was a Chinese bannerman). Qianlong saw nothing wrong with the literary ideal—he embraced it himself—so long as it did not mean the neglect of one's skills as a Manchu. But there were plenty of indications that martial standards were in fact slipping. He took these signs to heart, issuing edict after edict exhorting bannermen to keep their self-respect and hold on to native ways. Riding and archery—especially mounted archery—he said, amounted to the "family training of our nation," basic skills that all Manchus must possess. Allowing them to slip would betray ancestral trust: "From the time of its founding, our nation has placed great importance on shooting from horseback. The old practices and institutions should be respectfully followed by practicing and accustoming oneself to rigorous exertion."

Qianlong was particularly passionate about Manchu officials executing their duties in a way that honored the accomplishments of the dynasty's seventeenth-century heroes. If they did not, they were liable to be executed themselves. Such was the fate of Necin, a prominent noble and military leader active in the early part of Qianlong's reign. A true Manchu blueblood, Necin's grandfather had been one of Kangxi's right-hand men, and his great-grandfather was a famous general of the Qing conquest. When in 1746 Qianlong chose him to head the Grand Council, Necin had already compiled an outstanding record of service to the dynasty and seemed a worthy successor to the eminent Ortai. His appointment signaled the emperor's complete trust in his abilities. Two years later, in June 1748, Qianlong placed him in charge of the campaign to restore central control in western Sichuan, where the Tibetan peoples of the Jinchuan River region were in open rebellion. This was a mountainous and remote area, notoriously difficult to govern. Villages occupied the heights and were defended by sturdy stone forts surrounded by palisades and moats. "Necin is the only one who can chart a strategy forward and who can adjust and take advantage of such opportunities as present themselves," Qianlong said. "In commanding the entire army, his standing is such that everyone from general to soldier will shape up and pay attention." As Qianlong's man on the ground, his performance would reflect directly on the throne.

It is not hard to imagine the emperor's outrage, then, when he learned a few months later that, far from proving himself a shining example of Manchu omnicompetence, Necin brought shame instead. The abject failure of his original plan for a frontal assault on the rebels' mountain strongholds left Necin hopelessly stymied. Unable to develop any alternate strategy, Necin took to his tent and refused to meet with his staff. Instead of dealing with the present reality, he sketched ideas for future campaigns, each plan different from the one before. Though the emperor grew increasingly frustrated as he read these memorials, he still held out hope for news of at least a small victory to save face. But reports of defeats in successive skirmishes piled up, until by the end of the summer, incensed at the news that Necin had failed to capture and execute a known spy on his staff, Qianlong had had enough. Recalling his erstwhile favorite to the capital, the emperor excoriated him: "Even with a ten-to-one advantage you fail! Not to mention that with a massed force of three thousand men you cannot defeat a few score Tibetan bandits. This defies all reason!" In Necin's place Qianlong dispatched his brother-in-law, Fuheng, who quickly put things back on track. Within nine months, Fuheng had secured victory, the first major military success of the Qianlong reign, and returned with his triumphant army.

The receptions that awaited Necin and Fuheng could hardly have been more different. Back in Beijing by the late fall, Necin languished in house arrest for two months, unsure of his fate. After interrogating him repeatedly, Qianlong found him guilty of gross negligence and dereliction of duty, and condemned him to death. Once the hope of his generation, the disgraced Necin was brought to the parade ground where, before the assembled army, he was beheaded in January 1749. In a dramatic gesture meant to reinforce the point that Necin had failed not only him, Qianlong, but also his own ancestors, the emperor specified that the executioner should use the very sword that had once belonged to Necin's famous grandfather. When Fuheng got back a couple of months later, on the other hand, Qianlong ordered all noblemen and officers to the outskirts of the city to greet him. Ten days later, the emperor feted him and his officers at a special banquet in their honor at which he lavished all with food, drink, and gifts. As a clear sign of his favor, Qianlong also elevated Fuheng to the rank of duke, with the epithet "loyal and brave."

In these different ways, Qianlong made examples of Necin and Fuheng. His aim in doing so was not just the short-term goal of winning a battle, but also the long-term goal of rekindling Manchu fighting spirit. This was a never-ending job, however. Since local officials were always more willing to report good news than bad, the only way Qianlong could check to see whether his instructions on upholding Manchu military traditions were being followed was to inspect soldiers' skills himself. Sometimes he was pleased, other times horrified. In 1752 the emperor dropped in unannounced during archery practice in time to observe a number of high-ranking officials fire their arrows into the dirt, completely missing the target. He punished them severely, fining them one year's salary and depriving some of their ranks.

Hunting for Real Men

Spot-checks like this were well and good, but they did not go far enough. Qianlong struck upon a more systematic method for sharpening martial skills in 1741 when he reinstituted the annual hunt. Held late each summer at the Mulan hunting ground, the imperial hunt was a nod to dynastic precedent and may have satisfied Qianlong's wish to relive the "good old days" he remembered from the time he accompanied Kangxi there as a boy. To justify himself to court critics who pointed out that emperors a millennium before had rejected hunting as an extravagance, Qianlong explained, "The hunt as a martial display originated as an old Manchu practice. Every year during the sixty years my grandfather was on the throne he would go north to hunt." Though this wasn't quite true (Kangxi first began hunting there in 1681, after he had already been emperor for twenty years), Qianlong's point—that the Mulan hunt "really was the best way to train Manchus" and that filial obligations required him to observe established practice—carried the day.

The hunts went on, more than fifty of them during Qianlong's reign, the last one in 1795, when he was eighty-four years old. These were proving grounds for Manchu virtue and shows of dynastic vigor on individual and mass scales. Han Chinese were as a rule excluded. On the basis of their martial skills, each year Manchu and Mongol bannermen from the capital and several major garrisons were selected by competition to accompany the imperial party north from Beijing to the frontier. Once encamped at Mulan, they remained there for the month of September and sometimes longer, engaging in a continual series of hunts, archery contests, and sporting events. They were joined by non-banner Mongols from the north and west and by other nomadic subjects of the Manchu dominions like the Kazakhs, for whom this was an opportunity to reaffirm their ties to the throne, and to do so without the risk of contracting smallpox.

The highlight was the grand battue hunt. Three thousand soldiers were divided into small squads that fanned out at dawn to encircle a several square-mile area of the hunting preserve. At the proper signal, they began to close the circle, beating the bush (hence the French name *battue*) to drive the game forward before them. Within a few hours, animals of all sorts—hares, badgers, deer, boar, bears, sometimes even tigers—were forced into a clearing roughly one-half-mile in diameter, the perimeter of the clearing closely guarded by the now-weary beaters, joined by marksmen at the ready. Protected by sharpshooters from any sudden charge (any tigers would first have been taken care of by the "tiger gun brigade") but otherwise unaccompanied by his usual large ceremonial retinue, and armed himself with bow and arrows, Qianlong entered the scene. Riding out and taking careful aim at the largest buck, which had been specially selected for him, he shot and killed the animal, bringing it down before his admiring subjects. At this point, marksmen staked out around the perimeter were free to pursue game on their own (see Figure 4.1). At the end of the day, the meat would be prepared for cooking and divided up among everyone present; a few choice pieces, such as fatty deer tail, might be sent by express messenger to imperial favorites around the empire. All guests would be invited to a large banquet featuring entertainments such as wrestling, acrobatics, show-riding, and the music of lutes,

Figure 4.1   Court artists. *Qianlong Hunting at Mulan.* ca. 1750. Handscroll, ink and colors on silk. Musée Guimet, Paris. The grand hunts at the imperial hunting grounds north of Chengde were a regular part of Qianlong's annual schedule and provided him and his court a chance to practice riding and shooting in a relatively informal environment. © Art Resource.

Mongolian fiddles, and drums. Gifts were exchanged and honors bestowed, reaffirming the vitality of the vast Manchu empire.

The carefully stage-managed spectacle of the battue was balanced by numerous smaller-scale, informal hunts in which the emperor and a select party of companions took part. All these settings gave Qianlong the chance to demonstrate the virtues he insisted were integral to the Manchu national character: toughness, strength, bravery, robust health, and the sharp, "can-do" attitude of the hardened warrior. These qualities—what Qianlong sometimes liked to call "masculine virtue"—were contrasted, fairly or not, with the supposed softness of the effete Chinese man of letters. Qianlong celebrated these qualities in verse and song and, especially, in art. During his reign, numerous paintings of the Mulan hunt (and related subjects, such as rare hounds and prize horses) were commissioned. Over and over again, the emperor had his Jesuit-led salon of court artists paint scenes of the hunt, some on long scrolls that unrolled to reveal splendid tableaux of the wild northern landscape, some in stunning renditions on silk of nearly life-size leaping equestrians (and even the occasional equestrienne), others in murals to decorate palace interiors, still others on screens painted in oils according to Western techniques. The same martial ideal was echoed in portraits of veterans of the Dzungar wars painted in the 1760s and 1770s, described in Chapter 6, intended by Qianlong to commemorate the brave deeds of Manchu and Mongol soldiers.

Protecting the Roots

While for us today the impression left by all of Qianlong's various attempts to shore up the fading "Manchu Way" is deep, it is hard to know how effective this campaign was at the time. How widely disseminated, for instance, was the visual imagery Qianlong so vividly conjured up to amplify his message about the significance of Manchu "family training"? Given the limited circulation of paintings and scrolls, even in the capital, one is tempted to say that though they may have affected those who saw them as profoundly as they affect us now, this was a small audience, composed mostly of elites, not the mass of ordinary bannermen the emperor needed to reach if he was going to stop the steady slide of native Manchu customs. Likewise, though the spectacle of the grand Mulan hunt reached many eyes, this, too, was a select group. Dictionaries, because of their practical value, arguably had a wide circulation, but books such as the *Manchu Rites*, the *Researches of Manchu Origins*, and the *Ode to Mukden* were read by a limited few.

In the end, we are led to conclude that Qianlong's hard-fought campaign to uphold Manchu identity and preserve the dynasty's future by promoting and protecting ancestral ways was mostly a failure. Though there were always a good number of courageous men in the banner ranks, Manchu martial skills did not rebound across the board. The hunts in which Qianlong invested so much time and energy were carried on for only one more generation after his death and then discontinued forever in 1821. By then, the Eight Banners military machine was a shell of its former self. And while shamanic practices persisted—in fact, Manchus in Beijing were still performing shamanic rituals in the early twentieth century—the Manchu language, the most important marker of ethnic identity, continued to decline as Chinese took its place as the language of everyday discourse. It continued to be used in official communication as late as the 1920s, but by then few Manchus then spoke more than a smattering of words in their ancestral language. The last Qing emperor claimed that the only Manchu phrase he ever learned to speak was *ili*, "Arise!", which he would utter to officials kneeling before him.

In light of the ineffectiveness of Qianlong's nativist program and the disappearance of the Manchu language, one might likely reason that Manchu identity itself must have languished and disappeared. Yet this did not happen. Strange to say, despite many, many signs of acculturation, Manchus survived as an ethnic group into the nineteenth and twentieth centuries.

In no small measure, the credit for this belongs to Qianlong, who was as active on the institutional front as he was on the cultural front. His reforms of the Eight Banner system and his defense of Manchu economic, political, and legal privileges helped maintain a particular Manchu way of life. The reader will remember a reference earlier in this chapter to the "dual crisis" in Manchu identity, one cultural, one economic. By Qianlong's time not only were many bannermen forgetting how to ride and shoot, they were slowly becoming poorer. The steady deterioration of the standard of living of ordinary Manchus in the banners was every bit as alarming to Qianlong as the weakening of the cultural and performative manifestations of "Manchuness." Not only was it unseemly for the conquering people to be living in poverty, but unless some kind of solution could be found to the growing penury of the people on the banner rolls, people might begin to desert its ranks and the Eight Banners would disintegrate, dissolving with it the last institutional vestiges of the Manchu conquest regime and placing the future of the imperial house itself in jeopardy.

Qianlong seized the initiative by following up on reforms of the banner system begun by his father that restored a measure of fiscal stability and improved falling standards of living. He found ways to augment incomes in banner households both in the short term—by making gifts of cash (in the parlance of the twenty-first century, "bail-outs") and forgiving loans—and in the long term, by making grants of land and investing state money in real estate and pawnbroking and then earmarking the interest from such investments for the Eight Banners. One reason for Qianlong's success in this area was that it was easier for the state to intervene effectively in the economic and administrative spheres than in the cultural sphere.

Another important initiative was an inventory of the membership of every company in the Eight Banners in order to determine who was genuinely entitled to banner privileges and who was fraudulently claiming Manchu status. Every family was required to produce a genealogy and a brief account of the history of their affiliation with their banner company. These were collected, collated, and investigated, and in the process one's right to banner status was either confirmed or denied. In some cases, outright imposters were caught and summarily thrown out. In other cases, people who joined the banners under unusual circumstances were at first left on the banner rolls, but classified as belonging to a secondary status household; later they would be invited (or forced) to quit the banners and enter the civilian population, where they would have to make their own way. This helped whittle down the population that had to be supported in the banners and opened up more posts for "real" Manchus.

Qianlong pushed this purge of banner ranks slowly but surely from the 1740s through the 1770s. At the same time he also authorized the removal of tens of thousands of Chinese bannermen from positions in the provincial garrisons, making them back into ordinary Chinese (which is what he said they had been to begin with), and giving their livelihoods to Manchus who needed jobs. The materials of those who passed muster were later taken together and published as a kind of collective family history, titled the *Comprehensive Genealogy of the Eight Banner Manchu Clans*. This volume was yet one more example of the emperor's urge to codify and set in writing as much information about the Manchu people as he could.

Qianlong's success in upholding Manchu traditions was at best a qualified one. The easing of the fiscal burden borne by the state for the support of the Eight Banners brought by the reduction of the banner population made it possible for the institution to survive and to continue to mark a fundamental difference between Manchus and others in Qing society. This went a very long way toward sustaining the integrity of the conquering people and underwriting the dynasty's continued domination. But the emperor was unable to halt the economic slide of banner households. By the mid-1800s, poverty and idleness, not privilege and power, were the defining characteristics of "Manchuness." One can thus say that, despite Qianlong's efforts to save it, the old Manchu Way was irrevocably lost on his watch. At the same time, however, a new and distinctive way of living as a Manchu was ushered in. Frankly less vigorous, more urban, and more nostalgic, it continued to exist side-by-side with memories of the old days through to the end of the dynasty and beyond.

5

The Peripatetic Sovereign

As the discussion of hunting in Chapter 4 has shown, Qianlong was a vigorous ruler who enjoyed moving about. When he could, he would leave the walls of the Forbidden City for the more informal surroundings of the suburban palace just northwest of Beijing (where he first met his grandfather, Kangxi), or venture even further away to the bucolic setting of the Qing summer capital at Chengde or a rustic camp at Mulan. Indeed, Qianlong made traveling a signature of his ruling style. He personally visited scores of places throughout the realm, not just in the north but also in the east and, especially, the south (though not the far south). Most years he was gone from Beijing for at least three months, and some years as many as six months. Taking the lower figure as an average, and multiplying by sixty, we find that the restless emperor spent fully fifteen years—one quarter—of his total reign on the road. Few rulers in premodern world history have demonstrated an equal wanderlust. Plainly, if we are to understand Qianlong, we must grasp the importance these trips held for him and the effects they had upon his world. Following him on his travels will also allow us a glimpse into the China he ruled.

The Politics of Touring

Traveling to inspect the realm was an ancient aspect of rulership in China. References to kingly tours of inspection date from before the unification of the empire, when they appear to have evolved more or less as part of military campaigns and hunting expeditions. During the Warring States period (403–221 BCE), the philosopher Mencius idealized the practice as a cornerstone of benevolent governance, believing the sage kings of antiquity to have relied on it to confirm that the nobles were well regulated and the people happy. The first emperor, Qin Shihuang (r. 221–207 BCE), took advantage of this precedent when he went on a two-year tour of inspection just after unifying the feuding states into a single empire, and many later rulers followed in his footsteps, using tours to enhance their authority and check up on influential local elites. But over time, the perspective on touring gradually changed, as newly empowered bureaucrats came to regard the emperor's moving about the empire as mere pleasure-seeking that served to remove him from their influence. Rulers who proposed to leave the palace were accused of squandering resources that were better saved for a rainy day. Thus, from the seventh century on, imperial touring fell into disrepute (at least among some influential segments of officialdom) as the notion of a sequestered monarch surrounded by watchful and powerful ministers gained currency.

A few centuries later, however, something very like imperial touring was revived under the domination of northern peoples such as the Khitans, Jurchens, and Mongols, who, beginning in the tenth century, took control of parts (or, in the Mongol case, all) of what had been China. For these alien rulers, the rationale for imperial travel was not to be found in Mencius but in their own nomadic traditions. They kept multiple capitals, some in their ancestral lands in Inner Asia, some in formerly Chinese territory. Moving regularly between them according to the season and living in tents even after permanent buildings had been built, they devoted significant time as well to hunting exercises. Rather like the feudal kings of pre-imperial China, these non-Han emperors regarded the sight of a ruler on horseback as a sign of vitality and strength, viewing with contempt what they perceived to be the weak, "womanly" habits of Chinese emperors who remained forever trapped within their palaces.

With the appearance of these alternative models of rulership, debates over the propriety of imperial touring again emerged, debates that reflected the different strains developing within Chinese politics, including tensions between bureaucratic and monarchical power, between civil and military values, between northern and southern cultural styles, and between "native" and "barbarian" interests. When the Mongol Yuan dynasty fell in 1368, these same tensions flared up anew under the Han Chinese Ming dynasty that replaced it. Early Ming rulers favored the more active imperial model, and some emperors even dared to personally lead troops into battle. In one famous incident in the mid-fifteenth century, Mongols kidnapped the emperor and held him hostage for two years, engendering a major political crisis. After this, the pendulum swung the other direction, with later Ming emperors almost never leaving the confines of the Forbidden City. This weakened the emperor's position and led to vicious, debilitating power struggles between ministers and eunuchs, which historians then and now pointed to as a primary cause for the dynasty's decline.

Once the Manchu rulers took over, the pendulum swung back again the other way. Kangxi in particular was determined to refocus control in the emperor's hands and injected greater mobility into court activities. Some of his traveling, such as visits to Confucius' birthplace in Shandong Province, observed established Chinese conventions. Other trips, such as to Mt. Wutai in Shanxi, showed greater affinity to Inner Asian precedents. This was another way in which Manchu rulers combined classical Chinese precedents with Inner Asian ways.

Imperial touring reached its apogee under Qianlong, who brought the concept of touring to full fruition, emphasizing its importance to civil governance while simultaneously exploiting its military and strategic significance. Qianlong's tours were numerous—seventy-two in total, an all-time record. This does not include seasonal excursions to the small imperial hunting park south of Beijing or visits to the tombs of his father and grandfather, located in separate mausolea east and west of the capital. Many activities undertaken during the tours were highly structured rituals with deep historical resonances that provided Qianlong new ways to polish his imperial image. In practical terms, touring also allowed the emperor the chance to see for himself what circumstances in the provinces were like and permitted him to exercise authority in a more direct, less formalized manner than in the palace. Not that he left the palace entirely behind—a small army of ministers, guards, clerks, and functionaries accompanied him wherever he went—but he was able to break free of the usual constraints imposed by bureaucratic rote, since going on tour necessarily introduced an element of the unpredictable and the makeshift. In the eternal struggle between the arbitrary, mercurial power of the emperor and the more predictable, stolid power of the bureaucracy, the emperor could under these conditions expect to claim the upper hand. This may have been one other reason he so enjoyed being on the road (see Map 5.1).

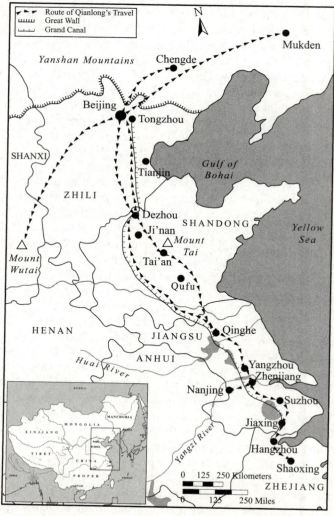

Map 5.1 Qianlong's Travels

You Can Go Home Again

We have already seen how, in 1741, Qianlong revived the imperial hunts at Mulan, turning the summer retreat into a proving ground for martial virtue in the hopes of strengthening a collective Manchu identity. The same hopes inspired a second visit to Mulan in autumn 1743, at which time the emperor went further afield, leading a pilgrimage from Mulan to the ancestral tombs in Mukden (modern Shenyang; the name referred both to Nurhaci's old capital, known in Chinese as Shengjing, as well as to the region generally), 400 miles (630 kilometers) away to the northeast. Mukden was an obvious choice for his first extended tour. It meant Qianlong could pay homage at the tombs of Nurhaci and Hong Taiji in a personal, unmediated fashion. (Ordinarily he sent someone in his place to offer sacrifices at the proper times of the year). The emperor was careful to stress this aspect of his visit, pointing out that, as with so many of his good ideas, the thought of going to Mukden occurred to him after reading the chronicles of the Kangxi reign:

> In former times, my august grandfather went three times during his reign of 61 years to pay his respects at the imperial tombs, thereby manifesting his filial intentions. When my father was on the throne, he undertook reforms on all matters that left him not a moment of leisure, on top of which he was occupied with military affairs in the west. When he was still a prince, he once was deputed by the emperor to visit the ancestral mausolea, but he was never able to do so again during the thirteen years of his reign. Now I, an unworthy one, have come to the throne and am fearful that their virtue will find no successor. I am deeply conscious of my ancestors' industry in building the empire, and never tire of daily honoring their spirits. If I were not to go to their tombs in Mukden to pay my respects in person, how would I be able sincerely to express myself? Accordingly, I have accompanied my mother, the empress dowager, departing the capital for our auxiliary capital, to extend my filial thoughts in admiration of my ancestors' military triumphs.

In going to Mukden, then, he was following the example of Kangxi, and making up for the long, though excusable, lapse that occurred under Yongzheng. This was a filial duty that, as a son, he could not have shirked.

The party moved from Chengde through Mulan and then into the southern portion of the Mongolian steppe. Qianlong was escorted by a select group of loyal Mongol princes and nobles, the latter no doubt pleased that the emperor could converse with them in their native language. They joined him in a few informal hunts along the way. The later arrival of Korean emissaries in Mukden gave the emperor the opportunity to accomplish additional diplomatic ends as well. Once he reached the suburbs of the city, Qianlong's main task was to offer the proper sacrifices of food and wine before the altars at each tomb, rituals that involved prostrations, the burning of incense, and the presentation of sacrificial texts extolling each ancestor. Certain rites he performed alone, while for others he was accompanied by his mother, his wife, other members of the imperial clan, and high officials; some of these rites were so elaborate that they required three days to complete. Once the entire cycle of rituals was concluded, the emperor made a grand ceremonial entrance into Mukden itself, heading for the old palace built by Nurhaci. There he held a great banquet, at which he bestowed gifts of silver, satin, saddles, and quivers to the over one thousand officials assembled, most of whom were Manchu. During his stay in the city, he ordered that promotions be speeded up for officers and salary bonuses dispensed to regular soldiers. He declared an amnesty for all but the worst criminals and forgave debts against the government. Special awards of textiles and silver were also presented to the thirty-odd women who took part in the ceremonies, along with gifts of cotton, rice, and silk to the elderly to show the emperor's consideration. The whole affair took on a carnival air. This lasted a few days, until the emperor at last departed again for Beijing, where he was welcomed after an absence of over three months.

Much the same routine applied in Qianlong's subsequent visits to Mukden in 1754, 1778, and 1783. Since another proclaimed purpose of these trips was to observe the beauty of the land and the "pure customs" of its inhabitants (this is purportedly what inspired the composition of the *Ode to Mukden* after the 1743 trip), it made sense to take different roads, and the itinerary varied somewhat with each visit. But the entourage did not enjoy much freedom in the choice of route, since the encampment was expected to be ready when it arrived, and setting up tents for 3,000 people required considerable time and planning (it required 800 wagons just to transport everything needed to shelter and feed those on tour). Coordinating all of this made an imperial tour similar in some ways to a military campaign. This was true whether the tour traversed a sparsely settled frontier area like Manchuria—which was officially closed to Han settlement and where, outside the largest settlements, cities and towns were still made largely of wood—or crossed the more densely populated areas of Shandong, Shanxi, and parts further south.

The Buddhist Pilgrim

Three years after his first visit to Mukden, Qianlong embarked on another grand tour, this time to Mt. Wutai in Shanxi Province, about 100 miles (160 kilometers) southwest of Beijing. Here again he was following in Kangxi's footsteps. Mt. Wutai (literally, "Five-terraces Mountain") was a site of great religious significance, designated since at least the seventh century CE as the Chinese home of the bodhisattva Manjusri, a principal Buddhist figure and spiritual avatar of righteous, benevolent kings, known in Sanskrit as *chakravartins*. Tang rulers regarded the peak as sacred, and in the thirteenth century the association of Manjusri with the Yuan emperor Khubilai Khan invested Mt. Wutai with new political meaning, which it retained even after the Mongols were driven from China. Then, in the mid-1600s, the Fifth Dalai Lama explicitly linked the new Manchu rulers to the chakravartin tradition, elevating their prestige among Mongol and Tibetan believers alike. This made Mt. Wutai an obvious choice for Qing imperial patronage.

Such favor was initially limited to gifts of money, but in 1683, one year after he had visited Mukden, Kangxi paid the first of four visits to the holy mountain. The stated purpose of these trips was to pray for the health of his mother and grandmother, who were both descendants of the Mongol imperial line, but he no doubt also aimed to reinforce his identification with Manjusri, "the savior of all living forms," and to demonstrate to potential Mongol allies (and enemies) his devotion to a major center of Tibetan Buddhist activity. We may also discern religious objectives, given that on later trips he traveled with his own personal lama to worship at Mt. Wutai's many temples, one of which, according to legend, held a lock of Manjusri's hair.

Qianlong's six visits to Mt. Wutai (in 1746, 1750, 1761, 1781, 1786, and 1792), each lasting a little over a month, were likewise shaded with personal, political, and religious motivations. They began with similar sorts of preparations as for his other travels, including the granting of tax relief and the appropriation of additional funds for road repairs to counties and provinces that would be affected by the imperial tour. This was done as much to mitigate complaints that touring imposed a burden on the local populace as it was to ensure an enthusiastic welcome when the imperial caravan eventually passed by. In 1746, 1750, and 1761, he was accompanied, as he had been to Mukden, by his mother. Stopping on the way first at his father's mausoleum west of Beijing, Qianlong also found time, as usual, to engage in a hunt or two during the week-long journey to Mt. Wutai, as well as to observe the situation in the villages he passed through, which he praised for their simplicity and tranquility. But he was not so busy that he did not remember to send one of the doctors traveling with him to attend to the Shanxi governor, his supposed host, who had fallen ill. Nor did he omit to take care of other routine business en route, including cases dealing with ginseng poaching in Manchuria, disaster relief in Anhui, a failed rebellion in Sichuan, general reforms in the examination system, and the suppression of a heretical religious sect in Yunnan.

Once at the mountain, Qianlong switched gears. Setting aside routine business for a few days, he moved between the several religious foundations situated on different parts of the mountain. Some of these had originally been non-Tibetan in orientation, but he and his grandfather had converted those, replacing Chinese monks with lamas, most (but not all) of whom were ethnic Tibetans. He made lavish donations of money for repairs and bestowed finely printed scriptures and gilt sculptures from the imperial workshops in Beijing, which, with generous Qing patronage, had by now become a major center of Tibetan Buddhism. There were also gifts of pearls, sables, satin robing, and white silken scarves, the last a traditional gift presented by Tibetan Buddhists in greetings and farewells. Local merchants supplemented these donations with cash contributions of their own.

That Qianlong spent some of his time in meditation as well would seem to be beyond dispute. Though most historians have long tended to dismiss Qianlong's identification with Manjusri as a ruse to entice Tibetans and Mongols into the imperial embrace, we now know that his interest in Tibetan Buddhism was anything but superficial. In 1761 his boyhood friend and mentor in all matters spiritual, Rolpai Dorje, accompanied Qianlong on his pilgrimage to Mt. Wutai. Six years younger than Qianlong, Rolpai Dorje (1717–1786) was a monk of the Gelug sect, to which the Dalai Lama also belonged. Like the Dalai Lama, Rolpai Dorje was an incarnate lama and possessed superior religious attainment; an earlier incarnation in his line had been a religious advisor to Kangxi. In 1745, having been appointed Qianlong's personal teacher, Rolpai Dorje led the emperor in the first of several tantric initiations and also taught him a little Tibetan. (It was Rolpai Dorje, too, who initially supervised the translation of the Buddhist Kanjur into Manchu.) In a clear manifestation of his religious convictions, in 1761 Qianlong ordered a copy made of a famous sculpture of Manjusri riding a lion that was housed in one of the Mt. Wutai temples. The copy was to be installed in a brand-new temple, Baoxiang ("Precious Form") Temple, that he would build in the Fragrant Hills just west of Beijing. A birthday present for his mother, this temple was erected adjacent to another religious foundation endowed by Qianlong in 1751 that was also modeled on one of the temples at Mt. Wutai. Both temples were staffed entirely by Manchu lamas.

In dedicating the Baoxiang Temple in 1762, Qianlong expressed his hope that he had brought the presence of Manjusri closer to the capital. A similar motive lay behind the restoration of another temple at the Yuanming yuan summer palace and the foundation twelve years later of a third temple at Chengde, with yet another copy of the same statue. Indeed, so powerful was the attraction of Manjusri—his name means "Smooth Lord," but Qianlong favored a more playful interpretation, "Lord of the Manchus"—that on several occasions Qianlong had himself portrayed as a quasi-incarnation of the bodhisattva. These images took the form of *thangkas*, Tibetan-style religious paintings rich with color and symbolism, which the emperor presented to temples in Beijing and Chengde, and Lhasa, where they were greatly appreciated. In all the versions that survive, the emperor is shown dressed in the robes of a lama. His right hand forms the usual *samadhi* sign, indicative of a state of enlightenment, while in his left hand he holds the Wheel of Time, signifying his status as a "wheel-turning king," which is what *chakravartin* literally means. He is surrounded by many figures, including (directly above him) Rolpai Dorje, as well as Tsongkhapa, the founder of the Yellow Hat sect, and a whole pantheon of teachers and deities proclaiming Qianlong's own spiritual heritage. In the background is a stylized depiction of Mt. Wutai (see Figure 5.1).

Such images would have been all but unintelligible, not to mention unpalatable, to his Han Chinese courtiers, for whom the Tibetan version of Buddhism was a distorted, even barbaric, version of the "true" teaching. More to their taste would have been Qianlong's poetic expositions on the scenery of Mt. Wutai:

> I have personally ascended to the mountain's peak,
> Come face to face with the southern moon.
> The brilliance of the cloud pavilions shines before me,
> The frosty woods dense with fog.
> In seven days I have toured the ancient sites,
> Picking up where I left off five years ago.
> They are telling me now that I must return to camp,
> The wind blows cold the sound of the distant bell.

However one looks at it, the geographical and spiritual landscapes of Mt. Wutai clearly offered Qianlong a welcome break from the concerns and pressures of his typical routine.

Figure 5.1 Anonymous. *The Qianlong Emperor as an Emanation of the Bodhisattva Manjusri.* Thangka, ink and colors on silk. Palace Museum, Beijing. Presented entirely in keeping with Tibetan Buddhist iconography, this religious painting and others like it reinforced Qianlong's claim to rule as a righteous "wheel-turning king," or chakravartin. © Palace Museum, Beijing.

The Ardent Confucian

Arguably less escapist in nature, Qianlong's eight visits to Shandong Province set yet another record. A coastal province situated southeast of the capital, Shandong claimed fame, not as the home of the Manchus, or of Manjusri, but of Confucius and Mt. Tai. Touring these sites conferred potent political legitimacy upon the emperor, so Shandong earned a regular place on Qianlong's itinerary.

As described in Chapter 1, Qianlong was educated in the manner of the day, steeped in texts connected with Confucius, a figure whose foundational status in the Chinese intellectual universe owed to what, by analogy, can be thought of as the combination of the intellectual authority of Aristotle and the moral authority of Moses. Ever since the first century CE, when Han-dynasty emperors announced their preference for the humane and vaguely liberal teachings of Confucius' followers, this school of thought (known as *Ru*) remained the cornerstone of political discourse and practical governance. The centrality of Ru beliefs, which stressed the sovereign's duties to Heaven and the people and underscored the importance of upholding ancient ritual practice as a guide to achieving virtue, was intensified in the eleventh century and then again in the fourteenth. By the time the Qing was founded, then, Ru doctrines had for seventeen centuries enjoyed an unchallenged preeminence among emperors and ruling elites alike.

Not that those doctrines were all homogeneous. Over time, Daoist and Buddhist beliefs, along with inevitable social and political change, had transformed parts of Ru thought sufficiently that any uniformity that ever existed had long since been lost. Indeed, one can say that Ru thought was subject to the same sorts of debates and ideological splits as influenced Christian doctrines in Europe. If it did not surpass them, the corpus of commentaries and explications of the Five Classics and the Four Books certainly equaled in abstruseness, profundity, and volume the body of Biblical exegesis and philosophical disputation formed in the West. There was thus not one monolithic "Confucianism," but many contending schools of interpretation that informed all higher thought. As they had come down to the eighteenth century, the complex formation of Ru beliefs thus constituted the very air one breathed; as the ruler of China, Qianlong had to learn to breathe that air together with the majority of his subjects. This meant joining the generations of emperors before him—including his own ancestors, who even before the Qing conquest had built a temple to Confucius in Mukden—in revering the great sage. To have done otherwise would have risked losing the support of the lettered and wealthy classes upon whom the dynasty depended to help govern the country.

Qianlong met this obligation with zeal, referring frequently to Confucian texts and doing what he could to encourage the principles enshrined in them, most notably (as we have already had occasion to observe) filial piety. He read and reread the classics and listened regularly to learned scholars expounding on their deeper meaning. His insistence on linguistic precision eventually provoked in him such dissatisfaction with the existing Manchu versions of the classic texts, which had been made in a hurry in the 1630s and 1640s, that he ordered completely new translations, to be published by the palace press. He issued his own preferred editions of the original Chinese texts and commentaries. Offerings at the large Confucius Temple in Beijing were a standard part of the ritual calendar, and Qianlong often went in person to officiate, substantiating his claim that "our dynasty venerates the Ru, treasures the Way, and honors the rites for the First Teacher." He also authorized the building of a new Confucius Temple in Chengde, visiting that temple when he was at the retreat, and bestowed honorary titles on the leading members of the Kong clan, direct descendants of the sage in whose care the family temple and graveyard had always been (and still is) entrusted. The most impressive tribute Qianlong made to the sage, however, consisted of personal visits to Qufu. Three of these visits were short detours on longer journeys to Jiangnan. The other five trips, sometimes called "Eastern Tours," were made expressly to pay homage to China's greatest philosopher.

Qianlong first came to Qufu in March 1748. Explaining his desire to make this trip, he noted that he had always been taught to follow the example of his predecessors. While his grandfather had visited Qufu in person and his father was responsible for rebuilding the temple after it burned down in 1729, he, Qianlong, had so far done nothing. Out of a sense of shame, and a wish also to satisfy his mother's longing to go to nearby Mt. Tai to pray, he set off from the capital for Qufu, arriving a little over two weeks later. The day he arrived he leisurely toured the precincts of the main Confucius temple, presenting the Kong family with wooden plaques carved in the imperial calligraphy. He also gave them a poem he had composed celebrating his visit to Shandong. A more formal visit to the temple followed the next day. In a sign of humility, the emperor descended from his palanquin and entered the main gate on foot, then proceeded to the main hall and prostrated himself before the portrait of Confucius. Adjourning to another building, he heard lectures on the classics given by two prominent Kong family scholars. He then went to the grave of Confucius, where again he kowtowed and made ritual offerings. The day was capped by a huge banquet at which he issued an edict praising Confucius and his descendants in effusive terms: "The First Teacher prepared the Way and established the Teaching; he is a man for all times and all the world." Before leaving, he ordered the erection of a large stone monument to commemorate the visit, noting the precedent set not just by his own ancestors, but by emperors of former ages as well.

Qianlong traveled to Qufu seven more times in his life, in 1756, 1757, 1762, 1771, 1776, 1784, and 1790. So common were these visits that rumors arose to the effect that Qianlong had secretly married a woman of the Kong family and that his frequent trips to Qufu were in fact to visit the daughter he had by an illicit liaison! While such tales were certainly false, there was no denying the extent of the largesse showered upon Confucius and indeed upon the entire population of Shandong, which could expect major tax relief with each imperial tour, along with special additional examination honors. In return, the emperor basked in the honor such visible patronage earned him.

When he left Qufu in late March 1748, Qianlong did not return straight away to Beijing. Rather, he headed for Mt. Tai (or Taishan), the other sacred Shandong landmark. Located two days' journey from Confucius' birthplace, and not to be confused with Mt. Wutai, Mt. Tai was if anything an even more meaningful site than Qufu. Looming high over the Shandong plain, Mt. Tai commanded awe from all who beheld it, not excepting Confucius himself, who had venerated the mountain as the source and symbol of kingly power, the place where Heaven and Earth met. For this reason, a successful visit to Mt. Tai, including an ascent to the peak and an offering to the spirit of the mountain, was seen as confirmation of a ruler's rightful place as the Son of Heaven. Again, it was the first emperor, Qin Shihuang, who had blazed the trail up the mountainside in the third century BCE. Emperors ever since had followed in his footsteps, and it would have been entirely out of character for Qianlong to have foregone such an opportunity, even though, as the chronicles show, he was quite preoccupied with developments in western Sichuan (the ill-starred Necin had just been sent to take over direction of the campaign).

Thus, after quitting Qufu, the imperial party trekked directly to Mt. Tai. Joined there by local officials, all first paid their respects at the temple at the base of the mountain. Proceeding partly on foot and partly in litters, the imperial party ascended the steep and winding path to the top. Once at the windy summit, the emperor and his mother made their way from temple to temple, staffed mostly by Daoist priests and nuns. In this and subsequent trips to Mt. Tai (1771, 1776, and 1790), Qianlong associated himself as closely with the mountain as possible by inscribing his calligraphy—in characters several feet high—on boulders looming along the path, proclaiming to Heaven, Earth, and History, "Qianlong was here." His writing still greets visitors today.

The Southern Tours

Of Qianlong's many travels, the longest, most expensive, and most famous were unquestionably those to the Jiangnan delta region. There were six such excursions, in 1751, 1757, 1762, 1765, 1780, and 1784. Qianlong considered these so-called Southern Tours of Inspection collectively to be one of his two greatest accomplishments, the other being the conquest of Xinjiang. Historians generally have had a much more negative opinion of the tours, arguing that the huge expenditures involved brought financial ruin to the country—a judgment that may exaggerate their economic impact. In any case, it is hard to argue with the impression that Qianlong's tours to Jiangnan rank among the most magnificent political spectacles staged anywhere in the world in the eighteenth century.

The name Jiangnan, meaning "south of the Yangzi River," is shorthand for the greater Yangzi delta area of modern Zhejiang and Jiangsu provinces. About 1,000 miles south of Beijing, it was and remains today the wealthiest part of China, in terms both of money and of culture. To draw an approximate analogy, the region was to China's economic development as England and Holland were to Europe's, and the living standards of its cities in the 1700s were probably not very different from those places, perhaps even slightly better. In Qianlong's day, Jiangnan accounted for 16 percent of the total agricultural land in the empire, but provided 29 percent of the government's land tax revenue in cash (paid in silver) and 38 percent of its revenue in kind (paid in grain), as well as 64 percent of the tribute grain sent to feed the capital. Apart from this, money generated from the salt monopoly operated by Jiangnan merchants under imperial license stood for more than two-thirds of all such revenue nationwide. China's thriving silk industry, which produced not only for the domestic market but also for markets in Europe and Asia, was concentrated in Jiangnan. Jiangnan cities were major transshipment centers for tea, porcelain, lumber, cotton, and other goods moving around the country.

Jiangnan's cultural dominance was even more lopsided. We can measure it this way: Of the sixty-one times the triennial metropolitan examination was administered between 1645 and 1795, fifty-one times the top-scoring candidate was from Jiangnan. Given the cutthroat nature of the competition, which ensured that only 1 percent of all candidates who took the lowest level examination could expect to make it all the way to the top, the success rate of Jiangnan scholars was astonishingly high. Since examination success translated directly into official appointments, the corridors of power were filled with Jiangnan men. Another measure of the looming presence of Jiangnan on the national cultural scene was the overwhelming number of famous places to be found there, including temples, monasteries, gardens, lakes, restaurants, and libraries. For eight hundred years the wonder of these sites had been sung in countless poems and essays by China's best known writers. No one could claim to be truly cultured unless he had visited the attractions in and around such Jiangnan cities as Hangzhou, Suzhou, Yangzhou, and Nanjing. Reading the guidebooks—of which there were many—would not suffice.

Qianlong was of course quite well aware of this. Given all of his hand-wringing over the harmful effects of Chinese urban life upon the pure and noble Manchu character, one might expect he would turn his nose up at its supposedly dissolute traditions. But Qianlong was a man of many cultures. As much as he enjoyed the excursions to Chengde and the Mulan hunting grounds, he also took great pleasure in the various refinements offered by Chinese poetry, painting, ceramics, and theatre. For someone with his cultural ambitions, the temptation to visit the promised land of Jiangnan was simply too great to resist. So as soon as he deemed it politically appropriate, he laid plans for the first of what would eventually be six grand tours.

Conscious as ever of the importance of precedent, and aware that some officials would be displeased with his initiative (recall that a few had already come forward to criticize his revival of the dynastic hunt), in 1750 Qianlong responded positively to an invitation that purportedly come from members of the Jiangnan gentry in terms none could impeach, employing separate but linked vocabularies of civil and filial duty:

> The land of Jiangnan is vast and its population is great; long have I eagerly attended to its affairs. Whether civil or military government, river control or coastal defense, or the many trials and tribulations suffered by the people, none have I not handled. But because the way is rather far, for more than a decade I have postponed traveling there. Many times, though, I have read the *Veritable Records* of my grandfather's reign in which the details of his Southern Tours are

recorded—how he accompanied his mother's processions, how the people, young and old alike, crowded the roadside to welcome them and acclaim the filial virtue of the royal house. This has impressed me very much.

Qianlong here presented three justifications for an expedition to Jiangnan. The first was to inspect public works and familiarize himself with local circumstances. Toward this end he would be inspecting bridges and dikes, looking in at imperial workshops, and calling upon provincial offices. The second was to introduce himself to the people of Jiangnan, a region which a century before had fiercely resisted Qing armies. Not only would he be inquiring after the welfare of local farmers and artisans, but he also granted them the privilege of gathering along the broader parts of the route and in the market places to observe him directly (normally, civilians were to bow their heads low when the emperor passed by). The third justification was the wish to show the sights of Jiangnan to his mother, the empress dowager. By insisting that filiality and not mere wanderlust inspired his wish to see Jiangnan, Qianlong made criticism of the tour difficult. Who could say he was wrong to try to please his mother? Or that he was acting imprudently, when his grandfather had gone on just such a tour of inspection not once, but six times? All the same, he was careful to insist that expenses be limited and that the privy purse (as opposed to public funds) would be used to pay for at least some. And so planning began. The trip was set for the spring of 1751, to coincide with the sixtieth birthday of the empress dowager. Fuheng, the hero of the Jinchuan campaign, was put in charge.

Preparations for Qianlong's first tour of the south followed the precedents that had been established by prior tours to other destinations. A route was laid out that more or less followed that taken by Kangxi, and roads were improved accordingly; where the party was to proceed by boat, canals were dredged, dikes improved, and barges requisitioned and properly outfitted. In places where encampment was impracticable, temporary buildings were erected to quarter the travelers. Qianlong ordered caution in instances where such preparations might inconvenience the peasantry, instructing, for example, that graves and farmland be left undisturbed if at all possible. Then there was the problem of horses. While the emperor's own mounts could be ferried across the Yellow and Yangzi rivers, horses for the rest of the party needed to be supplied locally. Finding and feeding the requisite 6,700 animals was no small task. Qianlong later reduced the number by 10 percent in response to petitions by local officials alarmed that a procession of so many beasts along relatively narrow roads would wreak havoc on the countryside.

Tax relief was granted in provinces affected by the imperial tour, and revenue that would have been sent to the capital was instead turned over to meet local expenses swollen by tour-related expenses. Additional forgiveness of taxes came when the emperor actually passed through, further alleviating the peasants' financial burden. Local officials in Jiangnan could expect to receive minor increases in rank as their part of the imperial beneficence, while examination candidates could look forward to special examinations that might allow them to win the coveted *jinshi* ("presented scholar") degree—the ticket to a successful career and high social status. Wealthy merchants, especially those who operated the harvest and sale of salt for the state, also obtained benefits from the court in anticipation of the emperor's arrival, and were in turn expected to "volunteer" their own substantial contributions toward local costs of preparation.

Despite Qianlong's efforts to minimize the disruption caused by his southward peregrinations, in 1758, just after the second tour, one foolhardy official submitted a memorial critical of the expenses involved, suggesting that the tours were too costly a form of entertainment and imposed too many hardships on the emperor and those who traveled with him. He asked that the emperor forego any further travel and cease the "extortion" such travel imposed upon local gentry. Qianlong was understandably angry at such charges. For one thing, he said, the tours were not undertaken for his amusement, but to inspect conditions in the provinces; they were hardly "entertainment." For another, forcing bannermen accustomed to an easy life in Beijing to undergo a little hardship was an important purpose of the whole exercise. In other words, as far as Qianlong was concerned, tours to Jiangnan—however beautiful its scenery and plentiful its pleasing distractions—were to be regarded principally as work, something the emperor had to do to properly discharge his solemn obligations as Son of Heaven, Son of the Qing, and Mother's Son. If this meant everyone had to spend a little money, so be it.

In this, Qianlong's Southern Tours were very much like the tours to Mukden, Mt. Wutai, and Shandong. There was one important difference, though, and that was one of scale. Where other trips involved journeys of no more than a few hundred miles, the Southern Tours covered a total of about 2,000 miles round trip. They were accordingly much longer in duration: the average length of a Southern Tour was 115 days, compared to 36 days for Western Tours to Mt. Wutai, 60 days for "Eastern Tours" to Shandong, and 88 days for visits to Mukden. At 3,250 people, the retinue for a Southern Tour was also larger than those for other tours; once horses, mules, camels, sheep, and dairy cows were accounted for, quadrupeds marching with the entourage numbered close to 10,000. In addition, there were the tremendous human resources involved behind the scenes. For example, in 1751 fifty thousand local laborers were contracted to carry out road repairs, and—since 45 percent of the route called for travel over water—something like 300,000 men were hired to haul boats and barges up and down the Grand Canal. This was indeed movement on an imperial scale. Little wonder that the same officials who were charged with organizing logistics for military campaigns were assigned the task of managing the organization of the tours.

Not surprisingly, an enterprise of this sort was very expensive. Estimates of the costs incurred by Qianlong's Southern Tours are necessarily rough, but it seems safe to say that each tour cost no less than 3 million taels of silver, possibly more. This was a considerable sum, to be sure, and Qianlong's critics then and now have on this basis criticized him for extravagance and egomania: Shouldn't this money have been saved up, or spent on projects that brought benefits to society generally? While one can easily imagine other worthy uses for these funds, the Qing polity, like nearly all early modern states, was a monarchy with a strong patrimonial heritage, not a government "of the people, by the people, for the people." Qianlong was emperor and had to behave like an emperor. Probably the most remarkable aspect of the stupendous outlay of resources associated with these excursions was that the Southern Tours did *not* in fact break the bank. Even after the last tour had been completed, the treasury continued to report a healthy surplus. In other words, given the enormous size of the national fisc, even a sum as large as 3 million taels—the equivalent of between 5 percent and 10 percent of the government's revenue surplus in an average year in the mid-1700s—was not an unbearable cost. In this regard, Qianlong's visits to Jiangnan offer a stunning testament to the wealth of the Qing state and his power to command it.

The "work" done on these tours to Jiangnan has already been described in part, since the emperor's numerous proclamations regarding tax relief, honors, rewards, and so forth counted as an important element of the tour, even before his actual arrival. Once there, he divided his time between keeping his mother company, meeting with local officials and members of elite Jiangnan society, presenting gifts, hosting banquets, observing military training, touring famous mountains and temples, inspecting dikes and embankments, investigating conditions at the salt yards and the imperial textile factories, visiting academies and libraries, viewing peasants at work in the fields, and making ritual offerings at the tombs of former emperors. This in addition to the regular business of the empire, which of course followed him.

It should be said that most elements of Qianlong's visits to Jiangnan were carefully scripted. Only occasionally was there the chance for an impromptu outing. Displays of the emperor's concern for general welfare balanced with shows of his cultural proficiency and feats of martial prowess: The same day (March 14, 1751) that he toured a famous island temple not far from Nanjing, he also issued an edict ordering that retired banner soldiers in the Jiangnan garrisons who were older than seventy be given special rewards. His attention was similarly divided in Suzhou and Hangzhou. Upon entering the former city on March 18, he noted in a poem, "The imperial procession alights in old Suzhou. This is for the purpose of taking measure of popular sentiments. How could it be for my own pleasure?" The emperor was then busy for days bestowing gifts to shrines dedicated to famous local poets and statesmen (again, many of these gifts were monumental samples of his writing to be hung prominently from the eaves), and on the 24th he paid a visit to a famous tourist site nearby. But on the 25th he spent the entire day reviewing military drills. In Hangzhou, the emperor toured the city in the morning with his mother, admiring the views of its famous West Lake, and then later in the day inspected troops, met with Eight Banner officers, and showed off his expert archery skills.

In this way, the tension between literary and military values, between pleasure and duty, ran through the entire tour. In 1751 during Qianlong's first Southern Tour, for instance, the emperor's crossing of the Yangzi River occasioned from him two very different responses: On the one hand, he wrote of seeing boats on the legendary Yangzi for the first time, emotional verse that echoed lyric poetry of the Song dynasty. On the other hand, he penned the essay, "A Record of Accompanying the Empress Dowager's Procession to Visit Jinshan," containing the line, "Our inspecting the provinces and observing the common people is in accordance with the ritual regulations for tours of inspection emphasized by the ancient kings." The first reaction revealed Qianlong as a sensitive, well-bred man of culture who could not but help be entranced by Jiangnan's striking scenery; the second depicted him as a historically minded, no-nonsense ruler, aware that all eyes were on him and curious to see whether his mother was really the only tourist in the procession.

As for remembering the tours and presenting them to history, Qianlong did not leave much to chance, either. Everything the emperor did was carefully noted by the imperial diarists who were always at his side, and Qianlong himself kept a separate record of his thoughts—or what he wanted people to know of his thoughts—in the form of poems. We have already sampled some of these. Some were inspired by memorable landscapes or famous historical or literary sites, while others were reflections on other aspects of his visit:

> We draw up the oars and moor by the canal;
> Taking up bowstrings, hands and bows coincide.
> Our troops go ashore in an orderly fashion;
> Need We be proud of scoring successive hits?
>
> Note in original: On this day We hit nine out of ten shots.
>
> We have come south to observe local customs;
> Drilling the troops is of great importance to this dynasty.
> Among the soldiers following in retinue,
> We are careful to encourage the diligent and outstanding.

(Translation by Michael Chang, *A Court on Horseback*.)

This and hundreds of other poems Qianlong composed can be found in a massive ten-volume compilation, *The Great Canon of the Southern Tours*, published in 1771 to commemorate his visits and distributed to top officials. In addition, Qianlong commissioned another kind of souvenir, a series of twelve paintings, each ten meters long, depicting the first tour of the south. Modeled on a 1714 series commemorating the celebrations of Kangxi's sixtieth birthday, as well as an earlier series celebrating the Kangxi tours to the south, these scrolls give us a sense of the pomp and ceremony surrounding Qianlong's activities. In addition to showing crowds on the streets, where tables have been set up, draped with brocade and furnished with offerings of incense in honor of the emperor, they also show scenes in courtyards, shops, roads, rivers and canals, all testimony of the plenty enjoyed by the subjects of the Qing ruler. They are also careful to depict the emperor engaged in the business of inspecting the realm, as in Figure 5.2, where he can be seen floating on a barge on the Grand Canal at Jiaxing, a town between Suzhou and Hangzhou.

It is perhaps worth mentioning that in almost every scene, Qianlong is shown riding on horseback together with his guards. For while the tours unquestionably were undertaken in part for the purpose of sightseeing, Qianlong himself was as much a sight to be seen as any that Jiangnan had to offer, and he was easier to see if he was in the saddle. The image of himself on horseback surrounded by

Figure 5.2 Xu Yang (active 1750–75) and court artists. *The Southern Tour of the Qianlong Emperor.* 1770. Handscroll, ink and colors on silk. Private collection, Boston. This scene, of the emperor on a barge, is taken from the seventh of the twelve immense scrolls (the shortest are nearly 32 feet, or 10 meters in length) painted to commemorate Qianlong's fourth tour of the Jiangnan region in 1765. © MFA Boston.

hundreds of mounted soldiers in their colorful uniforms, banners flying and weapons at the ready, was forcefully conveyed in city after city. His subjects were to know he had been there, and they were never to forget it. That people continued to talk about Qianlong's visits long after they were over—that the rumors, gossip, and wonder that swirled around them has lasted even to the present day (historical novels and TV movies about Qianlong's adventures in Jiangnan consistently attract large audiences in contemporary China)—is evidence that Qianlong accomplished his purpose.

In Qianlong's frequent movements about the realm to Mukden, Mt. Wutai, Qufu, Mt. Tai, and the Jiangnan region, as in his family life, we find the political and the personal inescapably intertwined. The tours enabled him to promote dynastic interests and consolidate his personal authority, to put his mark indelibly upon the landscape. At the same time they provided opportunities for both structured and unstructured displays of imperial might, munificence, and magnanimity. While the emperor's travels were undeniably expensive, they were not ruinously so; besides which, he was able to legitimate them in several ways. Touring allowed him to manifest his filial sentiments, both as far as entertaining his mother was concerned and also in terms of pursuing the ideals left by his grandfather. It permitted him to visit legendary places he had read or heard about since childhood but had never been able to glimpse. It allowed him to dispense largesse, to exercise patronage, and establish personal ties of favor. It allowed him to go personally to inspect local conditions, to see with his own eyes what the flood dikes looked like and how the crops were growing, and to meet officials on their own turf where he could get a better sense of how they were doing their jobs, rather than in the massive audience halls of the Forbidden City. Perhaps most importantly, where hunting put him in touch with his Manchu and Mongol constituency, touring gave him an ancient Chinese voice, enabling him to identify at once physically and metaphysically with the emperors, sages, poets, and painters of the past; behind that voice one could hear, not so faintly, the echo of conquest, of a kingdom won by force of arms, of surrendered cities in 1640s Jiangnan, of battles in the distant west that continued still in the 1750s.

Though Qianlong may sometimes seem remote to us today, the tours made his person, his court, and his power tangible and real to all who beheld their passage. In this, Qianlong's peripatetic style bore some resemblance to the European custom of royal progresses—bearing in mind that Qianlong traveled many, many more miles than any reigning European monarch of the day. French kings traveled to assert sovereignty, and English kings to oversee the aristocracy (and live at their expense for a while). They and other rulers also used the vocabulary of caring for the lives of ordinary people as a means of justifying their departure from their palaces. But perhaps nowhere was the practice of sovereign tours as deep and complex as in China. One finds remnants of it even in the twentieth century, with Mao Zedong's tours of the countryside in the 1960s or, yet more obvious, in Deng Xiaoping's 1992 visit to the Canton delta and the Shenzhen Special Economic Zone just outside Hong Kong. Deng's trip, meant to confer his blessing upon the new capitalist-style economy taking hold there and to allow that new prosperity to reflect favorably upon him, was christened by the popular press quite deliberately as—what else?—a "Southern Tour."

6

Building the Empire

Unification has been a recurrent theme throughout much of China's recent history. The tension between Beijing and Taipei that has endured since the end of World War II makes this abundantly clear. But that does not mean that the idea of unity emerged in China only with the birth of modern nationalism. In fact, a preoccupation with bringing together "all under heaven"—interpreted minimally as the territories of the traditional Chinese heartland (the "lesser empire") and maximally as including all the lands claimed by the Han and Tang dynasties at their furthest extent (the "greater empire")—has surfaced at just about every period of Chinese history, from the third century BCE on. In between periods of unification, the empire was often divided between rival dynasties, but this only fueled expectations that it should and would be reunited eventually. By no later than the fourteenth century, an emperor's prestige depended greatly on whether he could claim to have restored or preserved the unity of the realm.

This remains true for China's leaders in the twenty-first century, and it was unquestionably true for Qianlong in the eighteenth. Indeed, to achieve and uphold the integrity of the greater empire represented for him the ultimate political goal. It showed that the Manchu claim to power was part of the *zhengtong*, or "true line of rule," and that the Qing occupied a legitimate place in the historic transmission of Heaven's mandate. Sometimes styling himself "Seigneur of the Realm Who Looks Upon All with Equal Benevolence," Qianlong greatly amplified the successes of Kangxi and Yongzheng, reinforcing Manchu suzerainty over Tibet and Mongolia, adding new lands to the empire through conquest in the far west, and staving off border challenges in the south. In fact, under Qianlong the geographical size of the empire increased by an astounding one-third, giving China its modern shape—an accomplishment that has won praise from many Chinese historians today. To understand this important aspect of Qianlong's reign, this chapter will describe his remarkable achievements as an empire-builder, focusing first on the military and logistical aspects of Qing imperial expansion and then on the ways in which Qianlong worked in the later 1700s to develop a culture of empire and to shape historical memory so that it accorded with his own perception of his accomplishments (see Map 6.1a and 6.1b).

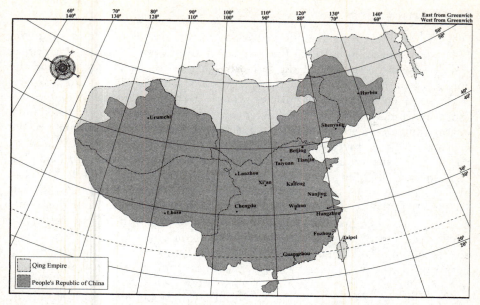

Map 6.1a Comparison of Qing Territory and the Territory of Modern China

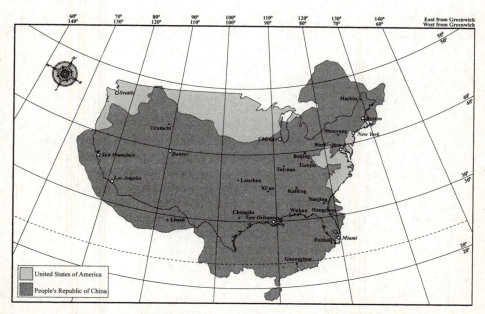

Map 6.1b Comparison of the Territory of Modern China and the United States

87

The Warrior King

Qianlong's military record on the frontier was a remarkable one. Beginning in the 1740s and continuing through the 1790s, his armies ranged across the steppes and deserts of the northwest, the forbidding heights of the Himalayas, and the jungles of the southwest. Expeditionary columns, supply lines, and caravans crisscrossed a territory second in compass only to the vast Eurasian empire established by Chinggis Khan in the thirteenth century. In terms of the projection of military might on a continental scale, a useful comparative standard might be the invasion of Russia by Napoleon. Of the 500,000 soldiers (some say 750,000) of the original expeditionary army Napoleon assembled in northeastern Poland in 1812, only 100,000 made it to Moscow; in the legendary retreat from Moscow, dwindling supplies, poor logistics, and bad weather doomed all but 10,000–20,000 men of the Grande Armée. The whole disastrous campaign lasted nine months. In comparison, Qianlong's three campaigns in eastern Turkestan, which took place fifty-odd years before Napoleon's invasion, involved smaller armies (about 40,000 men) but covered greater distances: where the march from Paris to Moscow was approximately 1,500 miles (2,400 kilometers), the distance from Beijing to the foot of the Tianshan Mountains was 1,900 miles (3,000 kilometers), and to the Tarim Basin 2,300 miles (3,700 kilometers). It should be said that smaller armies, numbering around 15,000, were sent on the latter campaign—though even at 15,000 men, Qianlong's professional forces equaled the size of the Continental Army led in the field by George Washington in the 1780s. The Qing campaigns also lasted longer, on average, than the French. While the first Dzungar war (1755) was over in just four months, the second Dzungar war (1756–1757) lasted fifteen months, and the succeeding conflict with forces loyal to the White Mountain Khojas (1758–1759) took a year and a half. Possibly the most important difference that emerges from this comparison is that Qianlong, unlike Napoleon, was able to consolidate his successes because he knew when to stop (see Map 6.2).

Qianlong was very proud of his military achievements. Late in his reign he titled himself "The Old Man of the Ten Perfect Victories," a reference to ten campaigns fought by Qing armies while he was emperor. It is noteworthy that among all the military actions he could have pointed to as evidence of Heaven's favor, Qianlong selected only these ten. All took place on the frontier. Unlike other fighting, such as the protracted wars led against millenarian sects in the remote hills deep in the Chinese provinces (see Chapter 9), or innumerable battles fought to quell smaller rebellions, the "Ten Perfect Victories" figured as part of the grand strategy of defending and expanding Qing imperial territory. That is to say, in Qianlong's view, "bandit suppression," as he thought of it, was one thing: any ruler had to be able to manage such an ordinary type of disturbance, so it was hardly worth mentioning. But conquest on the frontier was a glorious enterprise worthy of the ages, one that added luster to the emperor's rule and proved that he reigned with righteousness and humanity. As Qianlong himself put it in a testimonial he wrote in 1792, "The Record of the Ten Perfects,"

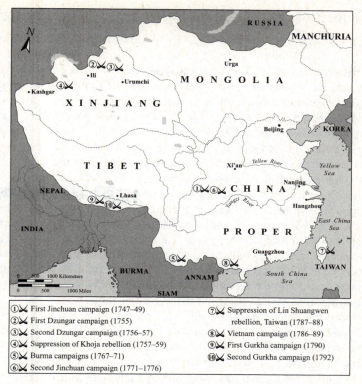

Map 6.2   Main Military Campaigns of the Qianlong Reign

The ten instances of military merit include the two pacifications of the Dzungars, the quelling of the Muslim tribes, the two annihilations of the Jinchuan [rebels], the restoring of peace to Taiwan, and the subjugations of Burma and Vietnam; adding the recent twin capitulations of the Gurkhas makes ten in all. Why is there any need to include those three trivial rebellions in the inner provinces?

There is no mistaking Qianlong's focus on the frontier as an arena in which the sovereign's mettle was most keenly tested and his reputation won or lost.

Not only because his victories on the frontier (some more clearly victorious than others, it should be said) formed an important part of his self-image, but also because they were major milestones in the expansion of the Qing empire, they merit our closer attention. In the following pages we examine three of these "perfect victories," all connected with fighting in Turkestan in the 1750s. We will then consider the various ways in which Qianlong sought to memorialize his victories and how he looked back on his successes near the end of his life.

The Conquest of the Far West: The First Dzungar Campaign

Qianlong's first major military adventure, culminating in the conquest of eastern Turkestan (modern Xinjiang), was in many ways his most impressive accomplishment on the frontier. Not only did it put an end to the Dzungar menace, which had been a threat to Manchu power since the time of Kangxi, but it also resulted in the incorporation of a new and significant population of Sufi Muslims into the empire. This created ties between China and the Islamic world stronger than at any time since the fourteenth century.

It does not appear that Qianlong had hungered for, or even planned on, the conquest of Dzungaria and Kashgaria.[1] For one thing, it was a staggeringly large swath of territory, spanning approximately twenty degrees of latitude north to south and another twenty degrees of longitude east to west—a total area of 1.46 million square miles, roughly equivalent to the western United States from the Rocky Mountains to the Pacific Coast. A historical crossroads of Eurasian trade routes, in the mid-1700s the region's varied mix of deserts, plains, and mountains were ruled by an assortment of princes, khans, and chieftains, its lack of unity a seeming invitation to ambitious emperors, sultans, and tsars. But one searches Qianlong's writings in vain for early declarations of something akin to "Manifest Destiny" or for pronouncements of a determination to extend the Qing map. On the contrary, the conquest of what would become the Qing Far West seems to have been the indirect consequence of Qianlong's desire to put an end to instability in the northwest and eliminate the possibility of a strategically disastrous Russian intervention, as well as a simple wish to punish those who had betrayed his trust. Many Qing officials opposed Qianlong's aggressive policies and argued against prolonged entanglements in affairs they perceived to be so distant from the court's proper concerns. Compared to the breadth of Qianlong's ambitions, theirs was a much more limited vision of empire. Not until the 1820s did Chinese elites come around to the view that in fact the conquest of what would be called Xinjiang made sense, either politically or historically (see Map 6.3).

As mentioned in Chapter 2, Qianlong had been content in 1739 to establish a treaty with the Dzungar leader, Galdan Tsereng, to buy peace in the northwest. This peace lasted only six years. The death of Galdan Tsereng in 1745 destabilized the political situation among the alliance of Choros, Dörböt, Khoit, and Khoshot Mongols, who together comprised the Dzungar confederation.[2] Leadership of this group passed first to a twelve-year-old son of Galdan Tsereng, but his dissolute behavior led to a coup five years later, when his older brother, Lama Darja (many Mongols took Tibetan-sounding names) took his place.

---

[1]Historically, the area of modern Xinjiang was divided into two broad regions: Dzungaria and Kashgaria. "Dzungaria" corresponds roughly to the area north of the Tianshan Mountains as far as the Altai Mountains, including the Ili Valley. "Kashgaria" corresponds to the area of the Tarim Basin, south of the Tianshan as far as the Pamirs and the Hindu Kush; it is sometimes also known as "Altishahr" (lit., "Six Cities"), because of the six main oases surrounding the Taklamakan Desert.
[2]These peoples are sometimes also referred to as the "Oirat" (sometimes spelled Oyirad). Strictly speaking, the Dzungars (the name means "left wing") were but one branch of the Oirat confederation, but from the time they achieved a dominant position in the early 1600s, their name was also frequently applied to the confederation as a whole.

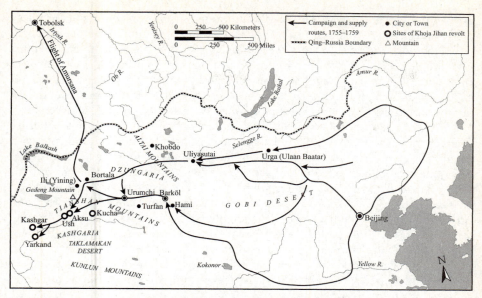

Map 6.3 The Conquest of Turkestan, 1755–1759 (based with permission on the map in Peter Perdue, *China Marches West*, p. 273)

Lama Darja proved to be even less responsible than his predecessor, prompting the formation in 1750 of an opposition coalition led by Dawachi, the grandson of a noted general, and Amursana, a Khoit chieftain. When their plot to unseat Lama Darja was exposed, they were forced to flee for their lives. Not long thereafter, having gathered a small force of 1,500 men to their cause, they staged a successful raid on Lama Darja's capital at Ili and seized power.

For the next three years, from 1752 to 1755, Dawachi remained as the nominal head of the Dzungar confederation. He enjoyed wide popular support and was backed by the Russian tsar. But his ally Amursana, who had provided most of the inspiration for the 1752 coup, was all the while making other plans. When Dawachi reneged on an earlier promise to share power with Amursana, relations between the two men grew openly hostile. Early in 1754, fighting broke out and soon spread to central and eastern Mongolia, as refugees from western Mongolia flooded into the lands of the Khalkha Mongols, who lived as loyal Qing subjects.

Alarmed by this turn of events, Qianlong sent representatives to deal with the crisis. Amursana, pursued by Dawachi's army of 40,000 men, also appealed to Qianlong for assistance. He may have guessed that Qianlong was unhappy with Dawachi and hoped to win the emperor's sympathy. If so, he picked an excellent moment. Qianlong was indeed displeased at Dawachi's having seized power from the legal heir and then—even worse—for having failed to approach the throne expressing his desire to maintain good relations with the Qing and asking for the emperor's blessing. Later that year, when Dawachi finally got around to sending an embassy to Beijing asking for Qianlong's understanding and cooperation in continuing good relations, Qianlong abruptly refused. One can almost hear him growling: "The majestic Great Qing holds unified sway over center and periphery alike, and now this renegade tribal usurper dares to see himself as our equal?!" Though most of his ministers were moved by Dawachi's humble language, Qianlong held firm, sensing an opportunity to insert Qing power decisively into the ongoing political struggles among the Dzungars. In an edict issued late in 1754, Qianlong lambasted Dawachi for his outrageous behavior, referring to him as yi, "barbarian," a term generally reserved for disloyal non-Han subjects.

By then, preparations for war had already begun. A few months before Qianlong had called up 30,000 of his best troops, mainly Manchus and Mongols, along with another 10,000 or so Chinese soldiers, ordering local officials to assemble stockpiles of food and supplies along the two main routes he and his advisors had mapped out. A huge support staff was assembled, equal in size to the actual fighting force, to cook, pack, maintain camps, mind the horses and other animals, and otherwise keep the supply train moving and the army going. 150,000 horses were readied, together with 100,000 camels for carrying burdens and 100,000 cattle and sheep for slaughter. This is not to mention the 1.75 million kilograms of noodles and bread gathered for feeding that half of the army that would march through Barkol on the way to Ili, or the ocean of grain required for feeding troops and staff.

Provisioning grain for the army presented special logistical challenges. Most of it had to be brought from the heart of China, where it was grown, out to the frontier, where it was needed, and it was impossible to expect soldiers to carry enough food with them for a long campaign. (One advantage Qing armies had was that their horses could graze on the grasslands of Inner Asia and did not require the shipment of fodder, as was the case in Europe.) Figures for the first and second expeditions to Ili show that on each occasion the Board of War requisitioned 100,000 piculs of grain (about 340,000 bushels—primarily millet, some rice), enough for the first six months. These amounts, it is worth noting, were but a small fraction of the country's annual grain production and were hardly a strain on the economy. So it was not that the government lacked the agricultural surplus to support military operations on a grand scale. The real expense was getting the grain to the battlefront. Once it was purchased, quartermasters organized enormous supply trains of porters, mule carts, and camels to move the grain some 1,700 kilometers. Transport costs came to ten times the original purchase price of the grain itself. Remaining focused on defeating the Dzungars, the emperor did not bat an eyelash.

On the diplomatic front, Qianlong kept busy feasting and entertaining loyal Mongol chieftains, explaining to them his reading of the situation in the west and the necessity of military intervention. The most dramatic moment came on January 23, 1755, when Qianlong received Amursana at the summer retreat in Chengde, hosting an enormous banquet at which the leading figures of the empire were all present. After inviting his guest to test his skills in archery against him, the emperor sat Amursana down and, speaking in Mongolian, queried him about events on the western frontier. Qianlong realized Amursana's political value to him as an indigenous noble, but was cautious about trusting him too far, aware that Amursana could well be playing a similar game with him. He decided to put Amursana and his Khoit troops at the head of the northern route army under the leadership of a trusted Qing veteran, Bandi, and saw the troops off as they departed for the frontier, proceeding with them a short way beyond Beijing's city gates.

The war began in late March 1755 and was soon over. By June, the bulk of Dawachi's forces, apparently unaware that a large Qing army was marching on them, was roundly defeated. Dawachi himself, having first fled south to seek refuge with Muslim allies, was betrayed, seized while drunk at a banquet and hauled before Bandi, who sent him to Beijing in chains. Qianlong did not execute his enemy, however. Instead, he accepted Dawachi's submission with mercy, granting him a title, entering him and his household into the Eight Banners, and giving him a residence in Beijing—with the understanding that he was not free to leave it. Dawachi lived there together with forty households of close followers until his death. The triumphant Qing army received liberal rewards from the emperor, who distributed titles and honors upon leading officers, including Amursana. As was his habit, Qianlong wrote a poem to express his elation:

> I called upon the whole army to bring peace to the Far West;
> Now they return, heaven-favored horses and men, reverently to receive felicitation.
> Every day, as evening fell, I sought news from remote lands;
> Gladly now I spread word that what I hoped for day after day has happened.
> Already in this campaign there is no more fighting;
> As it is often said, in leading, as in following, the thing is to be steadfast.

Leaving just five hundred troops under Bandi's command at the Dzungar capital of Ili, Qianlong called his troops home. All seemed in hand, but in fact, the real trouble was just beginning: One year later Qing armies were again on the march in the West.

The Second Dzungar Campaign

Qianlong's swift victory in 1755 led him to propose major changes to the political situation in the Altai region. He named new leaders of the different Dzungar tribes, confirming Amursana as head of the Khoit Mongols, and organized them on the model of the organization imposed upon the Khalkha (Eastern) Mongols, respecting the need to maintain existing social and legal institutions yet at the same time providing the court a means of supervision of local affairs. By keeping tribal leaders under his thumb, Qianlong's clear intention was to prevent the emergence of a renewed Dzungar confederation such as existed under Galdan Tsereng in the 1730s and 1740s. But as heirs to a tradition of resisting central authority, Dzungar leaders did not allow their ambitions to be so easily compromised. Whatever polite opinions he may have expressed as a guest in Qianlong's tent the year before, Amursana did not accept the new order being imposed by Beijing. He believed that his rightful place was as the new Dzungar khan, leading a reunified, independent confederation of the Western Mongols.

Flouting the emperor's command to appear in audience after the conclusion of fighting, and rejecting the seal he had been given, Amursana made clear his intentions to resist Qianlong's will. When other of the Dzungar leaders rallied to support Amursana's claim in autumn 1755, Qianlong ordered Bandi to make plans to arrest the would-be khan. But—as soon became distressingly clear—five hundred men were insufficient for such a maneuver. Having announced their will to rebel, Amursana and his allies rapidly concentrated their strength around Ili, determined to force a showdown with the Manchu troops garrisoned there. Facing certain defeat, Bandi led a party of sixty men on a breakout, which ended in disaster: On October 3, 1755, his makeshift camp surrounded by the enemy, Bandi committed suicide as every last man with him was killed.

These dramatic events made it plain that serious force would be necessary to bring Amursana to heel and assert Qing control of the Dzungar region once and for all. Qianlong wasted little time. Early in 1756, another expedition set out, this time to track down Amursana and root out any remaining Dzungar resistance to Qing suzerainty. As before, the army was split into two groups, a western route and a northern route. Amursana proved more elusive than Dawachi, however. After a year of inconsequential fighting back and forth across difficult and desolate terrain, in 1757 Qing armies set off again in pursuit of their quarry. This time they had more luck. Internal conflict had weakened the Dzungar cause, and an outbreak of smallpox created panic, leading many troops to simply abandon their posts and flee. In addition, the Kazakh leader who had earlier given safe haven to Amursana now signaled his wish to submit to Qing authority. Relentlessly pursued by the young Manchu general Joohūi, deserted by his supporters, and short of supplies, Amursana fled to Russia sometime in the spring of 1757. Still unsure of the outcome, the emperor put off performing the victory ritual at the ancestral temple just yet. When Russian authorities refused to abide by treaty agreements binding them to return fugitives, Qianlong wrote an angry note of protest to the tsar, which was ignored.

Events came to a close the next year, when Amursana died of smallpox. This time the Russians took the precaution of informing Qing officials of the fact and arranged for them to come to the border post at Kiakhta to inspect the body. Qianlong seemed satisfied and dismissed the matter, saying, "Whether or not the Russians surrender Amursana's body to us now is not worth our serious discussion."

The death of Amursana and the demise of the Dzungar confederation was a final blow to the ambitions of the Western Mongols. The Dzungar people themselves suffered catastrophic losses: of a population of 600,000, approximately 90 percent were either killed in fighting, died of disease, fled the area, or were taken captive. Even the name "Dzungar" was obliterated: After 1759, Qianlong prohibited its further use, insisting that the names of the separate remnant tribes be used instead. This move reflected his own profound sentiments, that with the completion of the task begun by his grandfather, Kangxi, a major historical milestone was passed. As he wrote after the initial surrender of the Dzungars in August 1755,

> In the past, my grandfather had on many occasions attacked the Dzungars, but the barriers separating those tribes proved too tough, and, lacking an opportune moment, he had to settle for a temporary truce and pull-back. In recent years, Dawachi and his ilk have been struggling and murdering each other, causing cease-

less internal disorder. [. . .] As universal lord of the lands under heaven, my authority covers all, so it is right that I should act to regulate the affairs of the nomads with an eye to the long run. [. . .] When the opportunity for quick victory presented itself, what would have been more unconscionable than to have appeased and temporized further or to have watched on hesitantly? What hope could one possibly have in that way of acquitting oneself bravely? Among we Manchus the old custom is for everyone to rally when there is a call to war; to shy away is to court shame. We do not intend to take advantage of the easy life, so that gradually habits of fear arise. Were we to do this, then rather having occasion now to celebrate winning a great triumph and returning the distant savage to the embrace of civilization, I would have had occasion to be very apprehensive.

This edict provides an excellent window on Qianlong's thinking as he pursued various military objectives. It also shows how closely linked his imperial ambitions were to the maintenance of those martial traits which, as we have seen earlier, he thought set Manchus apart.

The Conquest of the Tarim

By 1760 fighting around the Tianshan Mountains had emptied the region of most of its inhabitants. Yet large areas of fertile land remained, especially north of the mountains, which was well suited to farming or pasture. To leave the area unattended would invite further disorder, as one or another local tribe was bound to claim the land as its own. Qianlong weighed his options and, beginning in 1762, decided to implement a large-scale resettlement policy that offered military and civilian settlers various incentives to relocate to the remote western frontier. Several thousand households of impoverished Han Chinese farmers moved in response. At the same time, the state invested heavily in building new garrison cities to accommodate the thousands more Eight Banner and Mongol soldiers who would be stationed there permanently with their families to safeguard the border.

Before this colonization program could be implemented, however, Qianlong had to deal with the fallout of the Dzungar collapse on the southern side of the Tianshan range. Completely vanquishing the power of the Islamic elite in this corner of the empire proved an impossible task; but by 1759 an agreement was reached and arrangements made for the regular administration of the region under Qing auspices. In a way, Qianlong found himself reaching the same sort of compromise with these Muslim leaders that he had made with the Dzungars twenty years before. But unlike the Dzungar problem, neither he nor his descendants ever managed to find a lasting solution to the challenges to central rule posed by the Turkic lands of the Qing.

To understand these developments takes us in a different direction, one that, like the history of the Dzungars, ultimately traces its origins to the Mongol empire of the thirteenth century, when a son of Chinggis Khan, Chaghatai, ruled most of central and eastern Turkestan. His conversion to the Islamic faith helped it to flourish in the region, especially in the oasis cities encircling the Tarim Basin and the formidable Taklamakan Desert, which lay on the old Silk Road trade routes tying Central Asia to China. By the middle 1600s, the transmission of religious teaching there lay in the hands of Muslim clerical leaders known as Khojas (or *Khwajas*, from the Persian word for "master"). The Khojas were affiliated with an order of Sufi mystics called the Naqshbandi, one branch of which had moved eastward from Iran to the Tarim oases, where they came to assert their authority in the political sphere. Eventually the Naqshbandi split into two rival factions, called the Black Mountain (or Ishaqiyya, after their founder, Ishaq) and the White Mountain Khojas (also known as the Afaqiyya, after their founder, Afaq, a great-nephew of Ishaq). These dueling camps regularly sought outside military and diplomatic support to back up their competing claims to religious and secular authority.

A century into this continuing struggle, in the 1670s the White Mountain faction, who traditionally controlled the city of Yarkand, appealed to the Dzungar leader Galdan for assistance against their rivals. Seeing a chance to expand his influence, Galdan gladly intervened and ejected the Black Mountain Khojas from their capital at Kashgar, one hundred miles west of Yarkand. Thanks to this alliance with the White Mountain faction, the Dzungars held indirect authority over the southern Tarim for the next eighty years. To ensure the obedience of their Muslim clients, the Dzungars demanded not only that the White Mountain Khojas provide tribute, but also that they leave their sons in the Dzungar capital far to the north, where they were kept as hostages.

The total defeat of the Dzungars in 1757 threw this arrangement into turmoil. The Qing at first hoped to inherit the loyalty of the White Mountain Khojas, represented at that time by two brothers, Burhan ad-Din and Jihan, who had grown up as hostages in Ili. Qianlong offered to confirm their local authority as *begs*, or headmen, and to allow them to return to their ancestral home in Yarkand. First, however, Qianlong desired their formal submission, preferably in person, at his court. Their failure to report in a timely way to Beijing provoked growing worry, which proved justified when the brothers stood by in June 1757 as the Manchu officer charged with taking control of the town of Kucha was murdered. Within a month all the region was in open rebellion.

This turn of events seems to have taken Qianlong by surprise, for it took him one year to put together a military response. In part the delay owed to the emperor's decision to rotate new men into the field. He recalled his trusted man in the field, Joohūi, and replaced him with a distant relative of his own, Yarhašan. Not as talented a commander as Joohūi, Yarhašan set out with just over 10,000 men to lay siege to Kucha, where Burhan ad-Din and Jihan were hiding out. Despite a Qing attempt to bottle them up in the town, the two managed to escape to Aksu, where they enjoyed strong support. After three months Yarhašan had nothing to show for his efforts. Qianlong relieved him of his command and ordered him to await the arrival of Joohūi before returning to the capital for an inquisition. (Like Necin before him, he was later executed for dereliction of duty.) Joohūi, who had not yet returned to Beijing, now turned around. Taking with him what few troops he had remaining he proceeded to Yarkand, where the Afaqqiya leaders had since absconded.

A lack of reinforcements, however, almost proved his undoing. Joohūi's first attempts to move on Burhan ad-Din and Jihan were met with fierce resistance and brought heavy losses to his army. He retreated to the banks of the Blackwater River to regroup, but the enemy soon surrounded his position. Knowing that before long he would meet the same fate as his late comrade Bandi, Joohūi managed to sneak out an urgent request for aid; meanwhile he was forced to stay put. His luck turned when the Manchu troops found stashes of food buried underground that had been left there by Muslim irregulars, and an attempt by the Khojas' forces to flood them out of their camp fortuitously increased the Manchus' limited supply of water. In addition, Joohūi ordered his men to scour the trees and bushes around the camp for spent ammunition that could be reused, which replenished their own meager matériel. In this way, the Qing army held on for three months. Finally, in early 1759, fresh troops arrived from the north, and combined with a well-timed attack of Kirghiz cavalry from the east, the Siege of Blackwater was broken and the White Mountain attack dispersed.

The conquest of the rest of the region proceeded quickly after that. By midsummer the White Mountain leaders had been chased westward across the Pamirs to Badakhshan, in northeast Afghanistan. Jihan was killed. With most of his army taken prisoner by the Qing, Burhan ad-Din threw himself on the mercy of the local shah, who, though hesitant to betray his coreligionists by handing him over to Qianlong, at the same time worried about a possible Qing invasion. Qianlong wrote him in vaguely threatening terms:

> No doubt you will have heard of the military strength of our great dynasty. Stories will have reached you of our pacification of the Dzungars, and you have seen yourself how we have conquered Yarkand and Kashgar and sent thousands upon thousands of traitorous rebels fleeing in desperation. Sultan Shah, do not be misled by those around you whose views are intransigent. Convey Burhan ad-Din and the body of Jihan to my army, and I will certainly reward you generously.

In the end, the shah executed Burhan ad-Din himself and presented the Qing army with his body—minus the head, which he claimed had been stolen—along with the head of Jihan that Qianlong had requested. Joohūi accepted these grisly trophies and returned with them to the capital, where, before the assembled court, he presented them to the emperor in a grand victory ceremony. A generation later, the descendants of Jihan and Burhan ad-Din would return to fight again, but for now there was peace.

The Limits of Empire

The subjugation of the Islamic strongholds of Kashgaria brought a successful end to Qianlong's adventure in the Far West. What started out as a limited campaign to rein in an ambitious but minor Dzungar chieftain ended up in a five-year-long war that cost thousands of lives and a treasure in silver. What did Qianlong gain for his trouble?

Qianlong's conquest was in fact a watershed in world history. Not only did it add greatly, as noted, to Qing territory, but it brought to fruition years of efforts by the Manchu and Russian states to win control over the lands and peoples of Central Asia. In this connection, two points must be stressed. First, where contact between the two countries had previously been limited to the northern borders of eastern Mongolia and Manchuria, Qianlong's westward push sent a clear message to the tsar that, when it came to projecting force and playing the diplomatic game, the Qing were not to be underestimated. One hundred years would pass before the Russians felt strong enough to challenge the imperial borders set down by Qianlong in Central Asia. Second, the collapse of the Dzungars as a political entity after some 450 years signaled the demise of the last of the great nomadic confederations that had dominated the history of east and central Eurasia for two thousand years. The expansion of the Qing and Romanov empires signified the closing of the Eurasian steppe and their final triumph over their perennial nomadic enemy.

The momentous nature of the Qing conquest of all of eastern Turkestan, north and south of the Tianshan range, did not escape Qianlong's notice. In his writings at this time, he raised comparisons between the Qing and the Tang, the last dynasty to maintain stable rule over China and at the same time claim a view of the Pamirs from its borders. The following is taken from an edict to the grand councilor Fuheng, whose role as Qianlong's closest advisor put him second in command of the Turkestan campaigns:

> The military strength of the majestic Great Qing is at its height. So much surplus [. . .] had we stored up in the granaries, that not only did we not need to make extraordinary levies of corvée labor in the interior provinces, but thanks to the ceaseless remission of taxes in the two provinces of Shaanxi and Gansu, at first the villages did not even know that a military campaign was beginning! How can the Han, Tang, Song, or Ming dynasties, which exhausted the wealth of China without getting an additional inch of ground for it, compare to us? Adding it all up, within less than five years, our soldiers have covered more than 10,000 *li* on the western marches. No fortification has failed to submit, no people have failed to surrender.

Not wishing to tempt fate, though, Qianlong did not take all the credit, adding:

> In this, truly, we look up gratefully to the blessings of the blue sky above to proclaim our great achievement. To be sure, the accomplishments of men succeed so far as they accord with the moment; it would be most ungenerous not to recognize this.

One of the most interesting aspects of these comments is that Qianlong did not perceive the conquest of Dzungaria and Kashgaria—what soon came to be called by the unified name *Xinjiang*, "New Dominion"—as the affair of the common people. Indeed, he believed they should be as little troubled by it as possible. Rather, conquest was the business of the ruler and his minions—Manchus, Mongols, Han Chinese officials, and others involved in the imperial enterprise. From where Qianlong sat, it was therefore not the case that "China" conquered Xinjiang: *He* had. Nor did he feel the need to seek popular support for the campaigns to the Far West. The expansion of the empire was not done in the name of the "nation." It was done to extol his fame, to demonstrate that the business of the Qing dynastic house and its servants was also Heaven's business. It was also done in the name of strengthening the dynasty by hardening in battle another generation of young Manchu soldiers. For as we saw in Chapter 4, Qianlong worried that the "hereditary simplicity and bravery of we Manchus" had been softened by too many idle days, and he had no patience for those who, "when faced with military duty, try to suggest that they lack the skills." He sent them off to war instead.

The Qing and Islam

One further outcome of the conquest of eastern Turkestan that deserves mention was that after four centuries of relatively limited interaction, China entered a new period of direct and prolonged contact with the other major civilizational presence on the Asian mainland, Islam. This much was reflected in Qianlong's personal life, with the introduction of a Muslim woman into the palace. This was Consort Rong, whom latter-day writers of historical romance sensationalized as the "Fragrant Concubine." This young woman (we do not know her personal name) belonged to a prominent Khoja lineage whose leaders had ridden with Kirghiz cavalry to relieve Joohūi at the Siege of Blackwater. As a reward for their loyalty, Qianlong bestowed titles upon the men in the family, invited them to Beijing, and took their twenty-seven-year-old daughter as one of his own wives. Consort Rong became one of the emperor's favorites. He frequently included her on his travels and spoiled her with generous gifts of raisins, grapes, and melons imported from Kashgar. More noteworthy still, Qianlong showed considerable sensitivity toward Consort Rong's spiritual life, retaining for her a chef who could prepare dishes that accorded with Muslim religious strictures and which Qianlong himself grew to enjoy. She was permitted to continue wearing her own clothes, and occasionally Turkic-style entertainments were staged for her pleasure. In 1764 he even ordered a mosque built on the other side of the palace wall from Consort Rong's compound so she would be able to hear the muezzin's call to prayer. At her death in 1788 she was buried in a coffin decorated with Koranic verse written in Arabic.

Qianlong's respectful attitude toward Consort Rong and her family strengthened the ties binding his Turkic subjects to the throne. Yet Qianlong was unable to create a firmly grounded framework for the conduct of relations with the Islamic world. Apart from a new liking for Islamic sword design, he showed little interest in Islamic culture; nor did he appear inclined to acquaint himself with its ancient traditions of philosophy, science, and medicine. True, he ordered a revision of the imperial lexicon to include Chaghatai Turkish, the literary language of Islamic Central Asia, but as far as we know he never learned the language himself. This relative lack of curiosity in Islamic civilization stood in marked contrast to Qianlong's strong personal interest in Buddhism and Confucianism, or his lasting fascination with European visual art. Was it that the region was too remote from the capital, and too little understood, to warrant a sustained level of attention? Given the strong emphasis Qianlong placed upon Turkestan's economic value (in particular its jade deposits), this seems unlikely. Perhaps he felt that a monotheistic creed such as Islam did not offer sufficient flexibility as a ruling ideology, since it required the religious conversion of any ruler who sought the political advantages of posing as a protector of the faith.

Whatever the reason, Qianlong preferred that Qing control over the Tarim Basin remain indirect, conducted principally through *beg* headmen (equivalent to *tusi* chieftains in the southwest), with only small garrisons of Qing troops. This arrangement, which contrasted markedly with the large garrisons and intensive colonization of the territory north of the Tianshan, meant that Qing control here maintained a low profile. As a consequence, Xinjiang was less well integrated with the rest of Qianlong's domains. The limitations of this policy would be revealed in the large-scale rebellions of the nineteenth century.

Inscribing Victory

The conquest of Xinjiang gave Qianlong an enormous boost in prestige, which he did not hesitate to advertise at home and—as we saw in his note to the Badakhshani shah—abroad. He used all the media at his disposal to convey the message that the Qing was the most powerful state in the world, and that he, Qianlong, enjoyed the unparalleled favor of Heaven. At imperial behest, parades and reviews were held, banquets thrown, histories of the conquest were written, stelae erected, maps made, engravings produced, paintings commissioned, poems written, and songs sung. Similar celebrations followed the other seven of the "Ten Perfect Victories," though on a less grand scale. It is not much of an exaggeration to say that the second half of Qianlong's reign was a veritable orgy of martial revelry.

Some of this dynastic chest-pounding took poetic form. One tally holds that Qianlong composed more than 1,500 pieces on themes of war and battle relating to his ten campaigns, which typically were penned upon hearing a certain piece of news. They stand, therefore, as a kind of literary chronicle of his wars. Some of these works circulated in published collections, and he exhorted both officials and members of the imperial family to read and study his words for their edification. Continuing a tradition begun under Kangxi, Qianlong also produced authoritative military histories of the campaigns he supervised. The official history of the conquest of Turkestan was the *Record of the Pacification of the Dzungars*, published in the palace printing office in 1772. Totaling 171 volumes of printed text, it contains thousands of pages of recopied reports, edicts, and other assorted documents culled from the mass of materials relating to one of the great military enterprises in world history.

Formal histories took a long time to compile, however, and even then they would be read only by scholars. So other means were called upon to proclaim Qing power. Few were so powerfully symbolic as the engraving and exhibition of large-scale commemorative inscriptions. This was an age-old form of display, not unlike the use of decorated columns in imperial Rome. In the Qing, as throughout much of Chinese history, the use of a huge stone tablet, or stele, for such inscriptions was quite common. Up to fifteen or even twenty feet in height, each stele was mounted upon stone tortoises representing the mythical *bixi* upon whose back, legend held, the world rested. Standing before such an enormous monument, one could see the emperor's timeless words, in Chinese on one side, in Manchu on another, and—in the case of certain massive four-sided stelae—in Mongolian and Tibetan. Even if one could not read any of these languages, merely to gaze up at the impenetrable writing overhead was itself to perform a symbolic act of submission to the Great Qing. Like equestrian statues of Renaissance heroes, the idea was to honor personal bravery, enshrine political might, and inspire awe in the observer.

Beginning in 1755, Qianlong ordered the disposition of stelae all over the country to commemorate the winning of Turkestan. Some of these were in or near the Qing capital, while others were placed in the conquered cities of Xinjiang. All were large and expensive. The emperor himself often took the trouble to approve the choice of stone used, and of course was primarily responsible himself for the text that would honor the weighty slab. As a result of the great care that went into their production, many are still in place today. In the main, the inscriptions upon them consist of brief narratives of the particular battle they commemorate, to remind officials and soldiers of the past glories of their friends and relatives and the right-thinking of their imperial master, and to remind locals of the risks of running afoul of Qing authority. The stele raised in 1758 after the defeat of Amursana, thirteen feet (four meters) tall, starts out by proclaiming the identification of the Qing cause and the will of Heaven using a naturalistic analogy: "That which Heaven nourishes, though it be upset by human force, still, it cannot be killed. That which Heaven overturns, though people may replant it, still, it cannot flourish." The text then goes on to emphasize the perfidy of the Dzungars ("they have always been a wicked and cunning people") and the righteousness of the war against them.

Mapping Victory

Another way that Qianlong chose to immortalize his triumphs in Xinjiang was by having maps made of the new territory added to the empire. The production of maps and charts had, of course, accompanied the war effort itself, as generals and ministers exchanged views over strategy and tactics. However, among the general educated population, geographical knowledge of the Far West was extremely limited because most maps of the Chinese empire simply did not have any information on the Tianshan region. Usually this area was left nearly empty. His conquests meant that Qianlong was in a good position to fill in these blank spaces. In 1756, he appointed a small surveying team consisting of a Chinese court astronomer, two Manchu officers, two Jesuits, and two Tibetan lamas, and sent them to chart the latitudes and longitudes of Dzungaria and Altishahr. Enough of their work was completed for some to be included in a general 1760 geography of the empire. More detailed maps awaited a later expedition in 1769, which used the latest surveying techniques to produce all kinds of new maps, some on a spectacular scale, including one that ran to twenty feet in length and required an entire room to be exhibited. Because Jesuits were involved at all stages of the cartographic process, the information they gathered about the new lands added to the Qing empire was soon transmitted to European capitals, sometimes surreptitiously by missionaries, other times openly by the emperor himself, when he presented maps to foreign envoys.

Along with maps came the compilation of gazetteers, a typically Chinese form of local history that included maps, pictures, descriptions of geography, topography, flora and fauna, and biographies of native sons and daughters. The first of these, the *Polyglot Gazetteer of the Western Regions*, was published in 1763. This was mainly a list of place names in six different languages and scripts, intended as a standardized glossary for the compilation of the *Record of the Pacification of the Dzungars* and as an aid in local administration. The *Polyglot Gazetteer* was followed nineteen years later by the more complete *Illustrated Gazetteer of the Western Regions of the Imperial Domain*. This had maps together with lengthy descriptions of the land, cities, and inhabitants of Xinjiang. Both works were funded and published by the emperor and helped to illustrate the unity of the empire. As Qianlong wrote in the preface to the *Polyglot Gazetteer*,

> Now, in Chinese, "Heaven" is called *tian*. [. . .] In the Muslim tongue it is called *asman*. Let a Muslim, meaning "heaven," tell a Han Chinese it is called *asman*, and the Han will necessarily think this is not so. If the Han Chinese, meaning "heaven," tells the Muslim *tian*, the Muslim will likewise certainly think it is not so. Here not so, there not so. Who knows which is right? But by raising the head and looking at what is plainly up above, the Han Chinese knows *tian* and venerates it, and the Muslim knows *asman* and venerates it. This is the great unity. In fact, once names are unified, there is nothing that is not universal.

Qianlong here displayed to the reader his impartiality as universal sovereign. One is again struck by his dependence on language to emphasize the similarities, such as a reverence for Heaven, that despite disparities of culture and place bound his subjects to the imperial center. The publication of these materials, which circulated fairly widely among officialdom, and their promotion of a frankly pluralist agenda abetted the ideological integration of Xinjiang with the rest of the Qing empire. Apart from this, Qianlong's studied inclusion of earlier Chinese terminology that had applied a millennium or more before to certain of the areas and cities of Central Asia he now controlled emphasized his accomplishment of grand unification in ways that Chinese scholars could readily appreciate.

The Look of Victory

Images were yet one more resource at Qianlong's disposal when it came to spreading the news of the expanding Qing empire. Here, as with mapmaking, the emperor took advantage of the skills of the Jesuit missionaries at court to document this remarkable achievement. An outstanding example of this is a famous series of engravings of sixteen scenes from the campaigns in Dzungaria and Altishahr. The engravings were based on drawings made at the time by artists who accompanied the army to the frontier; these base drawings were completed in

1765 and then sent to Paris for engraving. The finished engravings were presented to the emperor in 1775, along with plates, so that more copies could be made.

Each engraving shows a famous scene from the 1755–1759 campaigns, typically, a scene of a dramatic battle or of enemy surrender. The siege of Joohūi at Blackwater is one in the series. The scale and size of each engraving is approximately the same, and the style—a distorted perspective based on Western techniques—is consistent throughout. More complicated events are narrated by dividing the image up into two or three sections separated by greenery or mountains, with a different sub-scene depicted in each section; in a way, they are like scrolls that have been compressed into one limited space. The engravings show definite influences of European traditions of showing battle, from the disposition of corpses to the way of showing exhaustion among men and horses. Typically, the center of the image focuses on the action of Qing cavalry moving decisively against the enemy, bows drawn, lances at the ready. In addition to movement, the engravings capture a tremendous amount of detail, such as might have been observed from a slightly removed vantage point: men falling from their horses, soldiers nocking arrows to their bowstrings (see Figure 6.1).

Many copies of these engravings were made. Complete sets were maintained at the emperor's different palaces and residences, and Qianlong made presents of other sets to certain temples where he had stayed. Unusually, we have some record of the individuals who received these inscriptions as gifts. These were mostly members of the imperial family, high civil officials in the provinces, military and political leaders who had themselves had a personal part in the Turkestan campaigns, prominent Manchu officers, as well as four private collectors in Jiangnan, as thanks for their contributions to the imperial literary collection project, then underway. Outside of China, one set was given to the Korean court, and sets

Figure 6.1 Anonymous. *Raising the Siege of Blackwater.* 1775. Copper engraving. Musée Guimet, Paris. One of a series of sixteen scenes celebrating the Qing conquest of the lands that would later become Xinjiang, these lively and detailed prints circulated widely both in China and Europe. © Art Resource.

circulated widely in Europe and, later, the United States, where they became collectors' items, along with engravings made of the emperor's victories later in Sichuan and elsewhere. Together with the explanatory legends Qianlong wrote to accompany them, these works have come down to us today as vivid documents of his efforts to bring order to this far corner of the realm.

At least as impressive are the many portraits of the valorous officers and soldiers who took part in these campaigns. Like the engravings, they, too, employed some Western techniques, and it may be that Jesuit artists were involved in painting some of them (none is signed). The images are also surmounted by brief legends, in Chinese and Manchu, stating the specific act of bravery for which the person portrayed was being commended. After the first Dzungar campaign, the emperor ordered one hundred such images, which became known collectively as the "Martial Worthies" series, and had them hung permanently in those buildings of the palace complex where foreign emissaries were usually received. Over time, following other military successes elsewhere in the empire, the series grew to accommodate more paintings, until there were 260 paintings lining the halls, a pantheon of Qing heroes. Most of these portraits have been lost today, apparently carried away as booty during the 1900 occupation of Beijing by foreign troops, but those that survive speak eloquently of the commitment to honor the spirit of bravery and sacrifice that contributed to the glory of Qianlong and the Great Qing.

Closely related to these images in terms of theme and production values are the many paintings of the emperor himself. The stories he had heard as a boy about the exploits of Kangxi, who personally led the hunt for the Dzungar leader Galdan, riding dangerously deep into the Mongolian steppe in pursuit of his archenemy, no doubt had a great influence upon Qianlong. Not that he took his grandfather's example so literally as to himself lead a military expedition off into the west, but he did ensure the impression that he *might* have done so, had he so wished. As remarked in Chapter 4, he was often painted returning from the hunt, looking quite comfortable on horseback, caught in a relaxed, almost casual mood. Other paintings show him in the act of shooting tigers, bears, and stags, evidence of his own personal bravery in the face of danger. The most famously martial of all is an equestrian portrait of Qianlong painted by Castiglione, done in the style of similar portraits of European monarchs, such as Philip II of Spain, with which the artist must surely have been familiar. In this painting, we see the emperor astride a beautiful pinto horse—a very different creature from the Mongolian tarpan known to the ordinary Qing soldier. Qianlong's moustachioed face appears noble and serene. Both he and his horse look to the viewer's right, as if deciding where to set their course. The emperor is in full battle array, quiver on the right, bow on the left. On his right thumb is an archer's thumb ring of jade; his left hand grips the reins firmly, while in his right he holds a riding crop. Imperial dragons swarm over his heavy embroidered coat with its oversized epaulets; a silver helmet decorated with *dharani* in gold relief and topped with a splendid horsehair tassel encases his head. This was a ceremonial outfit, which the emperor wore when reviewing departing troops or welcoming the return of a victorious army. We don't in fact know when he wore the armor, nor do we know where this painting hung in the palace. But we can easily imagine the impression the portrait—which is nearly life-size—must have made on the viewer. Its magnificence and splendor project the aura of a vigorous sovereign in full control of his imperial power, dominating the landscape (see Figure 6.2).

Figure 6.2   Giuseppe Castiglione (1688–1766). *The Qianlong Emperor in Ceremonial Armor on Horseback*. 1758. Ink and colors on silk. One of the best-known images of the many Qianlong left to posterity, this magnificent portrait is a good example of the hybrid Sino-European artistic style that prevailed in much 18th-century Qing court art. © Palace Museum, Beijing.

It was late in life that Qianlong reflected on his military record and gave himself the nickname, "Old Man of the Ten Perfect Victories." The immediate cause for this reflection was the successful repulsion of a second attempt by Gurkha (Nepali) troops to advance into Qing territory in southern Tibet. Interestingly, the mood in this short essay is not full of the same sort of elation as that found in his other war-related writings. Instead, it seems to represent the sober musings of an old man who is tired of fighting—tired, even, of conquest. In it he writes,

> As we had already demonstrated the overwhelming power of our forces, if we had said that it was essential to clean out and destroy the rebels' lairs, one by one, to smash them so that not one remained, this plan of action would not have accorded with the favorable intent of Supreme Heaven to the living. Therefore, saying that this region was completely taken over, we abandoned another thousand *li* beyond the borders of Western Tibet, giving up having it farmed and administered [within the empire]. In the end, there was nothing for it but to let it be taken by someone else. Having thus decreed, and learning of their [the rebels'] surrender, and taking pity on the troops, I called an end to the campaign.

The tone of resignation apparent in his words contrasts markedly with the confidence and bluster of his pronouncements of thirty-five years before, appearing to indicate as well a recognition that there were in fact some limits to his sovereignty. What is consistent, though, is Qianlong's reliance on, and belief in, the guidance and blessing of Heaven. He ends the essay this way, with a philosophical twist at the end, in reference to his having abdicated in 1795:

> By good fortune, in the space of my fifty-seven years [on the throne], ten times have our military efforts succeeded totally. How can one say this is not the favor of Heaven? For the greater Heaven's favor, the more sincere my reverence for Heaven. Not daring to presume to know how to express my thanks, I can only beg helplessly for Heaven's blessing with utmost reverence and trepidation. Having abstained from rule, I can only hope fervently for the time that I will become a completed person. What more is there to be said?

7

Renaissance Man

Given his overwhelming preoccupation with military affairs, the extent of his travels, and the great demands of ordinary business, it is more than a little surprising that Qianlong found time in his daily schedule to devote to activities as viewing paintings and writing poems. Yet he did—so much so, that in the minds of most historians, the image of Qianlong as a man of letters in fact greatly overshadows his image as a man of war. In part this is because of his own efforts to cultivate such a profile, evident in the many paintings in which he is shown as a cultured gentleman, in repose in his study, brush in hand (see Figure 7.1). Qianlong's reputation as a patron of high culture is also linked to the stunning assemblage of artwork in the Imperial Palace Museum, one of the greatest cultural legacies of premodern China, which owes its substance to Qianlong's passion to collect all that was fine in the world. Admiring this collection today, we can still take advantage of the detailed and accurate catalogues Qianlong had compiled over two hundred years ago. There is also the *Complete Library of the Four Treasuries*—at 10,000 titles, perhaps the largest single published anthology of writings in human history—which arose from Qianlong's wish to collect and review the entire canon of Chinese literary, philosophical, and historical works, from the earliest poems of the first millennium BCE to his own day.

Earlier chapters have already made clear Qianlong's urge to classify, rationalize, and regularize; it was entirely natural that this urge should extend beyond government institutions and language to the arts and letters. In so doing, he saw himself as contributing to a timeless artistic tradition, hoping to achieve the kind of immortality granted to collectors and patrons of the arts. Furthermore, by training himself as both a connoisseur and practitioner of the arts, Qianlong also sought to embody the ideal of the educated man, who in his words and deeds perfectly balanced *wen* and *wu*; literary accomplishment and martial virtue. Proficiency with a bow and arrow was not enough to win the esteem of learned officials, some from families that for centuries had been producing top scholars and who possessed libraries surpassing his own. To rule successfully, Qianlong needed to establish himself intellectually, to show himself as well versed in the poetry, art, history, and philosophy of the ages as the erudites over whom he presumed to govern. This was not an easy task. By certain measures he succeeded;

Figure 7.1 Giuseppe Castiglione (1688–1766) and Jin Tingbiao (?–1767). *Qianlong in His Study.* Before 1766. Ink and colors on silk. Palace Museum, Beijing. A highly idealized image of Qianlong as a Chinese scholar-poet stroking his beard in search of inspiration, surrounded by the "four treasures" of the literary man: brush, paper, ink, and inkstone. © Palace Museum, Beijing.

by other standards his efforts were marred by vanity, intolerance, and excess. Whatever one's opinion of his taste and talents, Qianlong's imprint on the cultural world of his day, like that on his political world, is impossible to overlook.

A Portrait of the Artist

The most direct of Qianlong's various connections with the creative arts were those in which he assumed the place of author. He tried his hand at different types of artistic endeavor, most notably painting, calligraphy, and, as we have already had occasion to see, poetry. These were cherished diversions, at once means of relaxation and forms of mental exercise. He pursued them religiously throughout his long life, leaving for posterity a considerable body of work. These efforts allow us to observe different aspects of his personality—though clearly, only those he wanted to reveal—and underscored the depth of his understanding of high culture. Being a "practicing artist," so to speak, had other benefits. For one thing, it made his frequent interventions in the creation of works by court artists, to whom he was not shy about offering advice and suggestions, more effective and persuasive, since he usually knew exactly what sort of results he wanted and could provide specific ideas about how to produce them. For another, the occasionally skillful line or poem might earn him the genuine respect of his main audience: the lettered elite of Beijing, Jiangnan, and the main provincial centers. Finally, his personal experiences as artist and poet enhanced his enjoyment and appreciation of the masterworks gathered around him, and made him a better critic.

To begin with the least successful of his accomplishments, we should consider Qianlong's efforts at painting and music. He began to paint when he was eighteen. Though he attempted much, usually subjects in nature (old, craggy trees were one of his favorites), the examples he left suggest only modest talent. He himself admitted as much, discouraging excessive praise and making little of his undertakings in this area. He could be sensitive to color, however: in the manufacture of court clothing, for instance, he banned the use of fabrics made of a certain shade of dark green that he apparently could not abide. And he often had definite ideas of how he liked things to look in the paintings executed for him by the forty-odd court artists he employed, paying visits to their palace workshop and giving detailed instructions as to the placement of trees, plants, and people. Vivid evidence of such direct participation comes from letters written by a Jesuit priest at the Qianlong court, describing the work of a fellow Jesuit, the painter Denis Attiret:

> On the morning of the third day, the Emperor honored him with a visit. He wanted to see all that had been done and found that the figure of his person, which had been drawn on horseback in one scene and carried on a chaise in another, leaned a little too far backward in both instances. He wanted this mistake corrected at once, and in order to facilitate this he sat on his throne, which was right there; he acted out what he had in mind and a drawing was made of his position.

Sometimes the emperor went so far as to indulge in joint composition with his artists, as on this occasion, again with Attiret:

> The mandarin told the painter that the intention of His Majesty was that he draw a certain Tartar gentleman on horseback pursuing a tiger, bow drawn, about to let the arrow fly; he added that the Emperor wanted to do the painting himself. Brother Attiret did what was expected of him. The Emperor returned the next day. A eunuch carried the painting His Majesty had done himself over the sketch [Attiret had made] of the Tartar on horseback. He displayed it before Brother Attiret and ordered him to retouch the posture of the rider. After that slight correction, the painting was returned to the chamber of His Majesty, who wanted to work on it some more. But that same evening it was sent to Brother Attiret, with the order to finish it. (Translation by Deborah Sommer)

Later that same week, having commanded the exhausted artist to paint his full portrait, Qianlong made a special request: to improve his appearance, his head was to be depicted slightly larger than life-size. Needless to add, the order was carried out.

Whereas his grandfather had dabbled at playing the clavichord, we have no evidence for Qianlong's ability at any musical instrument. In some paintings he is depicted as a classical scholar, sitting by himself in a clearing near a hut in the woods, the zither-like *qin* at hand, as if he were about to pick out a mournful tune to suit his lonely reverie. This, however, was mere fantasy, as the few remarks he left on the subject reveal that he had no real understanding of music. Nonetheless, he took great pleasure in it and was quite fastidious about what compositions were played at court. His tastes were catholic. In the early years of his reign he retained a couple of Jesuit music masters to train pupils at court, and even had them organize a small chamber orchestra to perform from the European repertoire. In a rather different vein, retreats to Chengde provided plenty of opportunities for the performance of Mongolian music, which, as can be seen in paintings of these scenes, accompanied banquets. Qianlong also enjoyed various kinds of singing and theater. Southern-style sung drama was a particular favorite. Under his patronage it grew to be the most popular sort of theatre in the capital, eventually becoming identified as "Peking opera." Even though he sometimes criticized such forms of entertainment as frivolous, in point of fact he rarely traveled without being accompanied by the court's professional opera troupe. Another of Qianlong's important contributions to musical culture was the codification and collation of court music, including not only titles but also, uniquely, scores. Music historians today have reason to be thankful that the emperor was so particular in this regard.

One area of artistic endeavor in which Qianlong could legitimately claim some personal accomplishment was calligraphy. To have lacked skill in this department would have amounted to a serious flaw indeed. For Qianlong, as for every gentleman in the eighteenth century, the practice of wielding brush and ink was not just an artistic, but a spiritual exercise, its quality a measure of one's character and moral fiber. He practiced this most important scholarly art without fail every day, coming to own a distinctive and handsome script, readily recognizable and regarded today by most art historians as quite admirable.

A true connoisseur, Qianlong could identify all but the most obscure allusions and wrote knowledgeably about various masters of the brush; indeed, his judgment in matters of dating and attribution, by and large, has stood the test of time. Among his favorite calligraphers were the immortals Wang Xizhi (321–379 CE) and Mi Fu (1051–1107). The former artist, whose influence on Qianlong's own style is most obvious, held a special place in the emperor's heart. Coming into possession of a rare sample of Wang's original work, he placed it in his favorite palace studio together with the works of two other master calligraphers named Wang, renamed the room for the rare treasures it held, and then wrote a poem about it. Every year he had the Wang Xizhi piece brought before him, set his seal on it in the way literary men were accustomed to doing, and wrote a short comment or poem on it somewhere, such as these lines, describing the pleasure this brought him:

In a long idling summer day, resting at the water pavilion,
The engaging breeze teases the flowering branches,
Moving the jade brush to capture the master's strokes,
The ink is pale and pale, the strokes flow and flow.
The Wangs are long gone, real works by Yan [Zhongqing] and Liu [Zongyuan] are rare,
Yet in copying their work to pass the time, they are companions who make me stay.
(Translation by Chuimei Ho and Bennet Bronson.)

By the time he died, he had filled the scroll with seventy-three such marks of his appreciation! He also had Wang's calligraphy copied out and carved onto stone so that rubbings could be made and distributed in booklet form for others to appreciate and learn from. These were but a few of the more than seventy such editions of calligraphy models he published out of the imperial collections.

Gifts of imperial calligraphy, as Qianlong learned from his grandfather, counted as a mark of great appreciation. Qianlong was more than willing to convert his talent to political capital, as on New Year's Eve, when he presented a gift to top officials of a commemorative inscription of the character *fu* (meaning "good fortune"), signing them personally in the presence of each gratefully kneeling recipient. In fact, he took such pride in his calligraphy that in 1770 he ordered officials to return to the palace these and any other such calligraphic gifts they had received from him before 1756 on the grounds that his style had improved so much that it was not suitable to let examples of his earlier hand remain in circulation. He promised replacements in exchange for the calligraphy that was turned in, even if it involved large wooden plaques and stone inscriptions. To judge from the large number of such monuments to be found today, Qianlong was true to his word. His only rival—the only other political figure whose calligraphy is so easily recognizable and so prominently featured in the Chinese landscape—is the Chinese Communist leader, Mao Zedong.

The Poet

More abundant even than his calligraphy was Qianlong's production of verse. Regardless of advancing age or the torrent of business surrounding him, the emperor produced a one-inch thick volume of poetry every year of his reign. Brought together and published in six successive editions in 1749, 1760, 1771, 1783, 1795, and (posthumously) in 1800, his 43,800 poems (counts vary) fill some 282 volumes (twenty-four volumes of poetry and prose written before he became emperor had already appeared in 1737). By this measure he stands as China's most prolific poet, writing the equivalent of two poems a day, every day, from the age of ten until his death at eighty-nine. Voluminous as it was, however, poetry was only one part of Qianlong's total literary output, which also included edicts, essays, prefaces, colophons, and inscriptions, of which there were many thousands more.

It is hard to believe that Qianlong really wrote all the poems attributed to him.[1] According to the testimony of one minister, each day after the conclusion of official business in the early afternoon, the emperor would first have lunch and then retire to his study, where he wrote at least one or two poems, an essay, or painted a picture. If true, this would suggest that Qianlong may indeed have authored most of the verse ascribed to him; or at least that the essential idea behind many, if not all, poems was quite likely his. Of course, he had help. Qianlong routinely asked Grand Council staff to recopy the drafts of his afternoon versifying and relied on top officials for editorial advice (a ticklish job, to be

---

[1]It is perhaps less exceptional than one might think for political leaders, even modern ones, to dabble in poetry. Among U.S. presidents, John Quincy Adams and Abraham Lincoln both wrote verse, and Jimmy Carter, the thirty-ninth U.S. president, published a volume of poems in 1995.

sure!). In the not uncommon instances when literary inspiration struck in the middle of an audience, Qianlong would pause to declaim his verse aloud, trusting that his minister/editor would remember the lines later on, when they could be written down and refined further. Should inspiration be lacking, he was not above asking court officials to look around in their spare time for material he could use, happy turns of phrase, memorable quotations, and the like. For such purposes, just as he maintained a stable of artists, he also kept a few literary types around at court, minor poets of the day. In the editing process, they would polish everything carefully before printing, so that the final versions might well depart significantly from the emperor's original.

As we have seen from various examples of Qianlong's poetry that have surfaced in preceding chapters, anything could be a suitable subject. Most of his work can be grouped into nature poems, commemorative poems (such as on the New Year, the occasion of a military victory, or a visit to some famous place), didactic poems, and encomia, which extolled the beauty of an item such as an ink stone or a jade (these would often be carved directly on the object). Much of this verse feels stilted, as though it were produced in a hurry for a certain occasion, which it often was. The following poem, translated loosely, exemplifies this well:

"Watching the Harvest: A Poem in the Antique Style"

> Wheat sprouts, come the summer, tassels yellow shroud,
> East west, 'cross the fields, paths run long and ripe.
> This day, to the land, aged peasants crowd,
> Sickles bent, cutting grain, joyfully they swipe.
> Smiles broad, as they see thin the morning clouds;
> Hands fly mid dense stalks wildly strewn askew.
> Hat brims burned by sun, backs and shoulders bowed,
> Soup bowls hardly touched, of hunger none do gripe.
> Child's cry gets no mind, naught but sparrows round;
> Spread word, harvest's done, at this all cheer and shout.

Written by a young Qianlong, this idealized celebration of the peasant's labor—the ultimate source, lest we forget, of the emperor's wealth—paradoxically emphasizes the emperor's separation from, rather than his closeness to, the backbreaking toil of his subjects.

More successful verse can sometimes also be found, however, in personal poems such as reminiscences about his old teachers and his grandfather. The sorrowful poem cited in Chapter 3, for example, written in memory of Empress Xiaoxian, is so intimate we can be sure that no one but the emperor could have written it. It must be said, though, that authentic, emotionally laden poems are rare in Qianlong's oeuvre. For him, composing poetry was typically not an arduous task involving deep contemplation, soul-searching, and the extended working and reworking of language. Really good poetry, after all, is almost always subversive, and it would hardly have done for Qianlong to have gone that route. Most of his poems were quick productions, which sometimes took shortcuts around the usual rules of rhyme and meter. Some were also for recreation. At the picnics and banquets he hosted, Qianlong liked to invent games in which everyone present would have to compose a suitable verse on a theme or rhyme set by him. More demanding amusements required longer rhymed quatrains; for these, officials would have prepared verses in advance and distributed them to all participants, lest anyone fear they would not be up to the task.

As casual as most of them were, they were still the emperor's work, so that once completed, his poems became subjects for scholarly commentary by the leading literary figures in the capital. Opinions at court were predictably generous, lauding his genius and talent; one official gushed that his lines flew "like dragons soaring in the sky." This opinion was shared by some in Europe. Voltaire, for one, thought very highly of the emperor's literary abilities. Writing to Frederick the Great of the *Ode to Mukden,* he said, "I declare that I was charmed by the tender morality and the wholesome virtue that courses throughout the emperor's works. How, I asked myself, could a man charged with the burden of governing such a vast kingdom find the time to write such a poem?" However, after reading the poem (available in Europe in French translation in 1770), Frederick replied halfheartedly that he found it "not to be in what one would call the European taste." Most modern readers would probably share Frederick's opinion on this point.

Overwhelmed by their sheer number, few modern literary critics have bothered to read any of Qianlong's poems; some lambasted his efforts as "nauseating." Though this may be a bit harsh, it is probably fair to say that the historical value of Qianlong's poetic efforts is greater than its literary value. This does not alter the fact that the emperor valued poetry greatly and took it quite seriously. He venerated the poems of earlier ages, most especially those of the Tang and Song dynasties, read them over and over, and could recite them by heart. In 1760 he ordered new editions and commentaries made of this most famous corpus of Chinese poetry. Later these would be gathered in his giant "Four Treasuries" anthology, discussed later.

The Collector

However opinions vary as to the merits of Qianlong's own creative efforts, there is no denying that as a collector of fine art, the emperor contributed greatly to the cultural traditions of the empire.

In China, as in Europe, India, and elsewhere, rulers surrounded themselves with exquisite paintings and priceless objects of various kinds, material evidence of their power and thus legitimation of their sovereign status. The Song emperor Huizong, for example, was famous for the art collection he assembled in the early 1100s, and was a kind of model for Qianlong (though it should be said that Huizong was a far more talented painter and calligrapher). The foundations of Qianlong's hoard were to be found not in the Song, however, but in the much more recent past. The dispersal of hundreds of works of art during the Qing conquest provided endless opportunities, even decades later, for connoisseurs. Qianlong took advantage of this to amass a fantastic treasure trove of hundreds of thousands of works, the bulk of which is divided today between museums in

Beijing, Shenyang, and Taipei, and with many examples in other museums and in private collections around the world.

Apart from calligraphy, which has already been mentioned, the main object of Qianlong's interest as collector was painting. He came to own more than 10,000 items, including most of the extant antique paintings by Song, Yuan, and Ming dynasty masters. Qianlong worshipped these works of art. He viewed a selection of them daily in his study, and would not infrequently compose short poems on the thoughts they provoked in him before returning them to storage or to wherever they hung in the palace. When he traveled—which, as we have seen, was often—he also brought paintings along with him, even very valuable ones. In true Chinese fashion, he had copies made of some favorites as a kind of homage to the original. If he were particularly moved, then, like many collectors, he might leave his seal on a painting to indicate to later generations both his ownership and his approval of the work as authentic and valuable. This seems to have happened rather often, actually; today we have hundreds of paintings bearing Qianlong's red seal, very often with more than one. In addition to seals, many also bear the poems he wrote praising their beauty or commenting on the pleasure they brought him on a cold and rainy day when he could sit himself down with them and lose himself in the scene unfolding before him. Though art historians sometimes wish the emperor had been less enthusiastic in his praise, they recognize that he had a good eye and seldom erred in his appreciation of a work.

Qianlong collected paintings by more recent masters, too, showing a strong preference for works belonging to the classic schools of Chinese painting, primarily landscapes. A great number of these artists were in residence in the palace, and their work is of very high quality. As a scholar, the appreciation of such "serious art" was his bread and butter, a mark of erudition and refinement. This was an image he was eager to project. As already mentioned, we have several portraits of him in the pose of a Confucian gentleman in his study, surrounded by tasteful scrolls and other objects that defined the man of letters—brushes, paper, arm rests, ink stones. Interestingly, in these portraits he is usually painted in the loose, flowing robes of a Chinese scholar rather than in Manchu court dress. Some of these paintings are literal "quotations" of earlier, well-known works, making Qianlong's identification as a participant in the high culture of the Han Chinese scholar-elite unmistakable. (Never mind the fact that he personally owned no such items as he is shown as wearing in these stylized paintings.) By entering the painting he transcended the role of art collector to become one with the cultured aristocrat of an earlier age. In identical fashion, Qianlong also inserted himself into a number of Buddhist paintings. These constituted a wholly separate part of the imperial collection, with its own detailed catalogues.

One consequence of Qianlong's obsession with image is that a large part of his collection of paintings in fact consisted of new work by his own court painters, of which we have already seen several examples. What is most striking is that Qianlong's preferences in this regard strongly favored European styles of representation. The several hundred such examples extant in Qianlong's art collection give it a distinctively cosmopolitan flavor. One part of Qianlong's attraction to Western-style painting was no doubt its exoticism, but even greater seems to have been its apparent veracity. The unusual use of color, perspective, and shadow to create life-like depictions of people and events, hybridized as it was with backgrounds of traditional-looking landscapes, fascinated and amused him. It is hard to say if Qianlong or anyone around him thought of these paintings as "art," though surely the renderings of horses, dogs, birds, and flowers by Castiglione and his studio must have been. More likely, it was their function as easy-to-understand portrayals of splendor and power that made them so appealing. Was it his early education and the simple but dramatic pictures he saw in the ancient Manchu chronicles he read as a boy, illustrating the deeds of his illustrious ancestors that fired his imagination so and produced such a strong attachment to visual imagery? The lively verisimilitude in the scores of depictions of personages, battles, and banquets that surrounded the members of the court wherever they were emphasizes the very important place this unorthodox artistic tradition came to occupy under Qianlong.

In addition to paintings, Qianlong acquired large numbers of other precious works of art, including especially ceramics and jades. He was a great connoisseur of ceramics, and prized above all the unparalleled productions of the Song period. Many of the finer examples in his collection bear his remarks on their bases, the results not simply of admiration, but of study and true expertise. These priceless pieces were displayed in palace rooms, where they could be enjoyed routinely. Qianlong also commissioned new porcelain of all shapes and sizes from the imperial kilns of Jingdezhen, which he royally funded. These were located far away in Jiangxi province, several hundred miles to the south, but he regularly inspected production and communicated closely with the kiln's director, advising him on design matters and complaining when colors were not to his liking or when he felt their quality was poor.

Somewhat curiously, many of the ceramics produced during the Qianlong period, though technically fine, appear garish in comparison with those of the Kangxi and Yongzheng reigns. For this reason, the label "in the Qianlong style" is frequently taken to connote extravagance and ornateness, not unlike European rococo. But this was only a partial reflection of his tastes. As he once expansively commented, "One may conclusively say that collecting can lead to the loss of one's life's priorities. But others may disagree. Antiquities are simpler than things made today, and things made today are more showy than antiques. But who can criticize when one prefers simplicity to ornament?" Or, to put it in more familiar classical terms, "*de gustibus non disputandem est*"—"There is no accounting for taste."

While eighteenth-century porcelain perhaps dims in comparison to the work of earlier times, the art of jade carving reached its height during the Qianlong reign. The examples that survive are impressive indeed. One carved piece, depicting an incident in the life of a famous Tang-dynasty poet, weighs over 1,800 pounds (820 kilograms); another, showing the mythical hero Yu controlling the floods, is six times more massive, weighing 11,000 pounds (5,000 kilograms). There are beautiful jade cups, plates, bowls, jugs, saucers, knives, handles, belt buckles, hairpins, headdresses, rings, jewelry, inkstands, brushes, brush pots, table screens, teapots, cabbages, insects, boxes, scepters, and seals, all of impeccable quality. Qianlong defended his large-scale sponsoring of working jade objects, saying that it was practical because jade lasted longer than other kinds of material; he was also proud of it in that much of the jade used by court artists (including the two gigantic pieces just described) were mined in the newly acquired territory of Xinjiang. Using jade was thus intended as an artistic expression of imperial conquest and triumph.

There is not enough room here to detail other parts of Qianlong's huge art collection, which also included antique bronzes, lacquerware, enamels, glassware, furniture, coins, and curios such as European clocks and watches. His love of the latter two items was well known. Western visitors to the court were encouraged to bring him examples of the latest designs when they visited Beijing. Ironically, much of what they brought was Chinoiserie, objects inspired by Chinese designs—or, rather, by what their European creators *thought* were Chinese designs. This was not serious art, but rather creations intended for fun. In the same spirit, Qianlong also liked to trick observers by having one material made to look like another. He had jades carved to represent bronzes, ceramics fired to look like lacquerware, and glass made to look like porcelain. He covered certain palace walls with life-size trompe l'oeil paintings representing garden scenes or young women in Western dress sauntering down shady arcades. For him, it was play to push his artisans (of whom there were hundreds) in new directions, and they responded sportingly. In this regard, the technical achievements of the Qianlong age have never been equaled.

Possessing the World

How did he come by all this treasure? One primary avenue was via gift-giving. Some of this came from abroad. In a 1761 painting showing the procession of foreign tribute missions to the palace at the New Year, we can see how heavily laden people are. Most gifts are wrapped in cloth, but a few are not: ivory tusks, fine horses, an enormous cloisonné vase tied onto the back of an elephant, and precious swords. At home, Qianlong's passion for collecting was widely known. Individual collectors who presented their sovereign with items they thought he would appreciate, knew their treasures would find a good home and that they themselves would earn Qianlong's gratitude. The emperor's birthday was a time when officials at all levels were obliged to send written greetings, and many sent presents, as well. A Korean diplomat, dazed by the noisy sight that confronted him at the celebration of the emperor's seventieth birthday, noted an astonishing 30,000 cartloads of gifts, not counting those carried on poles or on the backs of horses and camels.

The emperor had other ways of acquiring items with which people were not so eager to part. "Contributions" were sometimes suggested to the owners of particular paintings or jades that the emperor coveted. In more extreme circumstances, collectors in official positions accused of wrongdoing might find their entire households confiscated by the throne. In such cases, the emperor asserted his privilege to sort through the family heirlooms to select additions to the palace collections. Or, if there were no other way, the palace might actually buy something from a gallery or a private dealer. By all these means, the palace's holdings easily grew by an order of magnitude under Qianlong's rule.

With so many objects flowing into the imperial collections, some means had to be found to keep track of it all. The officials in Qianlong's court charged with the supervision of the art collection devoted enormous energy to the description and classification of every type of object in the emperor's possession, from bowls and bronzes to ink stones and seashells. They produced numerous catalogues of the main collections: Buddhist and Daoist paintings (appearing in 1744), bronzes (1749), secular paintings (1754), and ceramics (1775). Supplemental volumes were published in 1793 and 1816. Each entry was accompanied by a detailed verbal description, including its dimensions. In the case of three-dimensional objects, a drawing was made to facilitate its identification. If the item was inscribed with a poem, that was written out as well. Everything was numbered (the small paper labels used for this purpose can still be found glued to the underside of items today) and its location in the palace, whose interiors were deliberately and beautifully designed, was also noted down to facilitate inventory and prevent theft. The emperor was precise about what went where and did not tolerate capricious rearrangement of objects whose placement he had carefully overseen.

These dense and detailed catalogues reflect an almost obsessive comprehensiveness, a determination to own the world, or at least a few samples of everything in it. It is as if Qianlong wished to create a microcosm within the palace walls. Such were the demands of universality. Just as the expansion of imperial power in Europe led to the creation of museums in which "everything under the sun" was displayed, so in Qing China the expansion of central power resulted in the formation of a collection reflecting plentitude and magnificence. The chief difference, of course, was that in the former case museums were there for public consumption, to demonstrate to ordinary people (at least, the urban upper classes) how far imperial power extended, while in the latter, enjoyment of the unending variety of goods generated by the engines of the imperial machine was limited to those elite officials who were privileged to walk the palace's corridors and halls. There were smaller private collections that paralleled the emperor's own, but in China the idea of putting the country on permanent public display did not take hold until the 1920s.

The Patron of Letters

"A man without a scholar's bearing is a coarse fellow, a man of the marketplace, and cannot be grouped among the class of men of standing and refinement." So stated Qianlong early in his reign. In addition to being able to handle poetry, painting, and calligraphy with ease, to be considered a complete scholar, Qianlong obviously needed to know books well, too. This involved two distinct types of knowledge, one centered on their content, the other on the books themselves as material objects.

As with paintings, Qianlong's natural inclination to collect meant that he possessed a large library. The palace already had many books when he became emperor, but Qianlong added significantly to their number, built special rooms devoted to their storage and preservation, inventoried them carefully, and published catalogues. Pride of place went to rare volumes from the Song, when the art of printing reached its first apogee in China, but he avidly sought books from the Yuan and Ming dynasties as well. Plus, as we have seen in earlier chapters, he was an active sponsor of new publications and took great interest in the production of books in the palace. This interest corresponded to an enormous increase in the availability of publications across the country, as the cheap printing technologies and extensive distribution networks of Qianlong's day drove an insatiable demand for books of all kinds: classics, histories, poetry, plays, stories, novels, essay collections, and religious texts.

As for the texts themselves, Qianlong's early education provided a good start toward mastering their content. To achieve real familiarity with the vast corpus of literature in history and philosophy, there was no substitute for lifetime immersion in the classics. Qianlong applied himself toward this goal in much the same way that he sought to improve his knowledge of fine arts: by incorporating, as related in Chapter 2, time for serious reading and reflection into his daily schedule. Apart from his own private reading, the emperor participated in regular tutorials with senior court scholars. These sessions were conducted more or less in seminar style, with certain passages being selected beforehand for parsing and discussion between the emperor and the savants whose job it was to guide the emperor's thinking. As Qianlong grew more confident, he began to expound on important passages, stressing the link between moral rectitude and correct rule, the value of loyalty, and the path to peace and prosperity through the strict observation of social hierarchies. From here it was a short step to issuing new editions of the major texts, with an updated commentary that reflected the emperor's own understanding of political philosophy and history. These began to appear in the 1750s.

Encapsulating the dominant tone of high Qing Neo-Confucian orthodoxy, these imperially sponsored editions and commentaries advanced interpretations of the classics that shaped the minds of all young men preparing to sit for the civil service examinations for the next century and a half. Around the same time, to benefit hopeful Manchu students, Qianlong also ordered standardized, fully annotated translations of the Four Books and the Five Classics into Manchu. In addition, he also published his own views of history, including the *Comprehensive Mirror of Successive Reigns, Imperially Annotated* (1767) and new histories of the Ming dynasty (in 1775 and 1777), works which, among other things, set forth his views on the nature of imperial legitimacy, which we have encountered in previous chapters. In these ways, Qianlong's serious engagement with the Chinese canon—comparable in size and status to the Greco-Latin canon that was the sole basis of elite education in the West from the Middle Ages until the twentieth century—can be said to have outlasted him considerably. This is especially true when we consider the grandest of Qianlong's book collecting and publishing projects, the *Siku quanshu,* or *Complete Library of the Four Treasuries.* Moved by his twin interests in books and texts, Qianlong sought in the *Complete Library* to compile an anthology to end all anthologies, an authoritative compendium of everything worthwhile ever written in Chinese, regardless of genre, epoch, or length. During the preceding two millennia of imperial history, the great emperors of the Han, Tang, and Song periods had shown their respect—and fear—of books by ordering the collection and compilation of all known works. The *Complete Library* would be Qianlong's contribution to upholding the continuity of China's long love affair with the written word and a further means of reinforcing his own power. As one historian has observed, "Writing and ruling [were] opposite sides of the same coin, characteristic and interrelated expressions of landed literary dominance of imperial China."

The history of the *Complete Library* project sheds considerable light on the workings of power and the limits of imperial authority. Ever since taking the throne, Qianlong had urged local officials to keep an eye out for rare or unusual books that might surface in the houses and collections of people in the district, recluse scholars who possessed, or had even authored, works worthy of a wider audience. Few, however, reacted to these calls. In 1771 the emperor issued another appeal for the collection of rare texts. The response was similarly lukewarm. A third, more urgent, edict sent out in 1772 drew greater attention and discussion, out of which came the suggestion to undertake a revision of the *Great Yongle Encyclopedia*. This idea caught the emperor's imagination. The work in question was a compendium redacted in the early 1400s during the reign of the third Ming emperor, Yongle. Part book catalogue, part recopied texts of scarce works, the *Yongle Encyclopedia* was recognized as an invaluable repository of writings that would otherwise have been lost forever. But there was only one copy, which was known to contain many errors; much of it perished in the Ming-Qing transition, besides. A corrected and reconstructed version, it was argued, was needed.

Instead of naming it after himself, Qianlong christened the planned revision after the form of organization he adopted (the "Four Treasuries" referred to the four main genres of writing: classics, histories, philosophy, belles lettres). Before long, however, the conceptualization of the *Complete Library* began to shift. Rather than simply reworking the *Yongle Encyclopedia*, scholars were to produce an equivalent work but more comprehensive and of higher quality. One of the edicts authorizing the *Complete Library* reads in part:

> Now, to organize the books stored in the imperial household cannot but be a good thing. Similarly, the books of past and present authors, regardless of their number, who perhaps still live in the mountains and have not ascended to the ranks of the distinguished should also be collected from time to time and sent to the capital. By such means, the unity of scholarship past and present can be made manifest. Let the provincial governors be ordered to collect all books . . . that clarify the essential methods of government or concern human nature.

The emperor's instructions went on to specify that books should be bought at fair prices, that the government would pay for new prints from old blocks, and that rare manuscripts must be carefully copied and then scrupulously returned to their owners. The first order of business, he told them, was to make a list of proposed titles; these would be collected in Beijing and collated before a final decision was made as to what to include and what to leave out. Overworked officials around the empire now realized that they were not going to be able to avoid the task the emperor had placed before them. The search for books was on.

Once underway, the collection and compilation of texts for the *Complete Library* took nine years, from 1773 to 1782. The final production process, consisting mainly of correcting mistakes and making additional copies, lasted another ten, to 1792. Dozens of officials were engaged to plan and oversee the work, and dozens more scholars appointed in various capacities to read, edit, and rectify texts. Daily, these men checked the pages churned out by the project's some 1,400 scribes, who, chosen for their neat and precise calligraphy, were expected to write at least 1,000 characters per day. The emperor made it a habit to review the texts coming out of the special bureau created to manage the project. If he found any copyists' mistakes, he docked the pay of the editors responsible for the lapse and returned the text for correction. (He could not dock the pay of the copyists themselves, because they worked on a volunteer basis, receiving only their meals for free.) The final product was huge. Three times the size of the *Great Yongle Encyclopedia*, the *Complete Library* filled 36,000 volumes, taking up 4.7 million pages, in which roughly 3,500 different titles were reproduced in their entirety. (The digital version of the *Complete Library* requires 167 CD-ROMs.)

Like the catalogues of his other collections, Qianlong intended the *Complete Library* to be practically useful. Thus he insisted on the compilation of companion works. One was a detailed summary of the publication history and gist of every book copied into the *Complete Library*, as well as of thousands more books not selected for copying. The other was an exhaustive table of contents that worked as an index. These two works were printed and published immediately, but the *Complete Library* itself was too massive for blocks to be carved to print it all. Seven manuscript copies were made, of which four are extant. Each was stored in a special building constructed expressly for it. Made of brick, not wood, these fire-resistant structures were designed to allow the free circulation of air between the stacks, reducing the risk of damage by mildew and insects. Four copies were stored at imperial residences in the north, with another three stored in the cities of Yangzhou, Hangzhou, and Zhenjiang, where Jiangnan scholars could consult them more easily. Even to the present day, the *Complete Library* and its supplements remain standard reference works for every scholar of premodern Chinese literature, philosophy, and history.

It is hard to resist comparing the all-embracing intellectual activity surrounding this project to that of the Encyclopedists of contemporary France, which leads immediately to the question of motivation. We can identify at least four main goals behind Qianlong's *Complete Library*. Most basic, already outlined above, was a wish to secure his place in the pantheon of great men of letters. In 1772, having celebrated his sixtieth birthday, it seems that Qianlong had begun to think in terms of his own mortality. This may explain why, in his charge to the editors of the *Complete Library*, he indicated that they had to be finished in ten years' time. He recognized that, properly done, the anthology would be a work for the ages. To be sure it met his strict standards, he absolutely had to be around to see it to completion himself. A second aspect of the genesis of the *Complete Library* was Qianlong's bibliophilic wish to expand his library. While the palace collection was by no means poor, it was inferior in some respects to the celebrated libraries of Jiangnan, collections that had been built painstakingly over centuries and had miraculously escaped destruction by fire, the elements, war, and vandalism. Sponsoring a nationwide search for rare titles (many of which he knew were in these famous libraries because he personally had been shown them by their owners during his visits to the South) gave the emperor the chance, if not to own the originals, at least to have copies made of valuable old editions. In this way, his collection of books would grow by leaps and bounds. There would be no book he did not own, no volume he could not consult whenever he wished, as befit a universal sovereign.

A third goal was to provide accurate texts to the empire's men of learning. Many famous writings were passed down from generation to generation or from library to library by recopying, a process that involved a degree of error. Inevitably, some texts had become corrupted, presenting serious problems to contemporary readers who could make little sense of them. Their selection for inclusion in the *Complete Library* meant they came under the scrutiny of groups of philologically trained scholars who were able to reconstruct what they regarded as their archaic, original forms. This was in fact one of the most valuable aspects of the project. But just as issues regarding the meaning of certain Biblical passages resulted in major doctrinal conflicts in the European context, so in the Chinese context the matter of accuracy in classical texts also involved questions of "correct thinking," behind which lay serious differences of opinion as to the nature of truth (though not, it might be noted, regarding salvation and damnation, for Ru thinkers did not concern themselves with such questions). By giving the emperor authoritative versions of everything, the *Complete Library* aimed to settle once and for all the controversies surrounding problem texts or enigmatic passages. Modern scholars do not always agree that the versions Qianlong and his editors chose were the best, nor do they consider their interpretations to be final. Be that as it may, there is no denying that the promotion of texts that reflected Qianlong-era orthodoxy was a key motive behind the *Complete Library*.

The Censor

The fourth and final goal of the *Complete Library* project was to find and eliminate any remnants of anti-Manchu literature. The persistence of such a concern provides us with strong evidence that even 130 years after the conquest, the Manchu elite remained uneasy still about Han Chinese attitudes toward Qing rule. (130 years may seem like a long time, but American readers might reflect on the lingering sensitivities of the southern states where the history and symbols of the Confederacy are concerned.) Reading his early edicts, we find that Qianlong understood from the beginning that the broad search for books and manuscripts then underway would inevitably turn up materials of a questionable nature. He promised that no punishment would be visited upon the owners of such materials provided they turned them in promptly. Six months after shipments of books from the provinces began arriving at the palace, not a single dubious title had been unearthed.

By the fall of 1774, the emperor grew suspicious: "At the end of the Ming period many unauthorized historical accounts were written containing slander, unfounded rumor, and heretical opinion; some of this language is bound to be offensive to Our Dynasty. When this sort of thing is discovered, it should be completely destroyed in order to stem heterodoxy." He added that the failure to turn up such treasonous literature could only imply that people were complicit in hiding it, and that the retribution would be severe later on. These words seem to have motivated local officials, for within a few weeks the emperor began to receive the very kinds of writings he had asked for. Over the next decade, much material deemed offensive to the throne surfaced and was consigned to the flames. Though we do not know the exact number of writings that perished during this time, one widely accepted count is that 2,900 separate titles were destroyed and lost forever. Thus, though the primary objective of the *Complete Library* was to preserve the literature of past and present ages, it ironically led to the destruction of many works that might otherwise have survived.

Within a few years, the suppression of treasonous books began to spiral out of control. Anxious to please the court and worried about their own careers, officials began reporting on anything and everything they thought might be in the slightest way problematic. This expanded to include even Chinese translations of the Koran, which had been around for centuries (the emperor chastised the official responsible for this complaint). Many innocent people were implicated on flimsy grounds by lower-level officials in the provinces anxious to prove their worth to their court. Ordinary gentry families met misfortune when their neighbors took advantage of the increasingly hysterical atmosphere to accuse them of hiding seditious materials in order to throw suspicion on them and then profit from their misfortune, usually by seizing their land. Disregarding his previous promise of clemency, in fifty cases the emperor ordered that the authors (and/or their descendants), the owners, and sometimes publishers of works he deemed offensive be tried for treason. Some of these were hack poets whose only crime was the careless use of the characters *ming* and *qing* (as in the names of the dynasties) that mistakenly created the impression of sedition. But the penalty was severe for all: death, exile, or slavery.

The burning of books and the widespread persecution of those suspected of harboring anti-Manchu feelings created an atmosphere of heightened tension in the later 1770s and 1780s, which has earned Qianlong the reputation as a small-minded, conservative, and oversensitive autocrat whose meddling in literary affairs resulted in a literary inquisition worse than any in the preceding 2,000 years. Some go so far as to claim that the terror he imposed stunted innovative thinking and distorted the "natural" flow of Chinese intellectual and literary history. In these circles Qianlong is a villain, not a hero, and the entire *Complete Library of the Four Treasuries* is viewed as merely a cover for a mass campaign of censorship and destruction.

It is true that much injustice was committed in the name of upholding court-backed ideas of right and wrong, and it is also true that many works were suppressed (we have only their titles today, in most cases). But at no time does it appear that Qianlong himself instructed officials to act as censors in any broader sense. In fact, he rejected such a proposal when it was raised in 1780. So the conclusion that Qianlong planned the *Complete Library* from the outset as a way of censoring scholarly and literary opinion seems unjustified. Moreover, the confiscation of books on such a massive scale owed at least as much to the enthusiasm and ambition of junior officials and the petty quarrels of local landed gentry as it did to Qianlong's quest for vengeance. Though he probably could have been expected to do more, the emperor's inability to keep scholars from playing politics to settle personal or intellectual scores (and the difficulty he had in getting the project off the ground in the first place) reminds us of the real limits to imperial power in eighteenth-century China, even under as strong a figure as Qianlong.

Intellectual Agendas

The charge that Qianlong was responsible for perverting or stunting intellectual innovation is a serious allegation, deserving of special attention. What we find is that the emperor's intervention came at a time of serious philosophical crisis. The program championed by the court strongly emphasized the values of loyalty and filiality. This position was based primarily on the interpretations of the classics put forward by a group of Song dynasty scholars led by Zhu Xi (1130–1200), a figure in Chinese intellectual history whose status is comparable to that of St. Thomas Aquinas. Zhu Xi's interpretations, in turn, were based on certain versions of classic texts that he and other Song scholars believed most resembled the classic texts used by Confucius and other early philosophers. What those original texts were really like was a matter of some dispute, because they were destroyed during the reign of the first emperor of Qin in the second century BCE. Reconstructed afterward by scholars of the Han dynasty, these were the versions that Zhu Xi and his followers relied upon in the Song. By the seventeenth century, however, knowledge of the forms and sounds of the ancient Chinese language was far superior to what it had been during the twelfth century. Research in this area led an increasing number of scholars to the conclusion that the texts used by Song-era philosophers were unreliable. This position gained force when it was persuasively shown that one passage in the *Classic of History* that was key to Zhu Xi's entire philosophical stance was actually a forgery. For some, this meant that the interpretations offered by Zhu Xi and others were similarly mistaken and that a wholesale revision of the classical corpus was in order. The entire scholarly community of the Qing was thus riven into two factions, the "Song learning" school, which backed the traditional approach of Zhu Xi, and the "Han learning," or "New Text," school, which saw itself as possessing the necessary linguistic tools to probe more deeply into the true meaning of the classics.

The differences between these two different ways of defining and pursuing knowledge came to a head during the compilation of the *Complete Library*. Since only one version of a classical text could be included, the editors had to hash out which version it was to be. But they themselves were divided. Given that the weight of scholarly orthodoxy lay with the Song school and that the texts officially promoted by the court for study by examination candidates were those edited by Song scholars, one would have expected that it would be their versions that were accepted into the *Complete Library*. But this is not what happened. Many of the mid-level officials who carried out the hard intellectual labor, especially the writing of the annotated catalogue, were younger men whose sympathies lay with the philologically rigorous techniques favored by the Han school, developed most vigorously in Jiangnan. The intellectual dominance they won over the project ultimately changed in substantial ways the overall tenor of political thinking for the rest of the Qing. And it represented a delicate moment for Qianlong, who had to mediate the struggle between the two schools in order to maintain the balance between state interests and the participation of elite scholars in the imperial enterprise.

Influenced by the obvious elements of suppression and censorship in other parts of the project, some scholars have attributed the failure of Song learning to dominate the *Complete Library* catalogue to Qianlong's heavy hand. Close examination of draft versions, however, shows that it was the scholars themselves who were critiquing each other's views, not Qianlong. The emperor in fact helped find a compromise. He did not in the end impose a strict Neo-Confucian orthodoxy as indeed he might have, nor did he yield the floor entirely to Han learning scholars. In this light, the *Complete Library* stands as a great turning point in Chinese intellectual history—one of a new opening, not a closing, of doors. Ultimately, the movement begun by the Han learning scholars, who advocated a more active engagement in politics on the part of men of letters, led to the reemergence of a tradition of literati dissent at the very end of the 1700s that would have major implications for the future of Chinese state in the tumultuous century to come. Qianlong's interest in books, art, and connoisseurship should not be thought of simply as a love of "art for art's sake" or "knowledge for the sake of knowledge." In its proper context, we should see it, together with his love of travel and hunting, as part of his overall dedication to a model of imperial rulership according to which the sovereign should be master of everything. It reflected his desire to impose order—and, by extension, ownership—upon his world. Qianlong's wish to "inspect," as it were, artistic and literary endeavors was like his wish to inspect the different corners of his realm, to comprehend within his ken the entire range of creative activity known to his subjects and to put his stamp on it. In short, it mirrored the tendency toward universalism we have seen in other aspects of Qianlong's rule.

But there was more to it than this. To realize these goals required that Qianlong himself master certain bodies of knowledge and certain kinds of skills, without which his voice in cultural matters would lack weight. In other words, just as his insistence on the importance of old Manchu ways led to the expectation that he would embody those virtues and abilities, so his championing of the aesthetic and philosophic values cherished by Chinese artists and scholars led to the expectation that he would, if called upon, act like one of them. Hence Qianlong desired to be seen not just as a chakravartin, not just as warrior-king, but also as a sage-king who could be trusted with upholding the Way of the ancients. His trips to Mt. Tai, his command of the brush and his understanding of calligraphy, his mastery of artistic, literary, and philosophic traditions, his historical knowledge, his prodigious filiality—all combined to create an apotheosis of Confucian rule in the person of Qianlong. Authoring a new canon was another demonstration of his awareness of what made a ruler great. All of this may seem ridiculously self-conscious to the modern reader. But the imperial institution had so much history behind it and Qianlong so much insecurity about his legitimacy as a Son of Heaven, that we can hardly blame him if he took full advantage of the wide array of means available to him to build himself and the emperorship to new heights. In the end, though he perched but briefly upon those heights, his efforts culminated in much that was good and useful and beautiful to behold.

8

Qing China and the World

Much has been made in these pages of Qianlong's claim to universal rule. Lest it be taken too literally, the reader ought not conclude that such a claim translated directly into the conviction that the Qing emperor, even a great emperor like Qianlong, held sovereignty, or thought he should, over the entire world. Qianlong realized there were other countries out there—Holland, for example, India, or Russia—over which he did not hold power in any way, shape, or form. His recognition of the separate existence of other nations may be contrasted with the belief held by a conqueror like Chinggis Khan, who saw the entire world as his to rule; for as Mongol communications with medieval European kings and popes show, if certain countries were not yet part of Chinggis' empire, he firmly believed they were destined to be. One can say that Julius Caesar and Alexander the Great held roughly similar views in that there were no "natural" boundaries to the territories over which they believed they were destined to hold sway. Few were the challenges in those days to such pretentions to universality.

But this was not the case with Qianlong, who lived at a time when, around the world, frontiers were closing and boundaries were being drawn. He was no doubt familiar with the statement once made by his father that, "in the vastness of the nine continents and the four seas, China is only 1 percent." Qianlong's universality thus applied to those domains within the greater imperium whose lesser lords—by means of letters, gifts, and investiture missions—acknowledged the ultimate, if at times largely symbolic, sovereignty of the Qing emperor. Though Qianlong did not live to see what would become of the contradictions in premodern and early modern ideas of territoriality and sovereignty, his assumptions about how best to conduct affairs between the Qing state and outside parties set the tone for the eighteenth and much of the nineteenth centuries, when those contradictions finally did emerge, and painfully so for China. We may well ask, how, indeed, did Qianlong see the world beyond his borders? What did he know of the larger eighteenth-century world in which he lived? What were his views on how contacts with that larger world ought to be constructed? This chapter will try to answer these questions so that we can better interpret the interactions of Qianlong and his empire with strangers far and near.

Foreign Relations and the Tribute System

The reader has already become acquainted with the vast size of the Qing state, which, at 4.6 million square miles, was far larger than the present United States (about 3.6 million square miles—see Maps 6.1a and b). Understood in its broader sense, however, the Qing imperium extended over a much larger area, even, than this. Korea, for example, was considered a loyal subject nation whose fealty to the emperor was taken for granted; as Qianlong noted once (and not altogether correctly), "Korea has for generations been our dynasty's humble servant; among the tributary nations its significance is minor." Its independence from the Qing was ignored by some eighteenth-century maps. The same was true of Vietnam. Siam, Laos, Burma, Cambodia, Liuqiu (i.e., Ryukyu, modern Okinawa), and the islands of Luzon and Java were also considered to lie within the greater sphere of influence of the Qing emperor, as were a varying number of Central Asian peoples such as the Kazakhs, Kirghiz, Badakhshanis, and—before 1759, anyway—the Dzungars. The emperor did not rule these places in any direct fashion (that is, Qing officials were not posted there) and he was not really interested in changing this, unless he saw an urgent strategic need. In 1754, the king of Java requested that his lands be formally incorporated into those of China and its population entered into Qing registers; Qianlong replied that this was not necessary, because—at least in his eyes—the king's lands and people were "already within the compass of Our enlightened government."

The emperor's superior authority, his special relationship to Heaven, his position at the ritual and political apex of the dominant civilizational and economic force in their world, were widely recognized and celebrated. As such, Qianlong enjoyed an exalted status across East, Southeast, and Inner Asia. This fact meant that the line between "domestic" and "foreign" was sometimes difficult to distinguish. Other sorts of distinctions mattered more, perhaps none more important than the distinction between the "civilized"—those who accepted the nominal political and cultural hegemony of the China-based Son of Heaven—and the "uncivilized," meaning those who rejected it. The civilized were entitled to dignified treatment, while the uncivilized were abused, insulted, and threatened. If there was some question as to which side of the line someone fell, it seems they were usually given the benefit of the doubt.

We can think of this distinction also as that between "inner" and "outer." While there were many ways of being included on the inside, there was but one way of being outside, and that was to deny the emperor's authority. In visual terms, rather than thinking of a series of concentric rings revolving around the center (i.e., the emperor), it is probably more useful to think of Qing emperorship as a shady, all-encompassing, and infinitely expandable canopy. Some were seated nearer the middle and others farther out toward the edges. The grouping of family and close friends seated centrally was an essentially stable contingent, while those placed at the periphery (relatives, perhaps, but more distant) might move out of the canopy's shade without disrupting the party—aware, however, that they risked their host's potential displeasure, and that, in the event of inclement weather, they might not be permitted back again under the imperial shelter.

The lack of a strict division between domestic and foreign and the inherent relativity of such terms as "inner" and "outer" help to explain why there was no unified concept of foreign relations in the traditional Chinese political vocabulary. This fact often strikes Western readers as quite strange, as if the Chinese worldview were somehow deficient, or backward, or so turned in on itself that it paid no heed whatsoever to anything outside its borders. But it is worth remembering that a formal system of international relations involving sovereign states—the sort of system we are accustomed to thinking of as "normal"—came into being in Europe only gradually, between the Peace of Westphalia in 1648 and the Congress of Vienna in 1814. Before the Napoleonic Age and the emergence of the modern nation-state, relations between countries in Europe were still largely construed through the personal relationships between individual rulers, most of whom were related to one another. It is not an exaggeration to say that the framework employed by Qianlong to manage state-level contacts with those from abroad was not so wholly different from the same framework in early modern Europe, save that those personal relationships in Europe were on the whole far more the relationships of equals or near-equals than in China, where the relationship of a foreign ruler to the emperor was ritually and hierarchically more constrained.

According to this framework, instead of generalized foreign relations, there was the connection between the emperor and the Korean king, the emperor and the Siamese king, the Vietnamese king, the Russian tsar, and so forth. None of these necessarily stood as a model for any other, and though there were efforts to maintain parity and standard rules for receiving embassies, there was also room to discriminate between closer and more distant relationships. Missions from the Korean capital, for instance, arrived once a year, while those from Siam came only once every two years and those from Burma once every three; the reader may also recall the triennial visits to the capital accorded the Dzungars in the 1740s, when they had not yet been incorporated into the empire. The primary aim of such missions was to acknowledge the continued recognition of the emperor's greater authority and secure the emperor's recognition of the lesser, but still legitimate, authority of the king or prince concerned. Their secondary purpose—though sometimes it might have seemed to be the primary purpose— was commercial, as visits to the Qing capital afforded an excellent opportunity for trade. The volume of this trade was carefully regulated, along with the size of embassies, to avoid undue profit-taking. But a fair amount of illicit commerce was quite common, with well-run missions, such as the Korean mission, able through the private sale of ginseng to clear three or four times the amount they spent on sending the missions, which were not cheap.

One important difference between European and Qing diplomacy that should be pointed out is that diplomacy in the Qing context did not necessarily involve the sort of discussions of world affairs and deal-making that one typically tends to associate with such state-level affairs. True, missions occasionally made requests, such as for an augmentation of an embassy's trade allowance or to ask the emperor to send an imperial representative to officiate at the investiture of a new king. But these applications tended to take place more or less incidentally and were not part of the formal calendar of events. The true essence of any visit to the court by an outsider was concentrated in the guest ritual accompanying the imperial audience, which typically took place in special precincts on the west side of the Imperial City. Here, impressive paintings of war heroes, exotic prints of victorious battle scenes, and, one may presume, images of Qianlong himself in various distinguished poses were strategically displayed, serving as a backdrop to impressive ceremonies, which we might think of as falling into four principal stages, depending on the sort of physical activity involved: waiting, bending, giving, and eating.

First, there was waiting. Those summoned to an audience were required to arrive well before dawn and then wait—often for hours—for the emperor to appear, their remaining in attendance for absurd lengths of time a temporal expression of their humble rank before the Son of Heaven. Second, there was bending. Visitors were required to demonstrate their status as the emperor's subject physically, whether through genuflection (a salute usually reserved for members of the Eight Banners), kneeling, or the kowtow (a series of three kneelings and nine prostrations of the body). Third, there was giving. An ambassador to the Qing would bring with him any number of gifts for the emperor to present at court. Along with gold, silver, swords, and precious jewels, such gifts might include items that were hard to procure in China (ginseng, rhinoceros horn) or products for which the ambassador's country was famed (pearls, ivory, coral, rare incense, elephants, fast horses, superior strains of rice). At the audience, a eunuch would accept from the ambassador and then present to the throne a selection of the finest, most expensive items he had brought. In return, the emperor would have ready a few things to give to his guest, often objects wrought in jade or some other luxury material. Other presents for visitors—rolls of silk, satin, and damask, porcelain, fine tea—were stacked on tables flanking the audience space. Finally, there was eating. At the conclusion of the audience, the emperor hosted a grand banquet at which all partook of fine delicacies expertly prepared, listened to music, and enjoyed different kinds of entertainment. He himself sat separately on a dais; as a sign of his grace and hospitality, he sent down dishes and drink from his table to his guests, in this way cultivating the bond between himself and his visitors.

Because of the importance attached to the exchange of gifts during these ritualized visits, the constitution of foreign relations under the Qing is commonly referred to as the "tribute system," often understood as predicated upon a rigid hierarchy of relations between superior (the emperor, China) and inferior (other people, other countries), dictated unilaterally by the preferences of the former, and weighed down by hollow, ponderous ceremony. Such a view well suits an old-fashioned image of China as the "Middle Kingdom," with attendant implications of chauvinism, ostentation, arrogance, and isolation. For this reason, the tribute system has often been taken as a symbol of Chinese pride and intransigence.

It is worth considering a couple of objections to this characterization. First, the tribute system was hardly so rigid as it is sometimes made out to be. The system gets its name from the gifts presented to the emperor, called *gong* in Chinese. Following the precedent of the gifts presented by subject peoples to the Roman emperor, *gong* is usually translated as "tribute" in English. This custom has given rise to the assumption that *gong* and tribute correspond exactly to each other in meaning, which they do not. The word *gong* in fact referred to *any* gift presented to the emperor, not just to tribute items from foreigners. For this reason, we might more accurately think of the tribute system as a framework that structured relations between the emperor and any outsiders who might approach him, meaning just about everybody outside the court, not just those under the imperial canopy, and not exclusively non-Chinese. The system could be and was adapted to accommodate Dutch merchants, Mongol princes, Okinawan legates, Russian ambassadors, Muslim clerics, Tibetan prelates, and tribal leaders from Sakhalin, the Pamirs, and the Burmese border. As we will see later in this chapter, diplomatic ritual could even be tweaked to welcome the formal representative of the British crown.

It was a matter of course that the reception of visitors to the Qing court should be a hierarchical and ritualized business: no one expected anything else. Its purpose was to enact a vision, and to enforce a belief in that vision, of the way the affairs of men were to be ordered. Such order was perceived to bring prestige, honor, and material benefits to all who participated. But this did not perforce mean it was rigid and unbending, any more than kowtowing before the emperor was an act of personal humiliation. To demonstrate submission before one's own exalted lord was in fact a way of elevating oneself. It signified neither abasement nor the unilateral ceding of one's own interests before the Qing state. Qing dealings with Vietnam, for instance, show how participation in the tribute system could pave the way for an outcome favorable to the lesser state. At some point in the mid-1600s, Vietnamese farmers living on the Chinese border settled in a valley just to the north of the border, in Yunnan Province. When this fact came to light some seventy years later, Yongzheng at first affected outrage. But soft words from the Vietnamese ruler soothed his anger, and in 1725 Yongzheng good-humoredly ceded the disputed territory (about 260 square miles) to Vietnam, its tributary subject, and nominal "servant," saying: "From the time that Vietnam first submitted to our dynasty," he declared, "it has ever shown respect and obedience. It is not fitting that we should quarrel over a small bit of land." Chinese peasants on the land in question, Yongzheng added, were free to choose whether to stay as Vietnamese subjects or to be "repatriated" to China.

A second objection to the usual characterization applied to the tribute system is that the "Middle Kingdom" was not so isolated as is widely imagined. Contacts between the Qing and the rest of the world, while by no means unlimited, were frequent and regular in the 1700s. There was no official ban on contact with foreigners as there was in Japan, and though for most of the eighteenth century overseas trade was restricted to four coastal cities, this did not keep it from booming. Not only were European goods increasingly common in Chinese households, but Chinese goods were very much sought after in Europe. More on this is said later. First, let us concentrate on human flows.

In His Majesty's Special Service

The majority of foreign visitors to Qianlong's China were missionaries, diplomats, and traders, all of them male (there would be no female foreign travelers in China until the second half of the nineteenth century). Because their numbers were limited, managing their comings and goings was relatively easy.

The multiple roles of the missionary in eighteenth-century China have already been touched on in preceding chapters. The reader may remember the various positions they filled at court—as astronomers, mathematicians, geographers, surveyors, architects, painters, musicians, tutors, and translators. In addition to a small number of Russians, they were the only Europeans granted the privilege of permanent residence in Beijing. All others were restricted to living permanently at Macao, which had been granted to the Portuguese as a base in the late sixteenth century; located in the far south, near Guangzhou (Canton), this was the first port of call and entry point for nearly all visitors to China sailing from Europe. Another unique dispensation granted to missionaries—at this point exclusively Roman Catholics, primarily Jesuits or members of the mendicant orders—was that they were permitted to learn to speak, read, and write both court languages, Chinese and Manchu. In exchange for these privileges, missionaries became not just the emperor's servants, but also his subjects. Having come to China, they agreed never to return to their home countries, where it was feared they might betray too many confidences. Most of them honored this promise, and their tombstones can be seen to this day in Beijing.

Missionaries thus enjoyed something of insider status: they lived permanently in the country, they understood the local languages, and many were closely tied to the court (they took no part in the tribute system). As a result, their activities were closely overseen. This was as true in Beijing, where their connections with the political elite required them to keep a low profile, as in the provinces, where they were allowed to build churches and make converts among urban dwellers and peasants alike. Missionary work in China was tolerated until the 1720s, when the involvement of certain Jesuit residents of Beijing in the machinations surrounding Yongzheng's accession to the throne confirmed the suspicion of some that they could not be trusted. After this time, though churches in Beijing were permitted to continue operating, Catholic missions in the provinces were officially proscribed and churches closed. The few missionaries who remained in China worked at the emperor's pleasure, hoping for the day when they might once again be permitted to spread their gospel. But as long as the cautious Qianlong ruled, that day was still far in the future.

Qianlong was not so trusting of the Jesuits in his service as his grandfather. Kangxi had spent many hours in their company and struck up a particularly close friendship with the Belgian Ferdinand Verbiest, whom he invited along on trips into the country and on hunting tours. He seems to have valued the different Jesuit perspective on things and attempted in several areas to acquire some of their knowledge for himself. So great was Kangxi's trust that he deputed Jesuits to serve as translators in negotiations with Russian emissaries during the discussions that led to the 1689 Treaty of Nerchinsk, which established the first hard boundary between Russia and the Qing. He also relied on them to make maps of the Great Wall, greater Beijing, and later his entire realm (though he did restrict their access to distant frontier areas). Qianlong relied on missionaries for mapmaking, too, along with many other things, but does not appear to have become personally close with any of those men in his service, at least not so far as we know. He certainly did not employ them as diplomats, though he called on them to translate for him when Europeans appeared at court and would sometimes ply them with questions about politics abroad.

If Qianlong ever was close to any Jesuits, two likely figures would have been the Italian Castiglione and the Frenchman Michel Benoist, who between them shared much of the responsibility for the European accent that distinguished Qing imperial culture from its predecessors. Qianlong knew Castiglione from his youth and, as we have seen, delighted in his expertise. He added scores of Castiglione's paintings to the palace collection and put him in charge of an atelier where he could pass his techniques on to Chinese artists. The two men must have known each other fairly well. When Castiglione passed away in 1766, Qianlong bestowed on him a high official rank and contributed a significant sum toward his funeral. Benoist arrived at court later than Castiglione, but rose to prominence in part because of his skills at cartography and engineering. Qianlong turned to him for information on technical matters, and put him in charge of designing a number of European-inspired buildings and gardens that were built in the imperial retreat just north of Beijing, the Yuanming yuan. These palaces were in the best rococo style, adorned with Greek columns and ornamental façades, and were probably more authentic than any of the so-called Chinese pavilions being built at the same time in the gardens of European royalty. The grander among them had fantastic fountains built in their forecourts, with gardens laid out in classical French style, in imitation of Versailles or Fontainebleau. Like those places, and like the fabulous gardens of Delhi built by the Mughal conquerors of India, the landscapes of sites such as Chengde and the Yuanming yuan symbolized a fascination with the exotic as well as the expansiveness, order, and inclusiveness of the empire. Interiors were decorated in a quasi-Western fashion, displaying many of the emperor's European-made clocks, mirrors, music boxes, and knickknacks. In some rooms, false windows were painted with imaginary scenes of the European countryside.

Though they occupied but a small corner of the larger garden complex, these buildings were another reflection of Qianlong's interest in Western designs and fashions of representation. Their existence (unfortunately, they fell into ruins after British and French soldiers ransacked the Summer Palace in 1860) proves the keen awareness in Qianlong's mind, not just of the fact of Europe, but also of the technological prowess of Castiglione, Benoist, and others. Nonetheless, it must be said that, fatefully, this awareness did not lead him to investigate other types of Western technology or science, nor, as we will shortly see, does this curiosity seem to have persisted into his old age.

Guests from Afar

According to Qing custom, diplomatic activities were confined to Beijing and the imperial residences connected with it, the Yuanming yuan and Chengde. There being no foreign ministry or anything like it, visits of tributary nations were handled by the Board of Rites. This department maintained guest quarters in Beijing, saw to their various needs while they were on Qing soil (escorts were provided to and from the border), and instructed members of foreign delegations in the fine points of ritual and court etiquette. Visits from Inner and Central Asian domains were handled differently. For one thing, they were handled not by the Board of Rites but by the Bureau of Colonial Dependencies (*Lifanyuan*), mentioned briefly in Chapter 2. This was a specifically Manchu institution originally charged with overseeing the visits of Tibetan prelates and Mongol princes in the very early years of the dynasty. Later, when Kazakh chieftains, representatives of the tsar, and other visitors from overland began to arrive, the Bureau took over the management of those receptions, too. Another important difference between Inner Asian visitors and those from the Southern or Western Oceans (for such was the rough division made) was that the former were accorded greater privileges of negotiation. Especially early in his reign, the emperor would invite guests from Mongolia, Tibet, and Central Asia to sit down in his tent, explain their needs to him, and share their views. That such visits almost always visited in the summer at the imperial retreat in Chengde or the hunting grounds at Mulan facilitated this kind of informality.

With visiting Russian delegations, it was virtually expected that there would be lengthy and direct negotiations. In 1755, for example, Empress Catherine instructed her minister to ask if Russian ships could navigate upon the Heilongjiang River in northern Manchuria. This request, which took the form of a letter from the Russian Senate to the Bureau of Colonial Dependencies, was taken up by Qianlong and summarily rejected, his response carried back to St. Petersburg by a Qing emissary. As this episode suggests, relations between the two countries were more explicitly the relations between equals. After all, the Qing had entered into treaties with Russia, one in 1689 and the other in 1727, which required looking after. Added to a very active border trade was the worry of an eventual conflict with Russia over the Dzungar question. It was important to keep lines of communication open. Russian trading missions, limited to 200 members, were officially entitled to come to Beijing once every three years. Furthermore, Yongzheng had permitted the establishment of a permanent Russian ecclesiastical mission to look after their spiritual needs when they were in town. The Russian embassy occupies the site today. This mission—the only such foreign representation allowed in Beijing—was also charged with training small numbers of students in the Chinese and Manchu languages for future diplomatic service. In all this, one can see how Qing treatment of one group of "outsiders" could differ greatly from the treatment of another group.

All the Tea in China

Compared to missionary and diplomatic activities, the scale of commercial transactions involving traders from abroad was much, much greater. Indeed, trade was without question the primary channel of contact with the greater imperium and lands beyond. Some of this trade occurred on the overland trade routes from Russia. By the 1790s, between 5 and 7 million rubles worth of furs, silk, cotton, porcelain, tea, and rhubarb were traded annually between the two countries. A handful of Chinese families, most of them from Shanxi, earned fortunes in this trade.

But the bulk of foreign commerce moved by sea. All such trade was officially regulated: there was in theory no private commerce with overseas traders, who were required to deal exclusively through government-appointed brokers. These men, a number of whom came to possess huge fortunes, reported all transactions and revenues to local officials, who in turn transmitted these on to the court. Officials at each level took their cut, of course, and the emperor grew rich off the duties collected on his behalf, which varied widely depending on the scrupulousness of the brokers and officials on the job. Traders were further restricted in that, as mentioned, there were only four cities where foreign merchant vessels could legally put in to port: Guangzhou, Xiamen (Amoy), Ningbo, and Songjiang. If non-Chinese merchants wandered from these designated destinations, their movements were noted and they were turned back. Nor were traders permitted to enter the walls of the cities at which they trafficked, but were to remain in separate quarters maintained just for them, the idea being that the chances for misunderstandings and unpleasant incidents were thereby lowered.

The principle of separating foreign visitors from the general population ran very deep. In the early 1750s, when European schooners began showing up at Ningbo in larger and larger numbers, Qianlong worried that this Jiangnan coastal city would become "a second Macao." To forestall this, he ordered all ports but Guangzhou closed to Western Ocean ships. Henceforth they would only be allowed to trade during October to January and the rest of the time were restricted to Macao. This remained the rule for the next ninety or so years, until the Opium War of 1839–1842 brought major changes to the system of foreign trade. Other restrictions applied as well, such as a ban on all firearms, a strict prohibition on buying Chinese books, and a requirement that all communications and transactions pass through the foreign trade brokerages—there was to be no direct contact with tea growers or anyone else. It is worth noting, though, that this "Canton system" of trade, as it was called, applied only to traders from the Western Oceans. "Southern Ocean" traders from Southeast Asia were not affected.

One reason for Ningbo's popularity, as it turns out, was that officials there levied taxes more fairly and predictably. This suggests that trade was the least easily regulated aspect of foreign affairs, as most of it took place far from the capital in distant port cities. Though he might attempt to limit it, the emperor was unable to prevent extortion by local officials who were eager to line their pockets. He also had little power either to curtail efforts by foreign dealers to circumvent the restrictions placed upon them or to aid them when they found their money illegally tied up by the powerful brokerages with which they were forced to deal. There was no imperial navy, no overall agency of maritime affairs to coordinate between ports, and no central government office to keep track of their activities. Traders from abroad were the responsibility of local officials, who tended to regard such affairs as delicate and troublesome. The only time the central government came into direct contact with foreign commercial interests was when Dutch or Portuguese representatives came to the capital to present themselves at court under "tribute system" arrangements made by the Board of Rites. This occurred on seventeen occasions between 1655 and 1795. Like other visitors, mission members presented gifts and performed the kowtow. Their requests were accepted in an offhand manner, and were usually rejected. What leverage could they expect to have against the imperial throne? From the emperor's point of view, they were fortunate to be permitted to trade at all.

Qianlong liked things this way and often professed himself to be indifferent to the benefits of foreign trade. More than once he stated that permitting his subjects to trade with outsiders was a form of imperial graciousness, an act of benevolence on his part, and an activity wholly unconnected to the well-being of his people. Such statements should not be taken at face value, though. They were typically issued in direct response to some trouble connected with the southern ports. In this way, Qianlong asserted his authority over a situation in which the welfare of Chinese subjects had to be balanced against the claims of foreign merchants. For in fact he was well aware of what the foreign trade was worth, both to the court and to ordinary people. Between the time he had turned nineteen and the time he was forty-four, the tax on that trade brought roughly 7.5 million taels worth of revenues (£2.5 million at contemporary rates of exchange) into his private purse. Later in his reign, he could count on receiving over 850,000 taels of silver annually. Given that the volume of trade between Guangzhou and Europe increased at an average annual rate of 4 percent through most of the eighteenth century, Qianlong would have been foolish to have taken any action that put these handsome revenues at risk.

Foreign trade was no less important to the country at large. Millions of people, most of them living in the southern half of the country, were involved in industries directly connected to export markets in tea, porcelain, cotton, and silk. We find a clear demonstration of the emperor's recognition of the importance of exports to the national economy in the details of a ban on the export trade in raw silk that lasted from 1759 to 1764. The ban was first proposed in the interests of keeping the price of silk down. The argument was that the foreign demand for silk was putting inflationary pressure on the domestic market. The court approved this move, but changed its mind a few years later after receiving memorials from provincial officials pointing out that trade in this one item alone was worth between 800,000 and 1 million taels annually, that the ban on raw silk exports had not brought domestic prices down, and that instead the livelihoods of growers and spinners were being ruined. Qianlong explained his change of heart this way: "Since the ban on exporting [raw silk] abroad went into effect, the production of silk in Jiangnan has become unprofitable. This is of no benefit to those overseas and is a positive loss to the livelihoods of the people. Why should we not relax this ban? Let the goods of this world meet the needs of the world, especially when trade in them benefits the people." This is a very different view, indeed, than the one we are used to associating with the blasé Qianlong. However he might occasionally bluster about the peripheral importance of the empire's export-driven industries such as silk, porcelain, and tea, the emperor knew enough to let it grow. By the time he was an old man, one-seventh of all the tea in China was being exported to England.

The Macartney Mission

It was very much in connection with the tea trade that near the end of his life Qianlong received a visit from an ambassador from Great Britain. This episode, without doubt the most important diplomatic encounter of Qianlong's reign, deserves our closer attention.

As just mentioned, during Qianlong's rule, the scale of exports between China and Europe grew tremendously, enriching him personally in no small degree. The greater part of this trade was in tea, followed by porcelain (i.e., "china"), silk, and woven cotton. A number of nations were involved in this brisk commerce, including France, Sweden, Holland, and the United States, but their share in things was quite completely overshadowed by the proportion of the market that belonged to Great Britain. The demand for tea had skyrocketed since the beverage was first introduced to London society in the 1650s. Within fifty years tea had become the fashionable drink in English society, gradually replacing coffee; by the end of the eighteenth century, over 23 million pounds were being imported annually to satisfy consumer demand. This was all in "black tea," so-called because of the color the leaves had turned by the time they reached London wharves after the long voyage from Guangzhou.

The lion's share of this trade was in the hands of quasi-state monopolies like the British East India Company (EIC), which recorded a 4.5 percent annual rate of increase in shipping in and out of Guangzhou in the last half of Qianlong's reign and was making a handsome profit out of each shipment. For some people in British society, the import of tea, like oil imports in the modern world, came to assume real political importance. Not only was a disproportionate 90 percent of the EIC's business tied up in the tea trade, but in the late eighteenth century 10 percent of crown revenues derived solely from the tax upon the tea sold to market in England. As many at the time recognized, it was China that occupied the most powerful position in this commerce, since it controlled the world's supply of tea. The only other place in the world where tea was produced was Japan, which was essentially closed to overseas trade (the tea industry in India and Ceylon did not get under way until later in the nineteenth century). China also dominated the market for silk and had a monopoly on the production of fine porcelain. Nothing made by Josiah Wedgwood or by the craftsmen at Meissen could yet compare with Chinese wares. And because there seemed to be nothing produced in Europe that the people of China wanted as badly as Europeans wanted Chinese manufactures, a great deal of the profits from the sale of Chinese imports had to be plowed right back into purchasing next year's shipments of tea, porcelain, and textiles. China's balance of payments was thus overwhelmingly in its favor: for the roughly 31.5 million taels of British goods imported into China by the EIC during the period between 1775 and 1795, China exported to England goods worth over 56 million taels—almost twice as much—and enjoyed a net inflow of silver, which buoyed the economy. It was therefore out of a desire to foster a more advantageous balance of trade that the EIC, with the consent of the king, initiated the proposal of a British embassy to China.

The main goals of the embassy, as set forth by the British Home Secretary, were to expand the number of ports open to foreign trade; to secure a place of their own that, like Macao, could serve as a base for British commercial operations; to secure permission for a permanent British ambassador to the court in Beijing (and persuade the emperor to appoint a Qing ambassador to Britain); to "create new markets in China, especially in Peking, for British products hitherto unknown"; and to negotiate stable and universal terms of trade, including reduced tariffs, on all goods moving in and out of China. As it was doing this, the embassy was to gather as much information as it could about the land, its people, and its ruler, including economic, military, and political intelligence. The EIC, which footed the £80,000 bill for the mission, was all for these goals, but urged caution, lest existing trade arrangements be unexpectedly terminated altogether by an offended Qianlong.

The embassy was headed by Lord George Macartney, a veteran colonial administrator who had served in both the West Indies and India, and for a time had been ambassador to St. Petersburg. An Irishman, Macartney prepared himself for his mission by reading everything he could find about the current state of affairs in the Orient. He recruited secretaries, physicians, scientists, draftsmen, a botanist, and a watchmaker to the cause, and brought along a small military escort and a musical ensemble as well. Confident of his ability to persuade the Chinese government of the reasonableness of his terms, Macartney led the eighty-four-person mission out of London in the fall of 1792. They arrived in Guangzhou in June 1793. The three ships on which they sailed were loaded with gifts, including barometers, astronomical instruments, pocket globes, and an expensive glass planetarium crafted in England specially for the emperor. It was hoped that these would impress the Chinese court with English wealth and sophistication and perhaps fuel a desire for more mundane items as pipe lighters, knives, woolens, and scissors.

Once at Guangzhou, they made known to local officials their desire to travel to Beijing for a court audience. Macartney had learned enroute of the impending celebration of the emperor's birthday and decided to use this occasion as a pretext for his visit. Qianlong, informed of the arrival of men from the country of *Ying-ji-li* who had sailed around the world to convey to him the birthday greetings of their king, was very pleased. He welcomed them, ordering officials along the coast to provide them whatever provisions they needed (for which he himself would pay), and sent men from the court to receive the mission when it arrived at the northern port of Tianjin, to conduct his well-wishers on to the capital. There they would be permitted to rest before being led to Chengde, where the emperor would receive them. Dismayed as he was by the flags flying on his ship that read, "The English Ambassador Bringing Tribute [*gong*] to the Emperor of China," Macartney realized he could not complain about this or anything else, nor enter into negotiations on the mission's specifics, until he had been presented at court. After they had been comfortably quartered in Beijing, he and his men busied themselves with preparations for the upcoming audience, receiving occasionally contradictory instructions from various court officials. Efforts to confer with the Jesuits in the capital as how best to proceed were frustrated by the limits placed on the embassy's movements.

The chief sticking points in arranging for the imperial audience had to do with etiquette. As noted, previous deputations of visitors from European countries, chiefly merchants from Portugal and Holland, had agreed to follow Qing court custom by performing the kowtow, and the same expectation was made clear to the British. Macartney balked. His instructions were that, as the officially designated representative of his sovereign, he was to follow Qing ritual insofar as it did not compromise either his or his king's dignity. The kowtow, it seemed to him, crossed that line. He offered instead that he would go down on one knee, as he would have done at Westminster. Furthermore, where Qianlong's courtiers explained to him that no one was allowed to approach the throne directly, Macartney objected on the grounds that he was obliged to place the letter King George III had written to the emperor directly in Qianlong's hands.

In the end, after numerous exchanges, Macartney won the compromises he had sought. He would not be required to kowtow, and he would be allowed to approach the throne. The morning of the audience, Macartney, his companion, George Staunton, and others of the embassy arrived at the imperial encampment at 5 a.m., both having taken special care to dress in their finest regalia. Macartney wore the mantle and collar of the Order of the Bath along with a diamond badge, while Staunton wore "a rich embroidered velvet [cloak] and the habit of his Oxford degree, which is of scarlet silk, full and flowing." The emperor's arrival at around 6 in the morning was announced by a grand fanfare, as he was borne on a palanquin to the large Mongol-style tent in which audiences were held at Chengde (see Figure 8.1). Macartney's presentation to the throne was the first order of business, and it was carried out faultlessly: the British lord approached the throne, mounted the steps, and put into Qianlong's hands a diamond-encrusted gold box holding George III's letter. Passing the box to an attendant, Qianlong presented Macartney with two jade *ru-yi* scepters as a token of his esteem. After giving the emperor a pair of enameled watches that were his own personal gift, Macartney stepped down and took his seat at one of the low tables that were set up below the throne (all guests were seated upon cushions on

Houghton Library, Typ 705.97.807 P.

Figure 8.1   William Alexander (1767–1816). "The Approach of the Emperor of China to His Tent in Tartary." From George Staunton, *An Authentic Account of an Embassy from the King of Great Britain to the Emperor of China.* 1797. Engraving. Houghton Library, Harvard University. Qianlong is visible on the left, borne on a palanquin to the tent where he will receive Lord Macartney, who can be seen at the right, heading the line of dignitaries assembled for that morning's audience. © Harvard University Libraries.

the floor). The banquet then got underway. The emperor at one point did Macartney the honor of inviting him up to the dais where he sat to drink a cup of wine and converse briefly.

At the conclusion of this banquet, from Qianlong's point of view, the business of the embassy was over. To be sure, there would be further pleasantries—tours of gardens, palaces, and temples, and visits to the Yuanming yuan once the embassy returned to Beijing. There was even to be another audience on the emperor's birthday in which the English, along with hundreds of other guests, were included (historians continue to disagree whether Macartney did not in fact kowtow at this time). But the ambassador had been received, proper sentiments expressed, the rites of welcoming men from distant lands carried out. What else was there to do?

From the British point of view, on the other hand, the embassy had just gotten started. Naturally, they regarded the formal audience with the emperor as extremely important and suitable care had been taken to ensure a good impression. But now those formalities had been completed—auspiciously so, even. It was time to turn to the business at hand and open discussions of the British requests as concerned the future of their relations with the Qing empire. Time and again, Macartney attempted to fix a time for concrete negotiations with the officials (primarily Manchus) he had determined were truly powerful. Time and again he was rebuffed. He finally managed to press into the hands of lower-ranking mandarin handlers a written list of subjects for discussion, but this brought no results. Meanwhile, the grand display of gifts brought by the English had failed to spark Qianlong's interest, and the hoped-for desire to augment the scope of trade with Great Britain never materialized. By early October, the only thing that had become apparent was that—amid the sincerest protests of friendship—it was time for Macartney and his entourage to go home. The emperor would provision them as he had done before, and offer them every convenience (including a couple of milk cows and a boat to transport them on), but they had to leave.

The day he quit Beijing, he finally received a formal reply from Qianlong to the embassy's various requests. It carried the same sort of haughty rhetoric that Qianlong was prone to employ when discussing trade issues with foreign merchants:

> The Celestial Empire, ruling all within the four seas, simply concentrates on carrying out the affairs of government properly, and does not set value on rare and precious things. [. . .] We have never valued ingenious articles, nor do we have the slightest need of your country's manufactures.

Possibly anxious to divert attention from the vital importance that exports to Britain really bore to the Qing economy, Qianlong contrived here to trivialize the importance of British imports. What would Macartney have thought had he known that as a young man Qianlong had written three poems about the marvels of Western glass, which he so admired that he had the windows in the palace fitted for the first time with clear glass panes? Or if he had been allowed to see the true extent of Qianlong's collection of seventy English clocks (the one that played popular English tunes, for instance, or the one on which Cupid danced to the hours)? Qianlong focused his attention instead on the question of British diplomatic residency in China: There would be no permanent British embassy, no opening of more ports, nor any granting of the smallest bit of territory. Macartney was bitterly disappointed, and suspected court intrigues to have been the main reason for the failure of the mission.

It was only on the journey south to meet his ships, which by then were waiting at Guangzhou, that Macartney, to his pleasant surprise, began to make a little headway. Through informal discussions with his escort, the Grand Councilor Sungyun, he came to understand something of how Qing foreign relations were managed, and his interlocutor learned something of how European diplomacy was conducted. Macartney availed himself of the opportunity at last to speak openly to a listener who was both sympathetic and held a powerful position at court. Could the tariffs at Guangzhou be lowered and regularized? Could the brokerages be persuaded to desist from their extortionate practices? Could merchants be permitted to approach local officials directly to present their complaints, rather than go through the brokers who were themselves the subjects of those very complaints? Sungyun promised to convey his concerns to the emperor, and received prompt replies that these things would indeed be looked into and any irregularities rectified. At Hangzhou, Sungyun's place was taken by the governor-general of Guangzhou, also a bannerman, who continued to assure Macartney of the emperor's favorable disposition to the embassy and promised to do what he could to satisfy at least some of the embassy's requests as far as the trade at Guangzhou was concerned. But in the end, for all that, concrete results were few.

China in the World

The Macartney mission marked the last time that men of the Western Oceans could be managed at a distance using the traditional tools of ritual. (Twenty years later the next British embassy arrived, but because the two sides were unable to agree on protocol, there was no audience at all.) Two contrasting systems of diplomatic convention had come in contact. Each was backed by very different perceptions of the world that were themselves conditioned strongly by immediate historical experience. The contact was brief, but consequential. Macartney and his men knew about as much of the main events that had shaped Qianlong's world as Qianlong and his courtiers knew about the eighteenth-century British world. During their stay, the ambassador and his entourage made a determined effort to collect information, to record observations, to ask questions, and write down answers. Though the only British member of the delegation who could speak any Chinese was an eleven-year-old boy (Staunton's son), the mission returned much better informed about the Qing empire than when it left England. The same cannot be said for Qing knowledge of Europe, which hardly advanced at all. Where in England several accounts of the embassy written by its different members, including a volume of drawings by the embassy artist, were published in the years following, in China, the mission caused barely a ripple of concern among the Qing elite, and there were few published notices of the Macartney embassy.

This was not a result the British had anticipated. Expecting to find him as versatile as his grandfather, whose fascination with Western science, medicine, and mathematics they had read about in Jesuit accounts, Macartney's embassy was disappointed to find that their splendid gifts excited no special enthusiasm. (No one would permit them even to assemble the hot-air balloon they had brought along to demonstrate the latest European advances in flight.) Why was Qianlong, or indeed anyone at court, not more interested in the scientific and technological accomplishments shown him?

It is worth pausing for a moment to consider this question. It was not as though Qianlong lacked curiosity. His pursuit of religious enlightenment and artistic and literary experience, his delight in the natural world, his love of travel, and his fondness for Western forms of representation, all bespeak an inquisitive and active mind. So we should be cautious in assuming that Qianlong was really so disinterested in the outside world. True, the questions he put to Lord Macartney suggest a primitive grasp of European geopolitics: "He inquired how far England was from Russia, and whether they were good friends together, and whether Italy and Portugal were not near England and tributary to it." But Qianlong could have gotten the answers to these questions himself had he bothered to consult any of the maps made for him by missionaries in years past. He was unquestionably familiar with Western geography, and had even had Benoist paint a world map as a mural upon a wall in one of the Yuanming yuan palaces. He knew about the "great troubles in Europe," in other words, the French Revolution, and was aware of current intrigues at the Russian court. How could it be that he, who was never too busy to correct grammatical mistakes in the texts that passed before his eyes, could pretend to be uninformed of the relative location of England and Russia? If Qianlong persisted in asking naïve questions, it might have been that he did so deliberately. Was he hoping thereby to impress upon Macartney the limited level of interest one as magnificent as Qianlong might have in distant England?

Kangxi, of course, had not adopted this attitude and was never too proud to ask questions. But Qianlong was different, being both proud and insecure. Decades of responsibility for the affairs of so diverse and huge a realm, coupled with the many disappointments that plagued his personal life, perhaps had worn him out. Where a younger monarch might have sought out the secrets of Macartney's splendid instruments and machines, Qianlong may have been just too old and tired to care. In addition, the political atmosphere of the court in the 1790s, detailed in Chapter 9, was not conducive to bold initiatives or radical conceptual shifts. Factionalism had fairly paralyzed court policy-making: the few who had the political clout to go out on a limb and propose that the British embassy represented a departure from previous types of foreign missions were anxious only to use the opportunity to strengthen their own political hands and maintain the status quo. Had Macartney come twenty years earlier or ten years later, when the domestic political situation was not so polarized, perhaps things might have been different.

Ultimately, however, probably the best explanation for the relative absence of sustained interest in European matters at Qianlong's court is that there was no pressing reason to be curious about it—not so much because he thought the Western Ocean countries were devoid of interest, but because he did not *need* to be interested in them. On the face of it, this seems absurd. How, we might ask, could he not have seen that the rise of mercantilism, the growing power of parliaments, the advances in experimental science, the increasing confidence in what we call "Enlightenment rationality," and a newfound belief in progress would, within a century of Qianlong's death, lead the inhabitants of the westernmost peninsula of the Eurasian landmass to political and economic domination of nearly every corner of the world? How could he have been so obtuse?

From a post–twentieth-century perspective, the fact of Western prominence in commanding the resources of the world seems so obvious that we find it hard to comprehend it ever could have been any different, that it could have worked out otherwise. But in the later 1700s, no one—not the British themselves, not anyone—foresaw how the combination of technological breakthroughs, economic resourcefulness, and political ambition would ultimately drive Europeans and their protégés on the North American continent to take the risks they took to project their power wherever they felt it served what they regarded as the interests of science, civilization, God, and the "rational" use of natural and human resources. To believe that this was the necessary outcome of events—whether as the unavoidable consequence of environmental conditions, economic laws, the innate supremacy of the spirit of rationality, or divine will—is to overlook the decisive role of chance, ideology, and personality in producing change over time.

If instead we take a step back and look at the China of Qianlong's day and reflect for a moment on the sources of Qianlong's self-confidence—which we have already seen projected in the impressive paintings of him as a hunter, military captain, bodhisattva, and scholar—it may become a little easier to understand why Qianlong did not see what was coming. Internationally, the Qing empire was an impressive political achievement. It occupied a territory that dwarfed that of any individual European country, the nations of Europe appearing to be but individual provinces in comparison, and politically troubled, besides. Its population equaled about one-quarter of the world's total population and was three times the size of the contemporary population of Europe. The domestic economy was similarly enormous (Macartney estimated it to be at least four times larger than that of Great Britain). The flotillas of ships loaded with lumber heading for northern markets took one day to pass by a stationary observer. Interregional trade in tea, cotton, sugar, silk, and grain was the equivalent of the international trade in textiles and staple goods in Europe, for sailing the two thousand miles from a southern port such as Guangzhou to a northern port such as Tianjin was the equivalent of sailing from Lisbon to Hamburg—the difference being that, in China, one remained within the realm of one government. (Europe would not achieve anything like this degree of unity until the very end of the twentieth century.) Consumption of luxury goods in Beijing and the coastal cities of Jiangnan was as high as that in London and Amsterdam. What need had he to seek out Europeans, or any other foreigners for that matter, when they were willing to come to him with the most prized specimens of the most valuable items to be had anywhere on the globe? Without military or strategic considerations to think about, why send his courtiers on dangerous voyages around the world for the sake of mere commerce? After all, even without state support, thousands and thousands of Chinese merchants and their families were already undertaking the unofficial colonization of much of Southeast Asia.

In terms of Qianlong's domestic political position, by the time he reached the throne, the uncertainties that plagued the early Qing courts of Shunzhi and Kangxi were largely past, and, despite occasional flashes of ethnic resentment, Manchu power was well established. Unlike his fellow monarchs in Europe, Qianlong did not face competition over the division of power, nor was economic distress so severe. He faced no cultural crisis and no economic or political disaster befell him that might have precipitated a self-conscious turn to different models of political and economic organization, of which European states might potentially have been a source. In sum, Qianlong's reign was—at least during its first two-thirds—an age of remarkable social stability, economic growth, geographic expansion, military strength, political confidence, and cultural efflorescence. It is hard to blame him if he became convinced that he was presiding over a self-sufficient realm during an unprecedented period of peace and wealth.

We can wonder, however, whether he really thought the Qing heyday would endure forever, particularly given that by the time Macartney called on him there were plenty of signs of decay. Had he been more mindful of the plight of the landless and jobless who filled the ranks of rebel armies, Qianlong or his advisors might have anticipated that the trickle of opium the British brought to trade at Guangzhou would soon widen. By the 1830s the drug was streaming into the country in such quantities that the significant trade surplus it once enjoyed had been replaced by a huge deficit, realizing Qianlong's worst nightmares of economic imbalance. Only in our own day would the equivalent of the tons of silver drained from China's ports in those decades eventually return to the country, this time in the form of two trillion dollars' worth of currency reserves in Chinese banks.

9

Order and Decline in the Late Qianlong Era

In 1793, the year that Lord Macartney arrived to help celebrate his birthday, Qianlong turned eighty-two. For someone his age, Macartney remarked, the emperor looked quite well: "He is a very fine old gentleman, still healthy and vigorous, not having the appearance of a man of more than sixty." Indeed, Qianlong kept up a demanding schedule even in his advanced years and, physically at least, seemed to bear up well under the infirmities of old age. He boasted that he never needed glasses, and remained spry enough even at eighty-seven to go hunting one last time. But the outward glamor and vitality of the late eighteenth-century Qing order could not hide all the weaknesses that by then were present in the body politic, weaknesses that in many cases Qianlong himself could no longer see. The story of the later years of his time as emperor is not just the story of Qianlong's own personal decline, but also of the slow disintegration of the order he had presided over in its greatest glory.

The reasons for this deterioration were various. Perhaps the most insidious was the increased corruption and incompetence at all levels of the bureaucracy, which devastated the legitimacy of the political order. This loss of faith, combined with unprecedented population growth and the consequent social, environmental, and economic pressures, gave rise to numerous popular uprisings large and small. The seemingly endless effort to calm unrest among tribal peoples in the south further strained the ability of the imperial center to maintain control. Additionally, there was the heightened isolation of the emperor himself, which left him vulnerable to being used by those around him, something that even his abdication in 1795 did not change. This chapter rounds out our portrait of Qianlong by outlining the key social and economic trends of the age and Qianlong's efforts, as things began to unravel, to hold on to his accomplishments and illusions alike.

The Later Qianlong Empire

As the sunset of the "flourishing age of Kangxi and Qianlong" approached, the Qing regime remained imposing. Few of the trappings one would expect of a great imperial state were lacking. Capable ministers and generals aided a wise emperor, whose court—filled with able ministers, gifted scholars, beautiful women, and talented artists, musicians, and poets—occupied fabulous surroundings amid ornate palaces, splendid gardens, and extensive parks. Everything that was the best in the world was his, regardless of the expense required, prompting visiting Western visitors to liken Qianlong to "Solomon in all his glory." This impression was reinforced by the living standards of the empire's elite, for whom this was a time of invention, abundance, and indulgence. The very richest families lived in considerable luxury, their houses filled with fine porcelain, rare books, and expensive furniture, some of it imported all the way from Europe. Indeed, the taste among the Qing upper class for quasi-European styles makes a curious parallel to the fashion for Chinoiserie sweeping Europe at the same time. French maidens danced across their snuff bottles and Alpine shepherds and shepherdesses gamboled when their clocks struck the hour. Those who truly wanted to make an impression rented Western-style coaches for their children's weddings, just as today's status-conscious consumers rent stretch limousines.

Qianlong could look back with satisfaction on the many ways in which the empire had been transformed during the fifty-odd years of his watch. He took greatest pride in the military conquests that secured the incorporation of Mongolia and eastern Turkestan into the imperial map, already discussed in Chapter 6. In these regions, victory was followed up by successful administrative consolidation under trustworthy local nobles, overseen by officers of the Eight Banners, whose walled citadels dotted the northwestern frontier. Once these institutions were in place, colonization proceeded apace, as Han Chinese settlers, merchants, and traders soon found the new opportunities there irresistible. Similar processes of conquest and colonization occurred on the southern frontier. Climate and terrain here differed starkly from conditions on the steppe or desert, which cut the advantage enjoyed by Qianlong's well-equipped and supplied professional armies. The reader will recall the difficulty experienced by the unlucky Necin during the first Jinchuan campaign in 1747–1749, and Qianlong's pleasure in the relatively quick victory secured by Fuheng. Just one generation later, though, war broke out again in this forbidding territory. This time the campaign lasted over twice as long, from 1771 to 1776. Involving 100,000 men and costing upwards of 70 million taels, the scale of hostilities was as great as the Dzungar wars. The Qing triumph came as a consolation to Qianlong, who in 1771 had resigned himself to the failure of an ill-fated four-year campaign in Burma in which half of Qing forces perished of disease. And it was certainly preferable to the outcome of the 1788 attempt to intervene in Vietnam, when Qing troops, having temporarily restored the overthrown Lê dynasty king to power, were literally chased from the country by the army of the rival Nguyen family.

Qianlong and Tibet

Tibet was the main exception to the above pattern of consolidation by force. As explained in Chapter 2, earlier in the eighteenth century, the Qing had sent military forces to Lhasa twice to drive out Dzungar rivals who hoped to influence the political situation to their advantage by manipulating the succession of the

Dalai Lama, the most important incarnation in the Gelug order of Tibetan Buddhism. In 1728, the Qing court had placed Polhanas, a lay aristocrat, in the role of regent, in which position he enjoyed considerable authority. Although the Dalai Lama (whom the Qing had been holding in exile) returned to the Potala palace in 1735, real power remained with Polhanas. For twenty years he maintained good relations among the different religious hierarchies and with the Qing *ambans* (the name for the Manchu officials stationed permanently in Lhasa who acted as representatives of the emperor) to maintain stability across Tibet.

When Polhanas died in 1747, however, his position passed to his son, who was much more ambitious and whose loyalties were by no means so certain. Not only did he sow discord by openly favoring the Gelug over other sects, but his hunger for greater power and autonomy led him to murder his own brother and to renew contact with the Dzungars, possibly to collude with them against the Manchus. The two Qing ambans in Lhasa followed his actions closely, but were unable to persuade Qianlong of the seriousness of the situation; on the contrary, the emperor reduced the size of the Qing garrison in Lhasa from 500 to just 100 soldiers. The lid blew off this unstable situation when, in the fall of 1750, the ambans learned of plans for a rebellion. In a desperate act, but with Qianlong's tacit consent, they lured Polhanas' son into a trap and killed him. In the rioting that ensued they lost their own lives, while scores of others were injured and government granaries looted. Manchu authority in Lhasa, and Tibet, generally was imperiled.

In such circumstances, Qianlong faced the same challenge his father and grandfather had faced, of how best to structure the relationship between the imperial center in Beijing and Lhasa. He may, it seems, have briefly considered authorizing a punitive campaign, which was to have included the wholesale occupation of Lhasa and the colonization of central Tibet, but his religious tutor, Rolpai Dorje, convinced the emperor that, as a "protector of Buddhism," he should abandon such a drastic move. Qianlong's predicament was eased somewhat by the decisive actions of the seventh Dalai Lama, who quickly restored order and who, happily for the Qing, was favorably inclined to good relations with the Manchu emperors and so distanced himself from the Dzungars. In the negotiations that followed this incident, a new framework for the governance of Tibet was drawn up, known as the "Thirteen Articles." More authority was accorded the Dalai Lama and the Panchen Lama, the second-most powerful prelate in the Tibetan Buddhist hierarchy; the power of the Qing ambans was increased; and a council of nobles was formed in place of a single regent. It was hoped that such a coalition, based on an idealized historical model of patron and priest, would provide greater long-term stability. Qianlong's bargaining position was strong, given his longstanding interest in Tibetan Buddhism and the close association between Manchu emperorship and the bodhisattva Manjusri. This is not to say, of course, that his lavish patronage of Tibetan Buddhist art and architecture, his sponsorship of Buddhist translations and printings, and his visits to Mt. Wutai were merely political acts, only that they meshed seamlessly with his personal faith.

The revised system for the Qing governance of Tibet worked reasonably well, and sustained Manchu influence in the region into the early 1900s. It avoided the expense of a permanent large-scale garrison and allowed for a great deal of autonomy on the local level. At the same time, it acknowledged the sovereignty of the emperor and allocated a place for him in the Tibetan world order, especially in foreign relations, as became apparent in the late 1780s when the Gurkha kingdom, centered in Nepal, attempted to extend its influence northward and met resistance from Manchu, not Tibetan, soldiers. This intervention provided a further occasion to readjust relations between Lhasa and Beijing, with the Qing court for the first time asserting a statutory right to approve the selection of important new incarnations, including the Dalai Lama. In practice, however, the Qing emperors are on record as having exercised this prerogative only three times between 1792 and 1912—a good indication of how Qing power in Tibet gradually waned after the end of the Qianlong reign.

Population and Economy

Less trumpeted at the time than Qing geographic expansion, but of equal, if not greater, importance, was the demographic expansion that took place during Qianlong's long reign. Previous chapters have referred to the population boom of the eighteenth century, when the empire went from about 150 million people in 1700, to over 200 million by 1750, and well over 300 million by 1800. The rate of growth did not slow down appreciably until the middle of the nineteenth century, when the country's population topped out at around 410 million people. Such a fantastic increase seems suspicious, and the skeptical reader might be forgiven for thinking that it is perhaps the result of a previous underreporting of numbers. Some explanation is therefore in order.

Like previous dynasties, the Qing state stressed the importance of census-taking, and it is upon such surveys that the above population figures are mainly based. Also like previous dynasties, there were practical limits to the state's ability to ensure its accuracy, and—just as with modern censuses—one needs to factor in a certain margin of error. However, scholarly investigations into the question so far do not suggest that the census figures we have for the Qing are grossly wrong, perhaps because, unlike previous regimes, the Qing decoupled tax rates from household size, removing an obvious incentive to understate population. Plus Qing figures are generally corroborated by more easily verifiable census numbers from the early 1900s. In short, there is no getting around it: the population of China rose dramatically under the Qing, and particularly under Qianlong (a similar phenomenon occurred in the later twentieth century, when the population doubled between the 1950s and the 1980s). As yet, we do not entirely understand the demographic processes at work. One explanation is that fertility rates suddenly jumped in the eighteenth century. Research on the subject does not seem to bear this out, however, because fertility rates in China appear not to have been any higher than at another time in its history, or any higher than anywhere else in the world at the time. There is no firm evidence for decreased mortality, either, though improvements in medical care and in standards of living, especially in cities, may have brought about a decline in deaths owing to childbirth, illness, and disease. One factor that likely played a part in population growth was the appearance of new crops such as sweet potatoes, maize, and peanuts, nutritious foods that could be grown in relatively poor soil.

Whatever the reasons, the increase in population was widely observed and noted at the time, and cited as proof of the emperor's benevolent rule and of Heaven's blessings upon the realm. But commentators also had plenty to say about the problems brought on by increased population. Officials warned that villages were becoming too crowded and that there was not enough land for everyone. As a result, the soil was becoming exhausted, food shortages threatened, prices were rising, and poverty was spreading.

While the situation may not have been quite so dire as some believed—even late in the eighteenth century, British visitors reported "little serious poverty" in those parts of the country they visited—still, Qianlong realized that the responsibility fell to him as emperor to ensure peace and plenty. How to feed and clothe so many greatly preoccupied him: "How would I bear to dress in fine robes, knowing that there were people in the land shivering, without clothing?" he wrote. "How would I bear to eat with jade utensils, knowing there were people in the land going hungry, without food?" The emperor encouraged grain imports from Southeast Asia, and strictly forbade exports from grain-producing provinces. In the 1740s, continuing a policy his father also had pushed, Qianlong began to emphasize the importance of opening up new land to cultivation wherever possible, especially in marginal zones such as hilltops, mountainsides, and along riverbanks and seacoasts. Any piece of land, no matter how stony, barren, or remote, should be brought under the plow. To encourage farmers, he offered free land and extended permanent tax breaks to those who took the trouble to heed his call. In addition, in a reversal of longstanding policy, Qianlong relaxed restrictions on the movement of Han families into fertile frontier zones such as Manchuria and southeast Mongolia, even permitting the colonization of much of the area around his beloved Chengde, which saw the rapid loss of most of its forests as a result. The southern portion of the Manchu homeland began to fill up with land-starved families from Shandong, inaugurating a century-long process culminating in the peaceful conquest of fabled Mukden by Han farmers.

All around the empire, people sought out space for themselves and their families. In the southeast, Taiwan experienced major in-migration from Fujian Province and in the southwest Han colonists in larger and larger numbers bumped up against Miao, Tai, Yi, and other indigenous people. In the west, as mentioned, the state actively sponsored the settlement of Chinese farmers in Dzungaria after 1760. In the hope of relieving the burden on Gansu Province, which at first had to foot most of the bill for provisioning Xinjiang, it also established farming colonies for soldiers, and recruited Muslims from southern Xinjiang familiar with special Central Asian irrigation technologies to resume farming north of the Tianshan range. During the thirty-five years between 1740 and 1774, nearly 5,000 square miles of new farmland were opened up. But by 1785, the land reported to be under cultivation everywhere in the empire amounted to nearly 10 million *qing* (over 235,000 square miles), a 30 percent increase over 200 years before. If the tremendous surpluses of grain the government was able to store up are any indication, these policies seem to have worked, even if Qianlong's early wish to ban the production of alcohol—a wasteful use of grain, in his eyes—did not.

Of course, despite the state's positive intervention, the amount of land that could be cultivated was ultimately limited. Popular wisdom had it that it required 4 *mu* of land (about two-thirds of an acre) to feed one person. With rapid population growth, this ratio had worsened under Qianlong from 3.5 *mu* per person in 1766 to 3.33 *mu* per person in 1790. To improve peasant livelihoods, Qianlong authorized the publication and distribution of handbooks to educate farmers on the latest planting, irrigation, and fertilizing techniques. He instructed officials to pay attention to new crop strains and successful innovations in agriculture. Where land was unsuitable for growing food staples, he made sure that officials explained the advantages of cultivating cotton, mulberry trees (for silkworms), fruit trees, oil-bearing seed plants, sugar, tobacco, or other cash crops, and that they assisted them in finding markets for their produce. In most cases, this was not too difficult. Along the commercial networks crisscrossing Qianlong's China flowed goods of all sorts on an enormous scale. According to one long-time Jesuit resident, "the inland trade of China is so great that the commerce of all Europe is not to be compared therewith; the provinces being like to many kingdoms, which communicate to each other their respective productions. This tends to unite the several inhabitants among themselves, and makes plenty reign in all cities."

The reference here to regional specialization underscores what we know about the concentration of certain industries in specific areas: porcelain production in Jiangxi (1 million pieces per year from the kilns at Jingdezhen), textiles in Jiangnan, tea in Fujian, lumber in Yunnan, and rice in Hunan, to mention a few. Long-distance commerce in these and other items, along with the shipment, brokerage, and banking businesses that arose to facilitate it, accounted for a significant proportion of the national economy. Indeed, bearing in mind that the volume of the grain trade in eighteenth-century China was five times as great as the comparable trade in Europe, it more properly can be thought of as a continental economy. This should not blind us, however, to that part of the economy which was strictly local: estimates are that as much as 30 percent of goods and services circulated within just 100 miles of their place of production.

One of the reasons that trade thrived as it did in Qianlong's day is that, in keeping with Confucian tradition, the state hardly taxed local commerce at all. Though levies on domestic and international trade represented a significant source of national income, such exactions were minimal and often informal. To keep them that way, early in his reign, Qianlong reined in the practice of collecting taxes on small-scale exchanges: "In all of the larger markets in prefectural and county seats where trade abounds and where local officials are able to supervise matters, let the petty market tax be collected as before, but not so that it becomes burdensome. There should be no double taxation. In smaller markets in towns and villages, let the tax be completely abolished." Rather than commerce, revenue collection focused mainly on agriculture. Here, too, light taxation was Qianlong's guiding principle. The land tax averaged about 20 percent of household

production. This was payable in silver or in kind, depending on the p
country in which one lived (wealthier regions were more highly monetizeu
poorer ones). It was upon this tax, which totaled approximately 28.2 million
taels annually—about two-thirds of government revenue—that the fiscal well-
being of the state depended.

For this reason, Qianlong's refusal not to undertake a new cadastral survey or
to increase the land tax beyond levels set in the early 1700s had major implications toward the latter half of his reign. While the Qing tax system meant there
was no need to conceal the size of one's family, it did give people an incentive to
conceal the amount of land they owned. One practice, which became very common under Qianlong, was to falsely register land as belonging to a neighboring
gentry family, since degree-holders paid reduced taxes. Given that reclaimed and
newly homesteaded land was also exempt from state levies, as time went by, tax
burdens fell ever more disproportionately upon a smaller and smaller group of
people, forcing more and more of them into ruin. This in turn dragged the economy down and created new problems for the government. Though politically
costly, a general reassessment of taxable property might have cut short this
process of immiseration and put national finances on a firmer footing for future
generations. That Qianlong refrained from taking this step on filial grounds—in
1713 Kangxi had declared that taxes should never be raised—deprived the state
of income it could have used to cope with the greater demands made on it by a
much enlarged population.

Securing the People's Welfare

Behind these policies lay the belief, shared by most of the governing elite at the
time, that the country possessed a finite amount of assets and that as much of this
as possible should be dispersed broadly: "In maintaining peace and prosperity,
nothing matters more than that the people should not be in want. Since the
wealth of the empire is only so much, rather than gathering it all at the top, it is
better to distribute it at the bottom." A similar sort of concern characterized
other aspects of Qianlong's rule, especially early in his reign. "From ancient
times, the basis of successful government has been to nourish the people, and to
do that means to encourage gain while preventing misfortune," he once wrote;
"only when there is no worry over flood or drought will the storehouses be full."
In this regard, though the Confucian classics figured in the making of economic
policy under Qianlong, what mattered more to him was the bottom line: Were
results what they needed to be? What did the numbers say? For instance,
Qianlong was always on the lookout for pestilence or spells of bad weather and
forever inquiring about precipitation in different parts of the country. Few things
angered him more than when officials hid from him early signs of drought, or
cheered him more than when rain fell amply at the proper season. In spring 1744,
after the capital region received a particularly good soaking, the emperor greeted
his ministers one morning, saying, "I wonder whether now wouldn't be the right
time for the peasants to begin planting? Why don't you inquire and find out, so
that I may put my mind at ease?"

Despite these efforts, Qianlong was perfectly aware that crop failures were bound to happen, and saw to it that the government was prepared. The following edict, also from 1744, sums up his philosophy on this point:

> One can say that Our dynasty, which has lasted now for some one hundred years, enjoys tranquil, trouble-free days. But to conclude that because these are trouble-free days there is nothing for us to do is to court certain trouble in the future. Complacency is dangerous, and lazy government is the source of chaos. In my studies as a youngster I learned well the ethics of leadership. Daily since becoming emperor have I thought to bring happiness and prosperity to the realm. When I look around, I ask myself, "Are these the signs of perfect peace?" Seeing the growing numbers of people and the increasing difficulty of feeding everyone, if there were a sudden drought or flood, how would we cope? How can we be prepared if our ministers have not taken appropriate measures?

Chief among those "appropriate measures" was a remarkable nationwide network of government granaries, which doubled the size of its reserves during Qianlong's reign. Dubbed "ever-normal" granaries because of their alternative function of stabilizing grain prices, they fulfilled the task of providing food in emergencies remarkably well. For instance, during a famine in Hebei Province in 1743–1744 (one of the worst natural disasters of Qianlong's reign), officials on the scene surveyed the situation, classified victims according to degree of severity, set up temporary camps for those whom the famine had displaced, fed them from communal kitchens, and channeled grain relief to 1.6 million people. In addition, ever-normal granaries were sometimes called upon to furnish extra grain for military operations when the military's own network of granaries was unable to meet demand.

It should be said that by the middle of his reign, Qianlong seems to have had second thoughts on maintaining such a strong commitment to this kind of state interventionism, preferring to let markets do more and more of that work. This shift, plus mounting military expenses and rising corruption, weakened the civilian granary network seriously, meaning that flood and famine relief in the nineteenth and twentieth centuries was far less effective than it had been under Qianlong.

Needless to say, the best preparation for such disasters was to prevent them from happening altogether. Apart from offering special prayers and sacrifices (which Qianlong carried out regularly), not much could be done about earthquakes or droughts. Floods, on the other hand—then, as now, the most common type of calamity—were a different matter. For centuries a major responsibility of the state was the maintenance of dams and dikes to keep rivers flowing within their banks. A principal focus of these works was the Yellow River, which, because of very high silt levels, was historically prone to flooding; when this happened, the entire North China plain was liable to end up under a foot or more of water, ruining crops, carrying off livestock, and destroying homes and lives. Qianlong had an opportunity to observe such misery for himself during the Southern Tour of 1756, writing, "One saw the cadaverous and the hungry, their bodies barely covered in threadbare blue tatters, limping, some with no shoes; truly, the effects of the deluge spread all around."

Managing flood control was not simply a matter of coordinating the construction of dams, dikes, and seawalls. It also involved dredging waterways and required the timely regulation of reservoirs, overflow channels, and drainage canals linking dozens of rivers and lakes. Clever officials even figured out ways to divert excess water to irrigate new farmland. Because the consequences of failure were so catastrophic, hydraulic policy was one arena where Qianlong's skills as a ruler were most openly in evidence. Unlike losing a battle in a distant frontier, if the emperor and his men lost in the struggle to control the waters, ordinary men and women immediately felt the results. Little wonder that he routinely devoted about 10 percent of annual government expenses to the construction and upkeep of flood control projects around the country (the reader may remember that inspecting the results of these public works was one of the reasons given for the emperor's tours of the southern part of the country). As with his military triumphs, he erected stone monuments to mark victories over the elements. Most commentators agree that Qianlong's accomplishments in this regard were significant.

One common measure employed by Qianlong in response to drought or flood was to order tax relief for counties adversely affected. Granting those who had lost their farms dispensation for a year or two, or even more, was a way of directly easing the burden on strapped households. It also fit well with Qianlong's overall philosophy that the country's wealth should be concentrated in the people, and that therefore state exactions should be kept to a minimum. He did not even always wait for a natural disaster to extend this sort of relief. Four times in his reign—in 1745, 1770, 1777, and 1790—Qianlong decreed a nationwide amnesty of the land tax. In his judgment (which not all officials shared) the state treasury had sufficient surplus that it could safely do without its usual share of revenue, and still cover its expenses. Resulting in a grand total of over 12 million taels in forgiven taxes, these amnesties give us reason to pause a moment again to consider the scale of the later Qianlong economy. That Qianlong could get away with this not once, but four times, suggests a staggering level of wealth and confidence. This is not even counting the three times he canceled collection of so-called tribute grain (used to feed the capital) from the country's breadbasket provinces, the innumerable instances he forgave taxes on disaster-stricken counties and provinces, or the restraint he showed in his land reclamation policy, under which no newly cultivated farmland was to be taxed. Qianlong's magnanimity was impressive, but it also came at a cost, in that by limiting state revenues, Qianlong failed to foresee that the dynasty would require ever greater resources to deal with its increasing population and territory.

Limits of Authority

Qianlong's taxation policies owed not so much to a generous spirit or an overriding concern for the well-being of the mass of people. They owed more to the fact that he disposed of very significant resources, which accrued to the Son of Heaven as a matter of course, and also to the fact that the direct costs of government were relatively cheap. The only significant permanent costs the central government had to bear related to maintaining the military, which, at 60 percent or more, occupied by far the largest portion of the national budget. Officialdom itself was small in comparison. The enormous bureaucracies maintained by most modern governments were wholly unknown in the Chinese experience before the twentieth century. The state was there to guard the borders, keep the peace, enforce the law, and provide assistance in crises. Its representatives were supposed to set a moral example in order to win popular confidence ("There is no governing by laws; there is only governing by people," was one of Qianlong's refrains), and otherwise let the people go about their business. Officials were few in number relative to the population—on average 1 per 100,000 in the mid-eighteenth century—and grossly underpaid: a magistrate could count on a base salary of only 45 taels per year. He could govern only with the assistance of local elites, themselves often from degree-holding families, who provided much of the financial support needed to administer local affairs. Such support was vital, as magistrates typically needed to assemble what amounted to their own staff of secretaries, clerks, lictors, runners, and sergeants-at-arms. Plus, cultivating ties with influential families gave a newly arrived official access to the sort of detailed information about the area that he would need to govern knowledgeably.

The symbiotic relationship between officialdom and local society worked well enough so long as the imperial center was able to retain the loyalty of its servants and prevent abuses of power or improper dealings that might interfere with the state's basic objectives of collecting taxes and keeping the peace. Lest they become too familiar with the locals, officials served a rotation of only three years in any provincial office, and under no circumstances were they to take up a post in their home province. At the end of each term their performance was evaluated before the next assignment. But as the Qianlong reign wore on, a couple of disturbing trends became apparent. One was that ties between appointed officials and locally powerful figures grew cozier. The second was that connections between officials themselves began to outweigh those between officials and the emperor. Both of these represented an attenuation of the personal ties that bound individual men to the emperor, and signaled the weakening of Qianlong's power in the second half of his reign.

The first of these trends can be linked to the Qianlong demographic boom. For though the population doubled, there was no corresponding increase in the number of civil officials, which remained more or less where it had been under Kangxi. As a consequence, already overworked magistrates found themselves responsible for the administration of districts with double or triple the population of a few decades earlier. Without substantial additional financial assistance from the center, they grew exasperated and even more dependent on whatever help they could find locally, which drove a wedge between the imperial center in Beijing and different levels of local government at the prefectural and county level. The need for money became ever more urgent. This naturally made it harder to resist the temptation to take a bribe, impose an extortionate levy, or pursue the occasional crooked scheme. This, then, was the price to be paid for keeping government expenses to a minimum. Money for nearly everything—building bridges, erecting shrines, refurbishing temples—was provided for on a one-time basis, very frequently with the help of contributions from wealthy (and hopeful) donors, who were pleased to respond to the magistrate's, the governor's, or the emperor's call for help, especially when it meant receiving a low-level degree, which brought with it tax relief. So successful was this method of fund-raising that military campaigns came to rely on it. Indeed, there is growing evidence that the purchase of degrees was much more common, and constituted a much larger overall source of income for the state, than previously thought.

The second of these trends reflected what was probably an inevitable feature of the Qing bureaucracy, or indeed of any large organization invested with power and money, namely, factionalism. Earlier chapters have already discussed the general distrust in China for party politics of any kind. Yet factionalism seems to have been inescapable, if only because people rarely all agree on the proper solution to different problems, or even on what the problems are. In addition, in the Chinese case, young men eager to build their careers found themselves in intense competition with each other for the degrees that would enable them to take office. Later, if they were lucky, they competed to make a name and gain a position of authority and prestige. In such an atmosphere, one could never have too many friends; at the same time, one could never know for certain who one's friends are. This prompted different strategies for office-holders. Some opted to lie low and pass the buck, while others instead chose a riskier route, either proposing bold initiatives or blowing the whistle on perceived foul play. Qianlong tended to favor the latter sort, and dismissed the former as mere time-servers. Yet if he sensed that an official was acting mostly to win notoriety—or, worse, to cover up his own wrongdoing—he could be quick to punish. Either way, individual officials inevitably found themselves having to take sides. Those who steadfastly avoided such a choice usually found themselves friendless, marginalized, and without influence.

Hešen and the Perennial Problem of Corruption

As obvious a step as it might seem, it does not appear that the emperor ever seriously considered the need to enlarge the size of government, expand the number of magistrates, or undertake any basic alteration of the political model he had inherited. And he certainly was not going to abide by institutionalized political divisions: the only political party that mattered, in his view, was Qianlong. But one thing that Qianlong would not tolerate was gross corruption among officials. Ordinary people had to be able to trust those who had authority over them, for on a very basic level that represented their trust in him, the emperor. He grasped the lesson of the last years of his grandfather's reign: that excessive lenience only promoted deceit, fraud, and the gradual dissipation of imperial authority. Moreover, Qianlong believed that dishonesty among his officials threatened his legitimacy and weakened the ability of the imperial center to execute policy effectively. It amounted therefore to a kind of betrayal, making it among the most serious of crimes. Qianlong encouraged people to report to him confidentially on suspected cases of official misbehavior: bribery, fraud, nepotism, abuse of privilege, failure to report bad news. This would keep his men on a short leash and keep real power concentrated in his own hands. By the same token, accusing someone of corruption was an excellent way to remove a political enemy. It was up to the emperor to decide which accusations were false and which were true.

Literally hundreds of corruption cases were brought before Qianlong, most of them relating in some way to the embezzlement of state funds. Early in his reign, he decided that any case involving theft of sums larger than 1,000 taels would be punishable by immediate decapitation, a promise he kept at first when it became obvious to him that many officials understood his vow to depart from the draconian policies of his father as a license to pilfer and steal. Several tens of officials lost their heads. This seemed to get the point across, and the frequency of scandals diminished for some time.

However, by the second half of the Qianlong era, official greed reemerged as a serious problem, with major cases every few years. Uncovering malfeasance and tracking the culprits was difficult, owing to the tendency to conspiratorial action, whereby high officials agreed to protect each other should one of them be caught. As the risk of being discovered rose, so did the sums involved, often rising into the tens or even hundreds of thousands of taels. Qianlong tried to turn the tide, but at the same time he grew impatient when he sensed that the criticism was directed at him. In 1780 he lashed out at one grand secretary who had the nerve to allege— accurately, as it happened—that most provincial budgets were being shamelessly raided by government officials: "According to what Injangtu has reported, officials high and low alike are hypocrites and sycophants who will lie to your face. So I suppose that means I have been hoodwinked now for over fifty years?"

One famous case occurred that very year. Li Shiyao, a powerful governor-general from an illustrious and well-connected banner family, was discovered to have engaged in a whole range of illegal activities, including influence-peddling, fencing stolen jewels to junior officials at extortionate prices, pilfering state property, and hiding illegal profits in shady real estate deals. Hešen, the court minister assigned to investigate the case, reported that there was hardly one among Li's subordinates who was not implicated and that the accounts of the entire province needed to be carefully reviewed. In the course of these inquiries, many others also lost their reputations and their jobs. The 30,000 illegally gotten taels chalked up to Li's account ought to have resulted in his execution, but Qianlong hesitated, undone by the treachery of one of his most trusted officials. "Are there any among you I can really trust?" he asked his provincial officials. In the end, following Hešen's advice, he pardoned his old friend and reinstated him as governor-general.

This action sent a signal that the old emperor no longer had the nerve to prosecute official malfeasance with real dedication. Within the next few years, even more outrageous corruption cases came to light. In 1781, before Li Shiyao's case was even settled, the emperor learned that officials in Gansu Province, led by governor Wang Tanwang, had for three years colluded in a profitable ruse that redirected to their own private accounts money intended for the grain relief system. To maximize earnings, officials routinely exaggerated the amount of grain dispensed to areas purportedly affected by drought, justifying the need for ever greater contributions from aspiring local elites. Donors earned entry-level degrees that entitled them to stipends and the right to try for the higher degrees that might mean an official position—and a chance to author their own get-rich-quick schemes. For some time Qianlong was puzzled that a poor province like Gansu suddenly managed to produce so many scholars. And how was it that, in spite of such generosity, the granaries remained so low? When his initial inquiries failed to turn up the truth (the men he sent to investigate were themselves bought off), he let the matter rest. One can only wonder how Qianlong allowed himself to believe that the Gansu governor was not up to something when total reported grain contributions amounted to more than seven times the entire Gansu grain harvest. He even rewarded the governor for his outstanding work.

In the end, thanks to the persistent inquiries of other, more principled, officials, the details of the scheme were revealed. It turned out that the droughts were imaginary and that many donors were not from Gansu but Jiangnan men posing as locals to take advantage of lower examination standards to earn their degrees illicitly. The scale of corruption in this case was greater than any before. More than one hundred men were convicted of having defrauded the state of upwards of 10,000,000 taels, an amount equal to more than one quarter of the state's annual income. Sixty of them paid for their avarice with their lives. So many positions were left empty by the prosecution of this case that for a time there were not enough honest men left in Gansu to manage provincial affairs.

The next year yet another political scandal erupted, this one implicating the governor of Shandong and his cronies in a different scheme that also involved theft of money meant to stock the province's ever-normal granaries. Again Qianlong put Hešen on the trail, and again it turned out that the charges were true: several million taels were missing from the accounts. By the time the Shandong governor was executed, investigations had begun into similar peculation in Zhejiang Province, where accounts were over one million taels in arrears, and where more of Qianlong's handpicked men were found to have gone astray. For the rest of the 1780s and into the 1790s, hardly six months passed without some new scandal arising. Rumors spread quickly and were confirmed by arrests, confessions, more arrests, and indignant edicts published in the newspaper of record, the Beijing Gazette. From palace to marketplace, the rot in government was the common topic of discourse.

From Qianlong's point of view, there were a couple of bright sides to all this deceit and fraud, one of which was that the wealth confiscated from the households of all these corrupt officials was funneled to his own purse, enriching him tremendously. The officials who assumed the posts of those who had been cashiered were themselves charged with making up the deficit in silver and grain accounts. Another positive spin was that the guilt was spread between Manchu and Han officials alike; that is, the emperor did not need to worry that Han officials were secretly trying to sabotage the political system through corruption. But that was small comfort when Manchu officials, who owed even stronger allegiance to the throne, were wrecking it so effectively just the same. Qianlong could also reassure himself that there remained at least a few upright and incorruptible men in the empire upon whom he could rely, men who were above bribe-taking, who would always tell him the truth, who would never stoop to deceiving him for the purpose of self-aggrandizement. Mostly Manchus, these men included

Agūi (who broke the 1781 Gansu case) and Fuheng, both from prominent families, grand councilors with sterling credentials and impressive military victories to their names; another was Šuhede, known for his straight talk, strong opinions, and his willingness to challenge the emperor on key issues. But then, on the other hand, there was Hešen.

Born in 1750 to a Beijing banner family of no special distinction, Hešen was a bright lad who earned admission to the school for talented Manchu sons when he was nine years old. At the age of seventeen he married the granddaughter of a prominent official, a fortunate match that connected him with a wide circle of influential people, and before he was twenty he inherited a minor post in the palace guard. This provided him with only a modest salary, but it did place him occasionally in the emperor's retinue, where, two years later, he came to Qianlong's notice.

One story has it that Qianlong took an interest in the young Hešen because his delicate features reminded him of his beloved Lady Fuca; another relates how Hešen impressed the emperor by reciting from memory an examination essay he had written the year before. Whatever the reason, his address and manner evidently stuck in Qianlong's mind, and in 1771 he moved Hešen to the imperial bodyguard. Within the next few years, to widespread astonishment, Hešen rose in meteoric fashion to the top ranks of government, advancing in 1775 to the Grand Council, an unheard-of office for a twenty-five-year-old with no experience of the larger world (Agūi was sixty when he became grand councilor). From that time forward until Qianlong's death in 1799, Hešen could do no wrong. Unlike almost every other minister who served Qianlong, his career never suffered any reverses. He jumped from key post to key post effortlessly. By 1790, when he was but forty, there was hardly a position he had not held or an honor he had not received. To top it all, his son was married that year to the emperor's favorite daughter, Princess Hexiao, in unbelievably lavish ceremonies (described in Chapter 3), joining Hešen legally to the imperial clan.

Never before had the empire witnessed anything like the Hešen phenomenon. Many grew suspicious of his success and a brave few even tried to bring him down a peg, but the emperor was firm in his favor. The majority in officialdom, seeing Hešen's virtually impregnable position, sensibly decided to throw in their lot with his. As a consequence, for the last twenty years of his reign Qianlong effectively shared imperial power with Hešen. Had Hešen kept his master's interests above his own, this extraordinary departure from precedent might not have been so disastrous. But Hešen exploited his position for all it was worth. On the one hand, he fawned shamelessly over the emperor ("If his majesty needs to spit, Hešen is right there with the bedpan," went one popular catchphrase), and on the other hand he subverted the emperor's authority, stealing him blind. Qianlong's confidence in his right-hand man was such that he never saw the irony of sending him out to investigate corruption cases in the provinces when it was Hešen himself who set the pace for diverting public monies to personal coffers, Hešen himself who provided the cover for, and profited from, the nefarious activities of many of those whom he had to arrest later. This failure of judgment late in his life cost Qianlong, and the country, dearly.

How dearly only became clear once Qianlong died. Three days after his father passed away, the new emperor, Jiaqing, who had waited a long time before moving against his father's favorite, charged Hešen with twenty different crimes and ordered his arrest. A week later he was permitted to commit suicide, at which point his huge estate reverted automatically to the throne. When the accountants were done, the scale of Hešen's fortune stood revealed: a breathtaking 800 million taels, more than twenty years' worth of annual state revenue, and a bankroll big enough to have paid for another Ten Great Campaigns. The wags had it right when they said, "Hešen's fall, when it should hit, will fill up Jiaqing's purse a bit!" When we recall that, sixty years before, execution awaited officials who were caught having stolen so much as a mere 1,000 taels—a tiny fraction of Hešen's crime—we understand something of the degree to which imperial authority had weakened over time. We also see the limitations of Qianlong's reliance on personally cultivated ties with servants of the throne, which, lacking systematic checks, tended to extremes: witness the spectacular perfidy of his son-in-law, Hesen, compared to the exceptional fealty of his brother-in-law, Fuheng.

The Center Cannot Hold

The decreasing effectiveness of government and the increasing rapacity of officials, who, after all, were lower in the food chain and had to keep feeding Hešen and the other sharks at the top, were no secret in Qianlong's later years. Along with population squeeze and the increasing competition for scarce resources, they can be seen as factors contributing to the growing social instability of the time. Disputes over land rights skyrocketed, often ending in murder and mayhem that local magistrates, already stretched to the limit, had little time to handle. The continual drain of people—unmarried males, in particular—from ancestral villages to new settlements on the frontier created new communities where the usual institutions that knit the fabric of rural life were absent. In their place arose unofficial brotherhoods, millenarian cults, and bloody feuding, all beyond the reach of the state. The increasing commercialization of the economy, which brought wealth to many, also eroded older, more personal, and more stable patterns of exchange. Prices rose steadily beginning in the middle of Qianlong's reign: in some places, the price of rice in the 1790s was three times what it had been sixty years earlier. Property changed hands so often that tenants no longer knew who their landlords were, spawning conflicts over runaway rents. Even the better-off were not immune to the relentlessly escalating demands of tax collectors. Aggravating the situation further was the greater frequency of natural disasters, in part the result of excessive cutting of forest, reckless use of water, and loss of topsoil. When, as happened more and more, grain and funds intended to relieve the suffering of victims of flood or famine never materialized because officials in charge of relief efforts had stolen and sold it all, popular outrage was great. By Qianlong's later years, it erupted in frequent protests, riots, and uprisings.

To be sure, disturbances to the peace in the countryside were not unknown in the first several decades of the eighteenth century, but there is no mistaking their greater frequency and severity in the last thirty years, beginning with the Wang Lun uprising, which took place in Shandong Province in 1774. Though it was quickly suppressed, this revolt occurred right under the emperor's nose and is sometimes taken to mark another turning point in Qianlong's fortunes. This was followed by uprisings in Gansu in 1778, 1781, and 1784, Shandong in 1781, Henan in 1785, and Hunan and Guizhou in 1795. These latter involved the ever-recalcitrant Miao, with whom Qianlong had been wrestling since the first years of his reign. This is not to mention the two largest revolts of the period, one the Lin Shuangwen Rebellion of 1788, and the other the White Lotus Rebellion of 1796–1804. Both represented serious challenges to central authority, and were put down only at considerable cost and effort.

Historians know little about Lin Shuangwen, only that he was born in 1757 in Fujian to a poor peasant family and emigrated with his father in 1773 to Taiwan in search of a better life. The Lins settled near the town of Zhanghua on Taiwan's agriculturally rich west coast, where nearly all immigrants from the mainland were concentrated. Han colonization had begun with Qianlong's blessing a few decades earlier, but Taiwan was still very much a frontier zone, with a well-deserved reputation for lawlessness. Armed conflicts with the island's displaced aborigines remained common. Apart from a garrison of some 6,000 poorly disciplined soldiers, the Qing supported a very limited civil administration, meaning that settlers had to rely substantially on their own resourcefulness to get by. With no established system of village chiefs or lineage headmen as on the mainland, native-place connections emerged as a chief basis for broader community organization and for intracommunity rivalries, especially disputes over land. In addition, sworn brotherhoods such as the Heaven and Earth Society (Tiandihui), which promised mutual aid and fellowship, found fertile ground in Taiwan's "wild west" atmosphere. Along with many others, Lin joined. When in late 1787 the Zhanghua prefect decided to arrest a few troublemakers, violence quickly escalated out of control, resulting in the murder of the prefect and two other officials and the raiding of the granary and armory.

At this point, the rebellion came out into the open, with Lin Shuangwen leading the rebel cause. Exactly what their demands were never became clear. Qianlong called upon the recently disgraced Li Shiyao and other officials in Fujian to crush the rebels, but uninspired generalship left Qing troops stranded in the island's few walled cities, as control of most of the territory fell into the hands of Lin's force of some 100,000 men. After six months of useless exertions, Qianlong turned finally to a trusted Manchu commander, Fukang'an (Fuheng's son and the nephew of Lady Fuca), to wrest control of Taiwan back from the rebels. Arriving in late 1788 with a fresh force of some 60,000 troops, he immediately got to work. Aided by the formidable strategist Hailanca, a veteran of fighting in Xinjiang, Burma, and Jinchuan, the two subdued the main rebel force in less than one week. Lin saw that the odds were in the government's favor and retreated to the mountainous interior, where he was soon arrested. Transported to Beijing for trial, he was summarily executed in April 1789. Qianlong followed up with a clean sweep of his Taiwan administration, whose incompetence was revealed to have been responsible for the high level of popular unrest in the first place. Meantime, Qing forces spent the next few months hunting down anyone who had taken part in the rebellion, causing thousands to flee back to the mainland, unintentionally transmitting the ideas and organizational habits of the

Heaven and Earth Society to Fujian and other places, where they would reemerge in the nineteenth century as the underworld known as the Triads.

Even more shocking to the court than the Lin Shuangwen debacle was the outbreak of uprisings much closer to home, over a wide swath of central and north China, starting in 1796 and lasting for the better part of twenty years. Though only loosely connected with each other, each insurrection shared the same inspiration in the teachings of the White Lotus, a popular religious sect that combined folk Buddhist and Daoist beliefs. In addition to venerating a figure known as the Unbegotten Venerable Mother, White Lotus followers believed that the end of the world was imminent and prepared for the appearance of Maitreya, the Buddha of the Coming Age—such preparations often involving the proclamation of a new order, an act that the state quite understandably took to be defiance of its authority.

The origins of the sect remain unclear—elements of White Lotus theology can be traced to various groups that went by myriad names—but go back at least to the sixteenth century. Its appeal seems to have been strongest among the poorest, least privileged strata of society, for whom the promise of salvation and a life of plenty in the new age held out comfort and hope. Sect membership drew widely from different occupations and included women as well as men, most of them rural and illiterate, though over time more and more urbanites joined up. Leadership roles, also divided between men and women, fell usually to the somewhat lettered—herbalists, martial arts experts, healers, even the occasional acrobat—who could speak with authority on the few White Lotus texts that circulated and teach members how to chant the appropriate mantras. Because these scriptures and chants lay well outside the pale of the approved Buddhist canon, they were regarded as false and deceptive, requiring White Lotus adherents to keep their activities secret, lest they get into trouble. Additionally, by Qianlong's time there was also the added hint of pro-Ming, anti-Qing sentiment in some White Lotus teachings.

The same political, social, and economic problems that lay behind the other upheavals of the later Qianlong years also lay behind the White Lotus. People had plenty of reason to complain and plenty of room to develop connections with similar-minded people from other parts of the country and different walks of life. When the first uprisings broke out in 1796, the movement had already spread far more widely than officials could have guessed. The generally brutal and indiscriminate techniques that characterized official repression of the sect—such as locking up entire villages and freeing the "innocent" only upon payment of a bribe—predictably stiffened opposition and made uprooting the heterodoxy that much more difficult. Popular attitudes, even among the law-abiding, were entirely unsympathetic to the government. News of such tactics brought disapproval from the court, and even sympathy for the much put-upon peasant. But when rebels began occupying county towns, killing officials, and creating turmoil over much of western Hubei, northern Sichuan, southern Shaanxi, along with those parts of Anhui and Henan they bordered—marginal zones where hard-pressed settlers come to open new farms or illegal mines swelled the numbers of White Lotus faithful into the millions—the Qing state could not postpone action or soften its stance. Eight years and 200 million taels later, peace had been restored. By then Qianlong lay in his tomb.

The Final Act

Among Qianlong's many distinctions, one of the most memorable was that he abdicated the throne. This was something that, in all of Chinese history, only one other emperor had ever voluntarily done.[1] His stated motive, as it so often had been, was simple filiality, though we can be certain he once again had his eyes on the history books. When he took the throne in 1735, he declared then that, "Should I be so fortunate as to rule for as long as sixty years, at that time I will pass the throne on to my successor," the reason being that if he were to remain on the throne past that time, he would break the record set by his grandfather Kangxi, who had ruled sixty-one years. This was a milestone that, as a respectful grandson, he could not bear to surpass.

Most people probably forgot about Qianlong's youthful promise. It seems he may have brought it up again some thirty-six years later, telling his sons in 1772 that he would give up the title of emperor at the age of eighty-six. Only in 1778 did he repeat this intention publicly, at the same time announcing to the country that he had chosen an heir and had hidden the name in the usual place above the imperial throne. He added that if at some point after his seventieth or eightieth birthday he was no longer physically or mentally able to rule, he would step down before his reign had reached the sixty-year mark. As his eighty-sixth birthday approached, Qianlong referred more often to his upcoming retirement. Mention of it found its way into many edicts from 1793 on, as concrete plans for the transfer of imperial authority got underway. The date was set for a special ceremony at which he would formally transfer the imperial seal—New Year's Day of what would have been the sixty-first year of Qianlong. A new title, "supreme emperor" (*taishang huang*), last seen more than six centuries earlier, was recalled for use by Qianlong once he ceded the reins of power to his son and successor.

However, as his new title suggests, Qianlong had no real intention of letting go: "I absolutely cannot allow myself to be tricked or deceived before I abdicate," he wrote to officials early in 1795, "for even after I have abdicated, how could I then simply put state matters to one side and not attend to them anymore?" Indeed, in the edict issued on the sixtieth anniversary of his rule, in which he formally revealed the identity of the new emperor, Qianlong stated explicitly that he would remain responsible for all affairs of national importance. This, he said, would enable the new ruler to undergo a period of on-the-job training. Moreover, according to the new protocol, "Jiaqing" would be used in dating the country's calendar but "Qianlong" would remain in use at court. Qianlong would continue to live in the Yangxin Palace as before, he would still be empowered to issue edicts, he would still meet with the Grand Council, and newly minted coins would even bear both names.

---

[1] This was emperor Huizong of the Song dynasty, Qianlong's artistic exemplar, who reigned from 1100–1125 CE. Huizong abdicated when it became clear that the imperial capital would fall to the invading Jurchens of the Jin state. Emperor Gaozu of the Tang dynasty (r. 618–626) also abdicated, but not voluntarily.

In other words, for a period of about four years the empire found itself in the very strange position of having two sovereigns: Jiaqing reigned, while Qianlong continued to rule. Such a situation was far from ideal, especially as Qianlong grew progressively more feeble and his memory began to fail. The old emperor was unable to accept his inability to deal effectively with the rebellions then taking place across the country, yet he was equally unwilling to allow day-to-day management to pass to others. He never took up residence in the retirement quarters he had specially designed for himself, but remained lodged in the Yangxin Palace. Realizing that the whirlwinds of destruction tearing apart whole provinces owed ultimately to his failure to govern well, he remained as preoccupied as ever with his historical legacy, and desperately seized upon any successes as victories comparable to those of his storied ten campaigns. His empress was long dead, and all of his old advisors were gone, the last great man of the Qianlong era, Agūi, having died in 1795. This left him in the hands of the corrupt Hešen, who controlled three of the six government ministries and sometimes behaved as if he, and not Jiaqing, were the imperial heir. New policy matters or initiatives were set aside or postponed indefinitely as the top levels of the administration fell into a state of suspended animation. Jiaqing, himself a filial son, could do nothing unless bid so by his father, and waited patiently for nature to resolve his dilemma.

The welcome end to these aberrant politics came at last in early 1799. Just a day after receiving New Year's greetings from his son, grandsons, great-grandsons, and great-great-grandsons, and only a few hours after writing one last poem, in which he prayed for a quick end to the White Lotus rebellion, Qianlong suddenly weakened and took to his bed. Attended by the thirty-eight-year-old Jiaqing, just as he had attended at Yongzheng's death sixty-four years before, Qianlong uttered a few last words to his son and apologized for leaving him unfinished business. He died early the next morning, the chronicle says, "looking off toward the southwest." He was eighty-eight years old.

Several months later, in the fall of 1799, Qianlong was laid to rest in a magnificent mausoleum some distance west of Beijing, where his grandfather Kangxi also was buried. He himself had decided on its location and supervised the construction of the tomb. One can visit the site today, east of Beijing. The architecture above ground, all in Chinese style, is impressive: the stele marking the entrance to the mausoleum precincts towers thirty feet high, and the scale of the buildings is grand. Most notable, however, is the underground crypt. The twenty-foot-high walls, lined with huge slabs of stone, are covered with magnificently carved Sanskrit incantations, reflecting Qianlong's lifelong devotion to Buddhist practice. There is not a line of Manchu or Chinese writing anywhere. Atop his coffin was laid a shroud of orange silk embroidered in red with sacred mantras, also in Sanskrit. Next to the stone sepulcher that held his body was placed another sepulcher, with the remains of Lady Fuca. Theirs are the only two coffins in the chamber.

Conclusion

Son of Heaven, Man of the World

More than two hundred years have passed since Qianlong's death. For fifty years afterward, the events of his reign were all anyone could talk about, filling volume after volume of memoirs, private histories, and reminiscences. The afterglow faded in 1839 with the arrival of British gunboats that came to put an end to the trading system Qianlong had instituted and secured by force the diplomatic and economic concessions that Macartney tried to win nearly forty years before. Then, in 1850, the outbreak of the Taiping Rebellion, the most vicious civil war the world has ever seen, forced the glorious achievements of the preceding epoch definitively into the background. Following the triumph of the 1911 Revolution, which overthrew the Qing and instituted a republican system, Qianlong was reduced to something of a caricature, if not an outright villain.

The rapid failure of China's democratic experiment in 1915 and the turmoil that subsequently enveloped the country—militarism, fascism, the Japanese invasion, civil war, Communism—meant that for the following seventy-five years Qianlong, the very one who once held majestic sway over most of East Asia, seemed somehow almost irrelevant, too far removed from present circumstances, to be of much importance. If anything, he was part of a past that seemed to damn China to eternal backwardness and weakness. Qianlong appeared in history texts, to be sure, but emerged as either a small-minded tyrant with a persecution complex who threw a bomb in the garden of Chinese letters, or a friend of the landlord class who greedily enriched himself and his cronies and for decades permitted the systematic exploitation of peasants and tribesmen, crushing them when they opposed his will. It was Qianlong who permitted corruption to get out of hand, Qianlong whose arrogance closed off the country to the outside world, Qianlong who overlooked the need to acquire modern weaponry. In short, Qianlong came to stand for the Manchus generally, for foreign domination, for self-serving shortsightedness, and for all that a highly nationalist, modernizing Han people hated about their defeat-ridden recent history. In 1928 Chinese soldiers of one of the warlord armies then preying on the countryside even vandalized Qianlong's tomb, strewing his remains carelessly about as they searched for treasure and pillaged the mausoleum.

The end of the twentieth century brought about a remarkable change in Qianlong's position in history. The shift of the Chinese Communist leadership from political radicalism to economic pragmatism substantially altered the picture Chinese people saw when they looked back at the eighteenth century and at Qianlong's sixty-year-long reign. As China's economy charged ahead at breakneck speed, helping to transform the country into a major power, glances were cast back to the last moment of Chinese preeminence in the world, when its armies were strong, its people productive, and its culture the envy of many. (Some argue that this was more a Manchu than a Chinese accomplishment, a debate that will be difficult to settle.) For the first time, positive assessments of the period and the man began to appear in the popular press. Tourist literature and museum captions were rewritten in a more sympathetic light. Following the lead of newer scholarly accounts, television dramas and historical fiction of the 1980s and 1990s lionized Qianlong as a tireless ruler, the man who created the geopolitical blueprint of the modern nation, and who assembled one of the world's finest collections of art. His name began to appear in all sorts of places, even restaurants and cruise ships, wherever people wished to promote the idea of imperial splendor.

Qianlong's new popularity is not limited to China. Since the mid-1980s there have been countless major exhibits in museums in Europe, North America, Japan, and Southeast Asia dedicated to sharing with visitors the cultural magnificence and visual splendor of the Qianlong court. The millions of visitors to major tourist sites in and around Beijing can hardly avoid encountering him in one way or another. To be sure, his is not a household name in the West, at least not yet. But it is becoming gradually less obscure.

One of the difficulties in coming to terms with Qianlong and his era lies in scale. To sort things out, it may help to break Qianlong's life down into four periods. The first, 1711–1735, corresponds to the time of his youth, formal education, and preparation for the throne as Prince Bao. We see an earnest young man, full of promise, the dynasty's hope for the future. As the knowledge of what awaited him grew more certain, Hungli applied himself conscientiously to his studies; anxious to do well by the memory of his grandfather, he sought to absorb what lessons he could from his reading and from the experience of men in his father's service to arrive at a set of guiding principles.

The second period, lasting from his enthronement in 1735 to the death of the Lady Fuca in 1748, represents perhaps the most optimistic time of Qianlong's reign. Sorting through Yongzheng's legacy, the new emperor effectively asserted his own authority and established an atmosphere that was more tolerant and less permeated by fear. A raft of edicts issued from the palace exhorting dedication to the affairs of the common people and warning against complacency. The foundational assumption of this new regime was that all shared the young ruler's passion for the mundane details of governing: rainfall, harvests, grain prices, market conditions. The death of Lady Fuca not only deprived Qianlong of a close personal companion, but, in the revelations following it regarding the failure of so many leading figures—including his own sons—to follow proper mourning etiquette, demoralized him thoroughly. It was as if he suddenly realized that not everyone cared as deeply about the dynastic enterprise as he did.

This experience produced a new toughness and maturity, which distinguishes the third phase, lasting from 1748 to 1776. Vigorous and confident, yet ever the filial son, Qianlong enjoyed the collaboration of an unusually capable crew of advisors, generals, and ministers. It was then that Qianlong achieved his greatest successes. He initiated a series of well-publicized tours of the Chinese heartland, mixing with literary and cultural figures on their own turf and leaving his own stamp on the Jiangnan landscape in various forms: improved public works, his own calligraphy to be hung on the eaves of thousand-year-old gardens, the hoof-prints of the imperial retinue's six thousand horses on its roads. Pilgrimages east to Qufu and Mt. Tai cemented his claim to the Confucian legacy, while journeys west to Mt. Wutai allowed him to participate in the millennial traditions of Buddhist kingship. To reinvigorate the Manchu spirit and to keep himself in shape, Qianlong inaugurated the annual hunts at Mulan and built them into a central event of the imperial calendar. He combined with these an aggressive policy on the northwest frontier, which culminated in the permanent elimination of the Dzungar menace, the defeat of their Khoja allies, and the addition of hundreds of thousands of square miles of territory to his realm. Flexible diplomacy, creative institution-building, and the occasional armed intervention helped reinforce Qing authority over Mongolia, Tibet, and the southwest frontier. At a time of imperial expansion and consolidation all around the world, Qianlong and his men certainly contributed their part.

This period of his reign saw Qianlong in peak form, too, as a cultural patron. In this he behaved like a typical eighteenth-century monarch. Gathering to him a large group of talented artists, Qianlong ordered the visual documentation of the dynasty's daily life, leaving for history a vivid record of his time on the throne. Imperial workshops filled the rooms of his palace with paintings, carvings, ceramics, furniture, and curios of unending variety. When there was no more room, he built more palaces, some even in European style. Everything was inventoried and labeled. His passion for collecting brought priceless antiques and calligraphy into his hands as well, and Qianlong himself attended to the display of his favorite items. The emperor's printing presses could scarcely keep up with the flood of materials Qianlong wanted published: new editions of the Classics, Buddhist sutras, catalogues of art, administrative compendia, and endless volumes of history, philosophy, and poetry, including the emperor's own. Even the imperial presses were unable to handle the printing of Qianlong's epic *Complete Library*, the largest anthology of the written word in Chinese history.

With the 1774 Wang Lun rebellion, the 1776 appointment of Hešen to the Grand Council, and the death of his mother in 1777, Qianlong's life entered a fourth period, one of gradual alienation and worsening unease marked by frequent rebellion and incessant revelations of government corruption, ending with Qianlong's abdication in 1795. His four years as "supreme emperor" represent a bizarre coda to this last troubling period of his reign. The awesome difficulty of holding together such a diverse empire became painfully apparent during these years. The weakening of imperial authority in both its moral and political dimensions at the top was paralleled by the fraying of village and family institutions at the bottom. Material want and official greed meant that many came forward to exploit the vulnerabilities thus exposed; relatively few felt compelled to defend the principles upon which the order depended. The unprecedented doubling of the population, a driving force of eighteenth-century growth and expansion, was likewise the cause of rising social instability. Many people—especially single males with no prospect of ever marrying or starting families—found themselves cut loose from familiar moorings and turned to the new secret societies or popular religions for food and companionship. The more desperate found refuge in drink and, increasingly, opium. Thus here, in the waning years of the Qianlong era, originated the destructive nexus of social disintegration and economic decline that would lay waste to so much of Chinese society in the 1800s.

We should not be carried away by romantic notions of Qianlong or his times, lest we confuse legend and history. As with any major historical figure, there is plenty of good and bad to comment upon, and much that seems contradictory. It would be as easy to condemn Qianlong for the excesses of his reign as it would be to glorify him for its successes. More challenging is to arrive at a balanced understanding of his accomplishments and failures in their contemporary context and to see their long-term importance. Let us consider five ironies of Qianlong's rule with major implications for how we interpret the problems that China faced in the eighteenth century:

- Qianlong emphasized the importance of taming the wilderness and colonizing the frontier to increase the amount of arable land to feed his quickly growing population; in so doing, he contributed to the degradation of the environment that negatively affected the lives of Han and non-Han aboriginal peoples alike.

- Qianlong conscientiously spoke of the need to look after the welfare of the ordinary man and woman, and under him the overall standard of living improved and people could count on state assistance in times of crisis; at the same time, he presided over two of the worst decades of official corruption in history, which profited at the expense of precisely those ordinary people.

- Qianlong contended all his life with the need to balance the narrow concerns of the Manchu elite against the broader demands of Han scholar-officials, and stressed the importance of ethnic harmony; in his actions, however, he consistently favored Manchu interests and Manchu officials.

- Qianlong invested enormous resources in ambitious cultural enterprises, the fruits of which we still enjoy today; yet the realization of those projects also resulted in the loss of hundreds of literary and historical works and the large-scale expurgation from the record of views or ideas that did not accord with his own.

- Qianlong worked hard to create unity and impose control over what he saw to be the reconstitution of a great empire; many cheered this accomplishment at the time, but at the same time tens of thousands died or were killed in the process and many thousands more enslaved, their land taken, their cultures despoiled.

All of these paradoxes, and many others besides, are true. Some we can tie more specifically to choices made by Qianlong personally, while others over which Qianlong had less direct responsibility. Either way, they point to a series of questions that provided, as this study has shown, much for Qianlong and his ministers to consider:

- How to assess the costs of demographic growth and economic development?

- How to recruit talented individuals to government service and still keep civil servants honest?

- How to balance the particular and the universal to arrive at an all-embracing political constitution?

- What value to set by inclusivity and comprehensiveness, when cultural preservation also means destruction?

- How to assess the costs of imperial unification?

Not all these questions were necessarily new under Qianlong; the second question, in specific, was one with which Confucian statecraft had wrestled for centuries. But it is striking that these problems emerge for the Qing at the same time as they emerged in the countries of early modern Europe. It is equally striking that they persist in one form or another in today's China (and not just in China). In this limited sense we may perhaps venture to say that Qianlong was modern China's first ruler.

Not that Qianlong himself was a modern ruler. In reflecting on his rule and on the solutions that Qianlong tried to find to the problems he faced, we must remember that Qianlong was an emperor, not a president or prime minister. He owed his legitimacy not to any single constituency or to a popular election, but to Heaven. To him, this meant he had an obligation to no one and to everyone, to *all* constituencies—all peoples, all phenomena—taken together. As a universal sovereign, he interpreted the demands upon him as a call to master his world in all its complexity. Qianlong proudly assumed the role of the Confucian sage and gentleman scholar, of the art connoisseur, of the worldly wise statesman, and of the legitimate heir to the grand imperial tradition of the immortal Chinese rulers of the past. Simultaneously he projected the image of the model Manchu warrior—clever on horseback and a good shot, afraid of no man or beast—and that of a chakravartin king, a man of devotion who had acquired some of the wisdom of Buddhist teaching. All of this he did with panache and conviction, taking advantage of many different media and settings to communicate these images to the world. Yet Qianlong's wish to intervene positively and effectively in the operation of the empire's many institutions proved an impossible dream. In his zeal he often failed to see that pursuing one goal prevented him from realizing another. When conflicting visions meant pursuing apparently conflicting ends, he persisted, seeking along the way to reconcile the two; sometimes he succeeded, sometimes not.

As a universal ruler, Qianlong formed an opinion on everything, including, of course, on the subject of how a monarch ought to govern. Here we run into a final paradox, which is that the strengthened emperorship he inherited from his father weakened under him. Despite his emphasis on the sanctity of the Way and the responsibility of the sovereign both to ancestors and to generations yet unborn, the throne he left to his son was a shadow of what it had been. Qianlong's greatest failing was that as time passed he ended up ceding a great deal of his power to his ministers and lesser officials, who—as the decreasing efficiency and confidentiality of the palace memorial system attests—successfully reasserted their privilege literally to read his mail and control what he saw and heard. The emperor was sporadically still effective in getting what he wanted, but was not consistently able to rein in wayward officials. Moreover, his judgment led him astray as he misplaced trust in many people, most notably Hešen, whose actions severely compromised the emperor's authority. Indeed, we can say that the imperial institution never fully recovered from the effects of twenty years of cynicism at the top levels of government, which permanently deprived not only Qianlong, but all his successors as well, of the power to inspire the sort of selfless commitment to dynastic ideals that had motivated earlier generations. In that regard, too, it must be said that Qianlong left the emperorship, and the country, less able to deal with the challenges that lay ahead.

In fairness, the loss of central power was not entirely within Qianlong's control. It lay at least in part in the eternal tension between the centripetal and centrifugal forces present in the unified empire. From its beginnings in the third century BCE, the imperial center always had to contend with forces on the local level, which sought to assert a degree of autonomy or distance from central rule. Like the phases of the moon, at times the center had greater pull, at other times less. In large measure this explains the repeated pattern we observe of unification and disunification. This dynamic remains relevant in China today, which finds itself in a state of unification almost as great as the Qing, with which it closely identifies.

Putting aside the accomplishments, the image, the contradictions, the lingering doubts, we are left at the end with one last question: What kind of man was Qianlong? In the pages of this book can be found many parts of the answer: He was intelligent, industrious, and dutiful; vain, obsessive, and choleric. He was devoted to his family, especially the women around him. He loved theater, music, and grand celebrations. He generously rewarded bravery and dedication to duty and stood in awe of artistic talent. He could forgive poor judgment and mistakes, especially by otherwise meritorious men, but not could not abide stupidity, cowardice, or betrayal, and was by turns indulgent and vindictive. Above all else, perhaps, he was a visionary, convinced that a special place in history was reserved for him and determined—perhaps a little *too* determined—to do everything he could to make that a reality.

Pronunciation Key and Glossary

Chinese and Manchu names can be intimidating to those unfamiliar with the transcription systems used to write them in the Roman (Latin) alphabet. Readers may find this table of some help in determining the pronunciation of proper names and unfamiliar terms given in the text. Values in the middle column should be pronounced as in American English; syllables separated by apostrophes should be slurred together, while those separated by hyphens may be more clearly distinguished. Brief identifications are also provided as a convenience.

Name	Pronunciation	Identification
Afaqqiya	*ah-fah-kee-yah*	"White Mountain" faction of Naqshbandi order in east Turkestan
Agūi	*ah-gway*	leading Manchu general and grand councilor of the later Qianlong reign
Aksu	*awk-soo*	city on northwestern rim of Tarim Basin
Altishahr	*ahl-tee-shahr*	"Six Cities," one name for Kashgaria
amban	*ahm-bahn*	Manchu frontier administrators
Amursana	*ah-moor-sah-nah*	Khoit chieftain, Dzungar leader
Anhui	*ahn-whey*	province in central China
Ayongga	*ah-young-ah*	critic of Qianlong
Badakhshan	*bah-dahk-shan*	minor principality west of Pamirs (today's northeast Afghanistan)
Bandi	*bahn-dee*	Manchu general, perished in Turkestan conquest
Baoxiang	*bow-shee'yahng*	name of temple near Beijing

Barkol	*bahr-kohl*	garrison in eastern Xinjiang; modern Balikun
Beijing	*bay-djeeng*	imperial capital (Peking)
bixi	*bee-shee*	mythical tortoise-like beast
Burhan ad-Din	*boor-hahn ahd-deen*	Khwaja heir, co-leader of White Mountain faction; brother of Jihan
chakravartin	*chah-krah-vahr-tin*	Buddhist "wheel-turning" king
Changbai	*chahng-bye*	mountain range on China-Korea border
Chengde	*chung-duh*	mountain retreat of the Qing emperors
Choros	*choh-rohs*	western Mongol tribe, part of Dzungar confederation
Cixi	*tsuh-shee*	nineteenth-century empress dowager
Daicing	*dye-ching*	Manchu name for the Qing dynasty
Dawachi	*dah-wah-chee*	Dzungar leader
Deng Xiaoping	*duhng shee'yow-peeng*	Chinese Communist leader
Dezhou	*duh-joe*	city in Shandong on the Grand Canal
dharani	*dah-rah-nee*	Buddhist incantation text
Dörböt	*dur-bet*	western Mongol tribe, part of Dzungar confederation
Dorgon	*door-gone*	brother of Hong Taiji; regent to the Shunzhi emperor
Dzungars	*djoon-gahrs*	Western Mongol confederation and rivals of the Qing
Fengšeninde	*fuhng-shun-in-duh*	husband of Princess Hexiao
fu	*foo*	poetic form, "rhapsody"
Fuca	*foo-cha*	family name of Qianlong's first empress, Xiaoxian
Fuheng	*foo-hung*	leading Manchu general and statesman
Fujian	*foo-jee'yen*	province in southeastern China
Fukang'an	*foo-kahng-ahn*	Manchu general, son of Fuheng
Fumin	*foo-min*	Qianlong's first teacher

Galdan	*gahl-dahn*	Dzungar leader defeated by Kangxi
Galdan Tsereng	*gahl-dahn tseh-rehng*	Dzungar leader, nephew of Galdan
Gansu	*gahn-soo*	province in northwestern China
gong	*goohng*	tribute
Guan Di	*guwahn dee*	popular martial deity
Guangxi	*guwahng-see*	province in southwestern China
Guangzhou	*guwahng-joe*	southern Chinese port (Canton)
Guizhou	*gway-joe*	province in southwestern China
Gurkhas	*goor-khas*	ethnic group in northern India and Nepal
gūsa	*goo-sah*	"banner," highest-level military organizational unit in Manchu society
Hailanca	*high-lawn-chah*	leading Manchu military figure
Haixi	*high-shee*	early Jurchen tribal grouping
Han	*hahn*	Chinese dynasty, 202 BCE-220 CE
Hangzhou	*hahng-joe*	city in Jiangnan
Heilongjiang	*hay-lohng-djee'yahng*	river in northeastern China
Henan	*huh-nahn*	province in central China
Hešen	*huh-shun*	grand councilor, favorite of Qianlong
Hexiao	*huh-shee'yaow*	Qianlong's youngest daughter
Hong Taiji	*hoohng tye-jee*	second Qing emperor
Hubei	*who-bay*	province in central China
Huizong	*whey-dzoohng*	Song dynasty emperor, painter, and calligrapher
Hunan	*who-nahn*	province in south-central China
Hungli	*hoohng-lee*	personal name of Qianlong, made taboo after he became emperor
Hungpu	*hoohng-pooh*	cousin of Qianlong
Hungsi	*hoohng-suh*	cousin of Qianlong
Ili	*yee-lee*	garrison city in western Xinjiang; modern Yining

Ishaqqiya	*ishak-keeyah*	"Black Mountain" faction of Naqshbandi order in east Turkestan
Jiangnan	*jee'ahng-nahn*	Yangzi delta region in south-central China
Jiangxi	*jee'ahng-shee*	province in south-central China
Jianzhou	*jee'yen-joe*	early Jurchen tribal grouping
Jiaqing	*jee'yah-ching*	Qianlong's fifteenth son, seventh Qing emperor
Jihan	*djee-hahn*	Khwaja heir, co-leader of White Mountain faction; brother of Burhan ad-Din
Jin	*djin*	dynasty founded by Jurchens, 1115-1234 CE
Ji'nan	*jee-nahn*	capital of Shandong province
Jinchuan	*jin-chew'ahn*	region of eastern Tibet/western Sichuan
Jingdezhen	*jeeng-duh-jun*	porcelain production center, Jiangxi province
Jinshan	*djin-shahn*	scenic mountain island on the Yangzi
jinshi	*djin-shr*	highest examination degree
Joohūi	*joe-hway*	Manchu general, hero of Turkestan conquest
Jurchen	*djur-chin*	Manchurian tribe, founders of the Jin dynasty and ancestors of the Manchus
Kangxi	*kahng-shee*	fourth Qing emperor; father of Yongzheng and grandfather of Qianlong
Kanjur	*kahn-djoor*	main corpus of Buddhist texts
Kazakh	*kah-zakhs*	Turkic tribe of Central Asia
Khalkha	*hal-khas*	eastern Mongol tribe
Khitan	*kee-tahns*	nomadic tribe of eastern Mongolian steppe, founders of Liao dynasty
Khoit	*hoe'eet*	western Mongol tribe, part of Dzungar confederation

Khoja	*hoe-juh*	influential lineage of Sufi masters active in Islamic Central Asia
Khoshot	*hoe-shote*	western Mongol tribe, part of Dzungar confederation
Kiakhta	*kee-yakh-ta*	trading post on Qing-Russian border
Kirghiz	*keer-gyz*	Turkic people of Central Asia and sometime Qing allies
Kong	*kohng*	surname shared by descendants of Confucius
Kucha	*koo-chah*	city on northern rim of Tarim Basin
Lama Darja	*lah-mah dahr-jah*	Dzungar leader, son of Galdan Tsereng
Lê	*luh*	Vietnamese royal dynasty, 1428-1788
li	*lee*	measure of distance, approximately 1/3 mile
Lifanyuan	*lee-fahn-you'en*	Bureau of Colonial Dependencies
Li Shiyao	*lee shr-yao*	provincial governor under Qianlong
Lin Shuangwen	*lin shoo'ahng-won*	leader of 1788 Taiwan rebellion
Liuqiu	*lee'yoh-chee'yoh*	the Ryukyu islands; modern Okinawa
Lü Liuliang	*lee'you lee'yoh-lee'yahng*	critic of the Manchus reviled by Yongzheng
Maci	*ma-chee*	Lady Fuca's uncle
Maitreya	*my-tray-ah*	the Buddha of the coming age
Manchu	*man-chew*	non-Han ethnic group, founders of the Qing dynasty
Manjusri	*mahn-djew-shree*	Buddhist deity, avatar of righteous kings
Mao Zedong	*maow dzeh-doohng*	Chinese Communist leader
Mi Fu	*mee foo*	famous Chinese calligrapher
Miao	*miaow*	non-Han people native to Yunnan
Ming	*meeng*	dynasty preceding the Qing, 1368-1644 CE

mu	*moo*	measure of land, about 1/6 acre
Mukden	*mook-den*	secondary Qing capital in Manchuria, also known as Shengjing; modern Shenyang
Mulan	*moo-lawn*	hunting preserve, north of Chengde
Nanjing	*nahn-jeeng*	city in Jiangnan, former Ming capital
Naqshbandi	*nahksh-bahn-dee*	one of the major Sufi orders
Necin	*neh-chin*	Manchu official and general executed for incompetence
Nguyen	*new'win*	Vietnamese royal dynasty, 1802-1945
Ningbo	*neeng-boe*	Jiangnan port city (Ningpo)
Niohuru	*nee'oh-hoo-roo*	family name of Qianlong's mother
niru	*nee-roo*	company, smallest military unit in the Eight Banners
Nurhaci	*noor-ha-chee*	founder of the Qing dynasty
Ortai	*ore-tie*	grand councilor under Yongzheng and Qianlong
Polhanas	*poe-lah-ney*	Tibetan noble and regent
Potala	*poe-tah-lah*	palace of Dalai Lamas in Lhasa
Qianlong	*chee'en-loohng*	sixth Qing emperor
qin	*chin*	Chinese zither
Qin Shihuang	*chin shur-hoo'wahng-dee*	first emperor to unify and rule over China
Qinghai	*ching-high*	region of western China/northeastern Tibet, also known as Amdo
Qufu	*chyu-foo*	birthplace of Confucius, in Shandong
Rolpai Dorje	*rohl-pay door-jay*	Qianlong's instructor in Tibetan Buddhism
Rong	*rohng*	name of Qianlong's Muslim consort
Ru	*roo*	general name applied to philosophical schools associated with Confucius

ru-yi	*roo-ee*	talismanic scepter, commonly presented by Qianlong as a gift
samadhi	*sah-mah-dee*	in Buddhist iconography, hand gesture indicating enlightenment
Shandong	*shahn-doohng*	province in eastern China
Shaanxi	*sha'ahn-shee*	province in northwestern China
Shanxi	*shahn-shee*	province in west-central China
Shengjing	*shuhng-djeeng*	alternative name for Mukden
Shenyang	*shuhn-yahng*	modern name for Mukden
Shunzhi	*shoon-jer*	third Qing emperor
Sichuan	*suh-chew'ahn*	province in western China
Siku quanshu	*suh-koo chew'en shoo*	Complete Library of the Four Treasuries
Songjiang	*soohng-jee'yahng*	Jiangnan port city
Sungyun	*soohng-yewn*	Manchu grand councilor
Suzhou	*soo-joe*	city in Jiangnan
Šuhede	*shoo-huh-duh*	Manchu grand councilor
Taipei	*tye-pay*	capital of Taiwan
Taiping	*tye-peeng*	mid-nineteenth-century rebellion
Taishan	*tie-shahn*	Mt. Tai, in Shandong province
taishang huang	*tye-shahng hwahng*	"supreme emperor," Qianlong's title after abdicating in 1795
Tang	*tahng*	Chinese dynasty, 618-907 CE
Tarim	*tah-reem*	river in southern Xinjiang, name given to region generally ("Tarim Basin"), also referred to as Kashgaria
thangka	*tahng-kah*	Tibetan religious scroll painting
Tiandihui	*tee'yen-dee-whey*	secret society active in southern China
Tianjin	*tee'yen-djin*	coastal city in north China
Tianshan	*tee'yen-shahn*	mountain range in Xinjiang

Tsongkhapa	*tsohng-kah-pah*	founder of Gelug ("Yellow Hat") sect of Tibetan Buddhism
tusi	*too-suh*	chieftaincy (in southwest China)
Ula Nara	*oo-lah nah-rah*	surname of Qianlong's second empress
Wang Lun	*wahng loon*	leader of 1774 rebellion
Wang Shijun	*wahng shr-jyun*	Sichuan provincial governor
Wang Tanwang	*wahng tahn-wahng*	Gansu provincial governor
Wang Xizhi	*wahng shee-djur*	famous Chinese calligrapher
Wei	*way*	name of Qianlong's consort, mother of the Jiaqing emperor
wen	*won*	literary accomplishment
wu	*woo*	martial accomplishment
Wutai shan	*woo-tie shahn*	Mt. Wutai, in Shanxi province
Xiamen	*shee'ya-mun*	south China port city (Amoy)
Xi'an	*shee-ahn*	city in western China
Xiaoxian	*shee'yao-shee'yen*	Qianlong's first empress
Xinjiang	*shin-jee'yahng*	portion of Eastern Turkestan conquered by Qianlong
yamen	*yah-mun*	building compound where a public official lived and worked
Yangxin (Palace)	*yahng-shin*	name of the emperor's private study
Yangzhou	*yahng-joe*	city in Jiangnan
Yangzi	*yahng-dzuh*	the Yangtze, river in central China
Yarhašan	*yahr-ha-shan*	Qing general in Xinjiang campaigns
Yarkand	*yahr-kahnd*	important oasis city and royal town on southern rim of Tarim Basin
Yeren	*yeh-run*	early Jurchen tribal grouping
yi	*yee*	non-Han; non-Chinese; "barbarian"
Ying-ji-li	*eeng-djee-lee*	early Chinese name for England

Yongle	*yoohng-luh*	third Ming emperor
Yongyan	*yoohng-yen*	personal name of the Jiaqing emperor
Yongzheng	*yoohng-djung*	fifth Qing emperor; father of Qianlong
Yuan	*you'en*	dynasty founded by Mongols, 1260-1368 CE
Yuanming yuan	*you'en-ming-you'en*	palace and garden complex in Beijing suburbs
Yunnan	*yoon-nahn*	province in southwestern China
Zhang Tingyu	*djahng teeng-you*	grand councilor under Yongzheng and Qianlong
Zhang Zhao	*djahng jaow*	official sent in 1735 to suppress Miao rebellion
Zhanghua	*djahng-hwa*	county in Taiwan
Zhao Mengfu	*djaow muhng-foo*	Yuan dynasty artist
Zhejiang	*djuh-jee'yahng*	Jiangnan province
zhengtong	*djuhng-toehng*	"true line of rule"
Zhenjiang	*djuhn-jee'yahng*	city in Jiangnan
Zhu Xi	*djew shee*	Song dynasty philosopher
Zhuang (Prince)	*djew'ahng*	brother of the Yongzheng emperor and advisor to Qianlong

Timeline of the
Qianlong Era

1711	Hungli, fourth son of Injen (the Yong Prince) and Lady Niohuru, is born (September 25)
1722	Hungli accompanies Kangxi to Chengde; Kangxi dies in November; Hungli's father becomes emperor
1723	First year of the Yongzheng reign; Qianlong secretly named crown prince and heir
1727	Hungli and Lady Fuca marry
1730	Qianlong publishes the first of many collections of his poetry
1733	Named Prince Bao (Precious) by Yongzheng
1735	Yongzheng dies; Hungli ascends to the throne (October); Miao rebellion in Guizhou
1736	First year of Qianlong reign
1737	Grand Council is restored
1740	Signing of treaty with Dzungar Mongols
1741	Qianlong revives tradition of fall hunt at Mulan
1743	First "Northern Tour" visit to ancestral tombs in Mukden; Hebei famine
1745	Death of Ortai; first national tax amnesty proclaimed
1746	First "Western Tour" visit to Mt. Wutai
1747	First Jinchuan campaign begins (ends 1749); death of Polhanas, Tibetan regent
1748	First "Eastern Tour" visit to Mt. Tai and Qufu; death of first empress, Lady Fuca
1749	Execution of Necin; retirement of Zhang Tingyu
1750	Lady Ula Nara named empress; rebellion in Lhasa, Qing troops sent
1751	First of Qianlong's six "Southern Tours" to Jiangnan
1755	First Dzungar campaign; revolt of Amursana
1756	Second Dzungar campaign
1757	Flight of Amursana; Khoja rebellion begins; restriction of "Western ocean" vessels to trade at Guangzhou
1759	Return to Beijing of Joohūi after defeat of White Mountain Khojas
1760	Birth of fifteenth son Yongyan, future Jiaqing emperor

1761	Seventieth birthday celebrations for Qianlong's mother
1767	Burma campaign begins (ends 1771)
1771	Second Jinchuan campaign begins (ends 1776); celebration of empress dowager's eightieth birthday; return of the Torghuts to Qing rule; publication of revised dictionary of the Manchu language
1773	Work begins in earnest on *Complete Library of the Four Treasuries;* rebellion of Wang Lun
1775	Birth of Princess Hexiao; Hešen appointed to Grand Council; Paris-made prints of battle scenes from Turkestan campaigns presented to the throne
1777	Qianlong's mother dies, age 84
1780	Celebration of Qianlong's seventieth birthday (in *sui*); visit of Panchen Lama to Chengde; Li Shiyao corruption case
1781	Muslim rebellion in Gansu; Wang Tanwang corruption case
1782	Work on first *Complete Library* set is finished
1787	Lin Shuangwen rebellion
1788	First Gurkha campaign; Vietnam campaign begins
1790	Marriage of Princess Hexiao
1792	Second Gurkha campaign
1793	Visit of British emissary Lord Macartney
1794	Miao rebellion in Hunan
1795	Qianlong formally abdicates; Yongyan takes over as the Jiaqing emperor
1796	First year of Jiaqing reign; White Lotus rebellion breaks out
1797	Death of Agūi
1798	Last visit to Chengde
1799	Qianlong passes away, aged 89 *sui*; Hešen executed

Bibliographic Essay

When it comes to a major historical figure such as the Qianlong emperor, there is no shortage of relevant information available to the researcher, including both primary sources (i.e., material produced during Qianlong's day) and secondary sources (accounts written by later historians). Indeed, the volume of material is far too great for any single person, no matter how industrious, to possibly read all of it. Accordingly, while I have consulted a broad range of original materials, in writing this book I have of necessity also taken advantage of work by other historians. My debt to them, which ordinarily would be evident in footnotes and bibliography, will become apparent in the following pages, which introduce some important original sources for research on Qianlong and his times and provide an overview of existing scholarship.

Primary Sources

There is a very wide array of original sources available to anyone interested in the life of the Qianlong emperor and the era in which he lived. The overwhelming majority of these sources are in the Chinese language, mainly written in the classical style that was in wide use among all educated classes until the early twentieth century. Additional materials may be found in Manchu, Mongolian, Tibetan, and Korean, and there are supplementary sources in English, French, Russian, Latin, and other languages as well. Many of these sources are published (some were even available during the Qing), and more are published or put online every year. But the majority of original sources consist of unpublished documents kept in archival depositories and libraries in Beijing, Taipei, Shenyang, and elsewhere. A good general introduction to all the various kinds of original sources for the Qing may be found in the relevant sections of Endymion Wilkinson, ed., *Chinese History: A Manual*, 2nd ed. (Cambridge, Mass.: Harvard University Asia Center Publications, 2000).

The single most important published primary source consulted for this study is the *Veritable Records of the Qing (Da Qing lichao shilu)*, a detailed daily chronicle of affairs of state compiled by Qing court historians. For the Qianlong reign, the *Veritable Records* consist of 1,500 volumes, covering the period between 1735 and 1799. Each month is treated in two volumes, with the length of each volume falling anywhere between twenty and fifty pages; there is usually an entry for each day. In compiling the *Veritable Records*, editors consulted a wide variety of original documents gathered specifically for their purpose, some of which were destroyed when they were done, but many of which were preserved in the palace archives. Today, when we compare the original archival documents with what appears in the *Veritable Records*, we can see that what was copied into the latter is by and large accurate, although documents are often abbreviated in length and there is sometimes evidence of other kinds of editing. For this reason, scholars must approach these chronicles with some caution. Nonetheless, because of its comprehensive detail and chronological sweep, the *Veritable Records* is an important jumping-off point for all Qing historians.

It is worth mentioning that the *Veritable Records* were never meant to be published, but were intended solely for the use of the emperor and his ministers. Duplicate editions of the *Veritable Records*, which were copied by hand, were kept in five different locations in Beijing, Chengde, and Mukden, so that members of the court could consult them wherever they happened to be. In 1937, after the Japanese had taken control of Manchuria, the Mukden copy of the *Veritable Records* was discovered and published in Tokyo in a deluxe lithograph edition, making it available for the first time to scholars around the world. A small-format reprint of the Tokyo edition appeared in 1964, and a lithograph of the Beijing set of the *Veritable Records* was published in 1985–1987. The entire work is now also available online by subscription through Academia Sinica in Taiwan.

Apart from the *Veritable Records*, there are countless other types of primary sources for research on Qianlong, too many to list here. They include everything from original archival documents and manuscripts (for Qianlong's long reign, these number in the hundreds of thousands), both in Chinese and in Manchu, many of which bear Qianlong's writing. In addition, there are of course his thousands of poems, hundreds of prefaces, essays, and inscriptions, and lengthy court-sponsored histories of Qianlong's many military campaigns and of the Southern Tours. This is not to mention law codes, administrative regulations, quasi-official and unofficial historical works, catalogues, and the published writings of leading officials and generals, all of which provide unique perspectives on the emperor and his age. Non-textual materials include the numerous paintings of the emperor and his court (some reproduced here), maps, drawings, clothing, and the many material objects left behind in the palace buildings once occupied by Qianlong. In short, there is enough original material for research on the eighteenth-century Qing to last many generations.

Limiting ourselves to materials in Western languages, among the most valuable are the letters written by Jesuit missionaries at Qianlong's court, which are full of observations on the emperor and on imperial politics and life in eighteenth-century Beijing. The Latin originals are mostly in Rome, but French translations began to be published in the early 1800s as part of a large series documenting Jesuit missionary efforts around the world, *Lettres édifiantes et curieuses concernant l'Asie et l'Afrique* (Paris, 1838; letters from China are in vols. 3 and 4). Of interest also are the letters of Antoine Gaubil, S. J., collected in *Correspondance de Pékin, 1722–1759* (Geneva: Droz, 1970). Another set of extremely important sources on the late Qianlong period are the memoirs produced by different members of the Macartney mission. Foremost among these are Macartney's own diary, edited by J. L. Cranmer-Byng and published as *An Embassy to China: Being the Journal Kept by Lord Macartney During His Embassy to the Emperor Ch'ien-lung, 1793–1794* (Hamden, Conn.: Archon Press, 1974) and George Staunton, *An Authentic Account of an Embassy from the King of Great Britain to Emperor of China* (London, 1798). English translations of relevant texts may also be found here and there, including at the end of James Millward, et al., eds., *New Qing Imperial History* (London: Routledge, 2004), where Deborah Sommer's translation of the encounter (related in Chapter 7) between the painter Attiret and Qianlong appears; my thanks to her for permission to use it.

Secondary Scholarship

Biographies and General Histories of the Qing

Not surprisingly, secondary scholarship on Qianlong is also quite extensive; again, most of it is in Chinese. As mentioned in the preface, quite a few biographies have appeared since 1987, of which the following are representative: Liu Lu, *Guxi tianzi Qianlong* (1987), Bai Xinliang, *Qianlong zhuan* (1990), Zhou Yuanlian, *Qianlong huangdi dazhuan* (Beijing, 1990), Dai Yi, *Qianlong ji qi shidai* (Beijing, 1992), Sun Wenliang, Zhang Jie, and Zheng Chuanshui, *Qianlong di* (Changchun, 1993), Guo Chengkang and Cheng Chongde, *Qianlong huangdi quanzhuan* (Beijing, 1994), Tang Wenji and Luo Qingsi, *Qianlong zhuan* (Beijing, 1994), Gao Xiang, *Kang-Yong-Qian sandi tongzhi sixiang yanjiu* (Beijing, 1995), Zhang Jie, *Tianchao weifu: Qing Gaozong, Qianlongdi, Hongli* (Harbin, 1997), Chen Jiexian, *Qianlong xiezhen* (Hangzhou, 2003), and Guo Chengkang, *Qianlong dadi* (Beijing, 2004). Wu Shizhou, *Qianlong yiri* (Tianjin, 1999), offers an in-depth study of one day in the life of the emperor— January 28, 1765—which marked the halfway point in Qianlong's long reign. Also of great value are Chuang Chi-fa's comprehensive study of Qianlong's military campaigns, *Qing Gaozong shiquan wugong yanjiu* (Taipei, 1982), Gao Wangling's history of eighteenth-century Qing economy, *Shiba shiji Zhongguo de jingji fazhan he zhengfu zhengce* (Beijing, 1995), and the research into palace life by Wan Yi, Wang Shuqing, and Liu Lu, *Qingdai gongting shi* (Shenyang, 1990). Academic in style, these books are all based on primary research in the sorts of materials described above, and they have been extremely useful to me.

Apart from books, there are hundreds of scholarly articles on Qianlong and the Qianlong reign, and scores of popular histories and works of historical fiction centering on Qianlong and his court by well-known authors such as Eryuehe. Though based on fact, such books often stray from what is knowable from contemporary sources and are not reliable for the historian's purpose, even if they are fun to read.

In Japanese, there are two reliable, but outdated, biographies of Qianlong: Gōtō Sueo, *Kenryūtei den* (Tokyo, 1942) and Sugimura Yūzō, *Kenryū kōtei* (Tokyo, 1961).

In English, the best synthetic account of the Qianlong reign is the chapter by Alexander Woodside, "The Ch'ien-lung Reign," in Willard J. Peterson, ed., *The Cambridge History of China: Volume 9, Part 1, The Ch'ing Dynasty to 1800* (Cambridge: Cambridge University Press, 2002). Also well worth consulting is the chapter on Qianlong in Frederick Mote, *Imperial China, 900–1800* (Cambridge, Mass.: Harvard University Press, 1999). A much briefer, but still very good, narrative is that by Chao-ying Fang in Arthur Hummel, Jr., ed., *Eminent Chinese of the Ch'ing Period* (Washington, DC: US Government Printing Office, 1943–1944; look under "Hungli"). This book is a gold mine of information on all aspects of Qing history, and remains an indispensable tool for serious students of the Qing period. The article by Susan Mann and Philip Kuhn, "Dynastic Decline and the Roots of Rebellion," in John K. Fairbank, ed., *The Cambridge History of China: Vol. 10, Part 1, The Ch'ing Dynasty from 1800* (Cambridge, 1979) provides a superb synthesis of the achievements and problems of eighteenth-century politics.

The only book-length study of the Qianlong emperor in any European language remains Harold Kahn, *Monarchy in the Emperor's Eyes* (Cambridge, Mass.: Harvard University Press, 1971), an examination of the image-making process before and after Qianlong became emperor. Brilliantly conceived and written, it offers valuable insights on the institution of rulership, but it is of limited use to someone seeking the details of Qianlong's years on the throne. More recent is Philip Kuhn, *Soulstealers: The Sorcery Scare of 1768* (Cambridge, Mass.: Harvard University Press, 1990), a very accessible study of a fascinating, if bizarre, chapter in Qing politics and society set in the middle of the Qianlong reign, a story in which the emperor himself figures centrally. The lack of scholarly monographs is somewhat compensated for by a number of outstanding catalogues of recent museum shows, which contain beautiful illustrations of high Qing court culture accompanied by informative essays written by well-regarded specialists. Among the most noteworthy are Feng Ming-chu, ed., *Emperor Ch'ien-lung's Grand Cultural Enterprise* (Taipei: National Palace Museum, 2002); Zhang Hongxing, ed., *The Qianlong Emperor: Treasures from the Forbidden City* (Edinburgh, 2002); Chuimei Ho and Bennet Bronson, eds., *Splendors of China's Forbidden City: The Glorious Reign of Emperor Qianlong* (Chicago: The Field Museum, 2004); Evelyn S. Rawski and Jessica Rawson, eds., *China: The Three Emperors, 1662–1795* (London: Royal Academy of Art, 2005). For those who can read Chinese, there are two volumes on the Qianlong reign in the useful series edited by Zhu Chengru, *Qingshi tudian* (An illustrated encyclopedia of Qing history) (Beijing, 2002).

For general histories of the Qing period, the best broad introduction is the first third of *The Search for Modern China*, 2nd ed. (New York: Norton, 1990) by Jonathan Spence, the doyen of Western historians of modern China. Another trustworthy textbook, rather more detailed than Spence, is Immanuel C. Y. Hsü, *The Rise of Modern China*, 6th ed. (Oxford: Oxford University Press, 1999).

Though slightly outdated, Frederic Wakeman's *The Fall of Imperial China* (New York: Free Press, 1975) provides an outstanding overview of the high Qing order, as does Albert Feuerwerker's *State and Society in 18th-century China: The Ch'ing Empire in Its Glory* (Ann Arbor: University of Michigan Center for Chinese Studies, 1976). More current scholarship is showcased in the highly academic *Cambridge History of China*, mentioned previously. Worthy of note also is the debate over the Manchu contribution to modern China's historical development. See Evelyn Rawski, "Reenvisioning the Qing: The Significance of the Qing Period in Chinese History," *Journal of Asian Studies* 55.4 (November 1996), and the reply by Ping-ti Ho, "In Defense of Sinicization: A Rebuttal of Evelyn Rawski's 'Reenvisioning the Qing,' " *Journal of Asian Studies* 57.1 (February 1998).

Dynastic Transition and the Early Qianlong Reign

Kahn's biography, *Monarchy in the Emperor's Eyes*, is excellent on Qianlong's youth and education. For more background on the Yongzheng reign, the standard account is Pei Huang, *Autocracy at Work* (Bloomington, Ind.: Indiana University Press, 1974), but a more up-to-date view of the politics in the air when Qianlong was a young man is given in Jonathan Spence, *Treason by the Book* (New York: Norton, 2001). Spence's two books on the Kangxi era—*Ts'ao Yin and the K'ang-hsi Emperor: Bondservant and Master* (New Haven: Yale University Press, 1966) and *Emperor of China* (New York: Knopf, 1974)—remain excellent sources for understanding the historical currents under Qianlong's grandfather. Regarding the Qianlong-Jiaqing dynastic transition, a classic work is David Nivison, "Ho-shen and His Accusers: Ideology and Political Behavior in the 18th Century," in Nivison and Arthur Wright, eds., *Confucianism in Action* (Stanford: Stanford University Press, 1969).

Life, Ritual, and Religion at the Qing Court

The best introduction to the organization of the palace is Evelyn S. Rawski, *The Last Emperors: A Social History of Qing Imperial Institutions* (Berkeley: University of California Press, 1998), which is particularly strong on the place of women at court. Very useful, too, are the essays collected in Chuimei Ho and Cheri A. Jones, ed., *Life in the Imperial Court of Qing Dynasty China*, published as *Proceedings of the Denver Museum of Natural History*, series 3, no. 15 (November 1998). Norman Kutcher, *Mourning in Late Imperial China: Filiality and the State* (Cambridge: Cambridge University Press, 1999), is a close study of mourning ritual in the Qing, paying particular attention to the scandals that arose after the death of the Xiaoxian empress. Also focused on Qianlong's attitude toward and participation in ritual is Angela Zito's *Of Body and Brush: Grand Sacrifice as Text/Performance in Eighteenth-century China* (Chicago: University of Chicago Press, 1997). *Empire of Emptiness: Buddhist Art and Political Authority in Qing China* (Honolulu: University of Hawai'i Press, 2003), by Patricia Berger, casts new light on Qianlong's artistic and religious endeavors, in particular his (and his mother's) involvement with Tibetan Buddhism. For more on the Manchu religion, see Nicola Di Cosmo, "Manchu Shamanic

Ceremonies at the Qing Court," in Joseph McDermott, ed., *State and Court Ritual in China* (Cambridge: Cambridge University Press, 1999). On temples generally in Qing Beijing, see the pertinent sections of Susan Naquin, *Beijing: Temples and City Life* (Berkeley: University of California Press, 2000).

Imperial Institutions and Governance

For an authoritative explanation of the evolution of Qing governing institutions, the best place to turn is Beatrice S. Bartlett, *Monarchs and Ministers: The Grand Council in Mid-Ch'ing China, 1723–1820* (Berkeley: University of California Press, 1991). An introduction to the Eight Banners, the origins of Manchu rule in China, and the eighteenth-century solution to the problem of minority rule is given in Mark C. Elliott, *The Manchu Way: The Eight Banners and Ethnic Identity in Late Imperial China* (Stanford: Stanford University Press, 2001). A different perspective on Manchu rule and a complex critique of imperial thinking under Qianlong may be found in Pamela Kyle Crossley, *A Translucent Mirror: History and Identity in Qing Imperial Ideology* (Berkeley: University of California Press, 2000). Michael Chang, *A Court on Horseback: Imperial Touring and the Construction of Qing Rule* (Cambridge, Mass.: Harvard University Asia Center Publications, 2007), and Brian Dott, *Identity Reflections: Pilgrimages to Mount Tai in Late Imperial China* (Cambridge, Mass.: Harvard University Asia Center Publications, 2004), offer many insights onto the meaning of tours by both Kangxi and Qianlong, and a number of the essays in Millward, *New Qing Imperial History*, deal with the politics at the secondary capital at Chengde.

The workings of the provincial bureaucracy, its relation to the center, and the views of Qing officials on proper governance are the subject of Philip Kuhn's *Soulstealers* (already mentioned), as well as of William Rowe, *Saving the World: Chen Hongmou and Elite Consciousness in 18th-century China* (Stanford: Stanford University Press, 2001) and Pierre-Etienne Will, *Bureaucracy and Famine in 18th-century China* (Stanford: Stanford University Press, 1990). Of value also is the essay by R. Kent Guy, "Imperial Powers and the Appointment of Provincial Governors in Qing China," in Frederick P. Brandauer and Chun-chieh Huang, eds., *Imperial Rulership and Cultural Change in Traditional China* (Seattle: University of Washington Press, 1994).

Frontier Expansion and Military Campaigns

For a general overview of Qing military culture, see Joanna Waley-Cohen, *The Culture of War in China: Empire and the Military under the Qing Dynasty* (London: Tauris, 2006); also the special issue of *International History Review* on Manchu colonialism (June 1998). The wars against the Dzungars are recounted in detail and compellingly analyzed by Peter Perdue in *China Marches West: The Qing Conquest of Central Eurasia* (Cambridge, Mass.: Harvard University Press, 2005), and the extension of Qing control over Xinjiang is well told in James Millward, *Beyond the Pass: Economy, Ethnicity, and Empire in Qing Central Asia* (Stanford: Stanford University Press, 1998). There is no work in English that adequately addresses the complexities of the relationship between the Qing court and Tibet in the eighteenth century. Parts of this story emerge in Luciano Petech, *China and Tibet in the Early 18th Century*, 2nd ed. (Leiden: Brill, 1972)—this goes up only as far as 1750—and also in Berger, *Empire of Emptiness*; a fascinating chapter is narrated in Xiangyun Wang, "The Qing Court's Tibet Connection," *Harvard Journal of Asiatic Studies* 60.1 (June 2000). Qianlong's dealings with the Mongols form part of the subject of Johan Elverskog's *Our Great Qing: The Mongols, Buddhism, and the State in Late Imperial China* (Honolulu: University of Hawai'i Press, 2006).

For the southeastern frontier, Qing expansion and rule in Taiwan is treated comprehensively in John Shepherd, *Statecraft and Political Economy on the Taiwan Frontier* (Stanford: Stanford University Press, 1993). The story in the southwest is related in Laura Hostetler, *Qing Colonial Enterprise: Ethnography and Cartography in Early Modern China* (Chicago: University of Chicago Press, 2001), C. Patterson Giersch, *Asian Borderlands: The Transformation of Qing China's Yunnan Frontier* (Cambridge, Mass.: Harvard University Press, 2005), and John Herman, *Amid the Clouds and Mist: China's Colonization of Guizhou* (Cambridge, Mass.: Harvard University Asia Center, 2007); see also the several articles by Yingcong Dai on Qianlong's military exploits in the southwest, for example, "The Qing State, Merchants, and Military Labor Force in the Jinchuan Campaigns," *Late Imperial China*, 22.2 (December, 2001).

Eighteenth-Century Society and Economy

A very good general introduction to the society over which Qianlong ruled is Susan Naquin and Evelyn Rawski, *Chinese Society in the Eighteenth Century* (New Haven: Yale University Press, 1987). More details on political economy will be found in some of the books already referred to earlier, including Rowe's *Saving the World* and Will's *Bureaucracy and Famine*. Another important work is Kenneth Pomeranz, *The Great Divergence: China, Europe, and the Making of the Modern World Economy* (Princeton: Princeton University Press, 2000), which offers a bold comparative analysis of economic development in China and Europe focusing closely on the 1700s. Helen Dunstan provides a careful look at fiscal policy in *State or Merchant? Political Economy and Political Process in 1740s China* (Cambridge, Mass.: Harvard University Asia Center, 2006).

Other aspects of Qing society in Qianlong's day are treated in the following books: Susan Mann, *Teachers of the Inner Chambers: Women in China's Long 18th Century* (Stanford: Stanford University Press, 1996) opens a window onto the operation of gender in mid-Qing Jiangnan; David Ownby, *Brotherhoods and Secret Societies in Early and Mid-Qing China: The Formation of a Tradition* (Stanford: Stanford University Press, 1996) traces the origins of secret societies in mutual aid groups formed on the frontier and persistent state efforts to control them; Matthew Sommer, *Sex, Law, and Society in Late Imperial China* (Stanford: Stanford University Press, 2000) examines shifting notions of gender and their reflection in social and legal norms; Melissa Macauley, *Social Power and Legal Culture: Litigation Masters in Late Imperial China* (Stanford: Stanford

University Press, 1998), analyzes legal cases from the eighteenth century to arrive at a bottom-up perspective on social and economic life. This is a fraction of much important scholarship on Chinese society in the Qianlong era that has appeared in the last decade.

Intellectual and Cultural Trends

The major scholarly developments of the Qianlong era and their social and political implications are brilliantly covered in the work of Benjamin A. Elman, *From Philosophy to Philology: Intellectual and Social Aspects of Change in Late Imperial China* (Cambridge, Mass.: Harvard University Asia Center, 1984) and *Classicism, Politics, and Kinship: The Ch'ang-chou School of New Text Confucianism in Late Imperial China* (Berkeley: University of California Press, 1990). Though it spans a much longer range than just the eighteenth century, Elman's massive study of the examination system, *A Cultural History of Civil Service Examinations in Late Imperial China* (Berkeley: University of California Press, 2000) is a mine of valuable information. On the *Complete Library of the Four Treasuries*, in addition to the classic study by L. Carrington Goodrich, *The Literary Inquisition of Ch'ien-lung* (New York, 1966), there is a fine book by R. Kent Guy, *The Emperor's Four Treasuries: Scholars and the State in the Late Ch'ien-lung Era* (Cambridge, Mass.: Harvard University Asia Center, 1987). Antonia Finnane, *Speaking of Yangzhou: A Chinese City* (Cambridge, Mass.: Harvard University Asia Center, 2004) gives a vital sense of eighteenth-century urban culture, while the world of publishing that flourished at this time is addressed in Cynthia Brokaw and Kai-wing Chow, *Printing and Book Culture in Late Imperial China* (Berkeley: University of California Press, 2005).

Foreign Relations

A foundational study of Qing foreign affairs is John K. Fairbank, ed., *The Chinese World Order* (Cambridge, Mass.: Harvard University Press, 1970). A powerful, if controversial, challenge to some of the ideas presented there is James Hevia, *Cherishing Men from Afar: Qing Guest Ritual and the Macartney Embassy of 1793* (Durham, N.C.: Duke University Press, 1995). The place of the Jesuits at Qianlong's court is well covered in the exhibition catalogues listed above, and is also described at more length in Joanna Waley-Cohen, *Sextants of Beijing: Global Currents in Chinese History* (New York: Norton, 1999).

Index

Note: For ease of reference to external sources, transcriptions of the Chinese-character names used by Manchu individuals are provided in parentheses following their given names as transcribed from their Manchu-language forms (Manchus did not routinely identify themselves by family name).